THIS HAPPENED TO ME A WHILE AGO. WHEN I WAS TAKING A WALK THE OTHER DAY, I SAW AN UNUSUAL STREET STALL. AN OLD MAN WHO LOOKED LIKE THE STOREKEEPER WAS SMILING AT ME.

THE SIGN SAID "CHECKMATE SHOGI." (SHOGI IS LKE JAPANESE CHESS.) IF YOU COULD SOLVE THE SHOGI PROBLEM, IT SAID, YOU'D WIN 30,000 YEN! SO, OF COURSE I ROSE TO THE CHALLENGE! ONE MOVE, TWO MOVES...BUT I FAILED ON THE EIGHTH MOVE!

THEN THE OLD MAN HELD OUT HIS HAND AND SAID SOMETHING... *HUH?!* 1,000 YEN FOR EACH MOVE?! THE SIGN DIDN'T SAY ANYTHING ABOUT *THAT!* AND THAT'S HOW I LOST 8,000 YEN.

–KAZUKI TAKAHASHI, 1997

Artist/author Kazuki Takahashi first tried to break into the manga business in 1982, but success eluded him until **Yu-Gi-Oh!** debuted in the Japanese **Weekly Shonen Jump** magazine in 1996. **Yu-Gi-Oh!**'s themes of friendship and fighting, together with Takahashi's weird and wonderful art, soon became enormously successful, spawning a real-world card game, video games, and two anime series. A lifelong gamer, Takahashi enjoys Shogi (Japanese chess), Mahjong, card games, and tabletop RPGs, among other games.

Yu-Gi-Oh!
3-in-1 Edition
Volume 2

SHONEN JUMP Manga Omnibus Edition
A compilation of the graphic novel volumes 4-5-6

STORY AND ART BY Kazuki Takahashi

Translation & English Adaptation/Anita Sengupta
Touch-up Art & Lettering/Kelle Han
Design/Sean Lee (Manga Edition)
Design/Sam Elzway (Omnibus Edition)
Editor/Jason Thompson (Manga Edition)
Managing Editor/Erica Yee (Omnibus Edition)

Printed in the U.S.A.

Published by VIZ Media, LLC
P.O. Box 77010
San Francisco, CA 94107

10 9 8 7 6 5 4
Omnibus edition first printing, May 2015
Fourth printing, June 2020

www.viz.com

PARENTAL ADVISORY
YU-GI-OH! is rated T for Teen and is recommended for ages 13 and up. This volume contains fantasy violence, alcohol and tobacco use, and suggestive situations.
ratings.viz.com

www.shonenjump.com

Vol. 4
KAIBA'S REVENGE

STORY AND ART BY
KAZUKI TAKAHASHI

THE STORY SO FAR...

Shy and easily picked on, 10th-grader Yugi spent most of his time alone playing games…until he solved the Millennium Puzzle, a mysterious Egyptian artifact passed down from his grandfather. Possessed by the puzzle, Yugi became Yu-Gi-Oh, the King of Games, and challenged bullies and criminals to weird games where the loser loses their mind! But now, one of Yugi's past opponents has recovered from Yugi's "Penalty Game," and is preparing a special project of his own…

DARK YUGI

武藤遊戯

YUGI MUTOU

The main character. When he solved the ancient Egyptian Millennium Puzzle, he developed an alter ego, "Dark Yugi," which emerges in times of stress. Afterwards, the regular Yugi doesn't remember what happened.

城之内克也

KATSUYA JONOUCHI

Yugi's classmate, a tough guy who gets into lots of fights. He used to think Yugi was a wimp, but now they are good friends. In the English anime he's known as "Joey Wheeler."

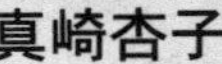

ANZU MAZAKI

Yugi's classmate and childhood friend. She fell in love with the charismatic voice of Yugi's alter ego, but doesn't know that they're the same person. Her first name means "Apricot." In the English anime she's known as "Téa Gardner."

海馬モクバ

MOKUBA KAIBA

Seto's little brother. He challenged Yugi to the collectible miniatures game "Capsule Monster Chess."

海馬瀬人

SETO KAIBA

An expert at the collectible card game "Duel Monsters." When he tried to steal a super-rare card from Yugi's grandfather, Yugi beat him at his own game, then trapped him in an illusionary world where he was eaten by the game's monsters.

本田ヒロト

HIROTO HONDA

Yugi's classmate, a friend of Jonouchi. In the English anime he's known as "Tristan Taylor."

武藤双六

SUGOROKU MUTOU

Yugi's grandfather, the owner of the Kame ("Turtle") game store.

Vol. 4

CONTENTS

Duel 25: The One-Inch Terror

AWRIGHT! TODAY I'M FINALLY GONNA BREAK THIS DUDE'S RECORD !!

THIS "KAI" HAS THE HIGH SCORE ON ALMOST ALL OF THE GAMES IN THIS ARCADE.
IT'S NOT JUST THIS GAME...
THE PUZZLE GAMES AND THE FIGHTING GAMES...
PLUS, THESE GAMES ARE CONNECTED ONLINE TO ARCADES ACROSS THE COUNTRY!
THAT MEANS THIS "KAI" DUDE IS THE NUMBER ONE GAMER IN JAPAN!
WOW!
HE MUST BE AWESOME!
I WONDER WHO HE IS?
DUNNO, NEVER SEEN HIM...
BUT GET THIS, YUGI!
IF I BEAT THIS GUY, I'LL BE THE BEST IN JAPAN!
YOU'RE RIGHT!
AWRIGHT! TODAY, I'M GONNA BEAT "KAI"!!
YAY!!
PFFT...
SHYEAH RIGHT! NOT IN A MILLION YEARS...
HUH...!
THERE'S NO WAY YOU CAN BREAK KAIBA'S RECORD!
WHAT WAS THAT, YOU LITTLE BRATS!?

READ THIS WAY

K...HEY, YOU GUYS! DID YOU JUST SAY "KAIBA?"
YEAH, KAIBA THE GAME MASTER!
HE'S SO TIGHT! HE'S LIKE A LEGEND!
THERE'S TWO BROTHERS, THE OLDER ONE'S THE GAME WHIZ!

IT'S HIM... KAIBA!
KAI

HE'S NOT JUST A GENIUS AT DUEL MONSTERS ...
HE'S AN EXPERT AT ANY GAME!

BUT... THEY SAY KAIBA GOT BORED WITH NORMAL GAMES...
NO SURPRISE! NO ONE CAN BEAT HIM!
AND THEN, THERE'S THIS RUMOR ...

HE'S WORKING ON THIS SUPER SECRET PROJECT ...
THEY SAY HE'S BUILDING THE ULTIMATE GAME...

THE ULTIMATE GAME ...!!

LATER! HAVE FUN CHALLENGING HIS RECORD! FOREVER!
WA HA HA HA HA!
GRRR ...

LET'S PLAY, YUGI!
OKAY!
ARRGGH! I SUCK AT THIS ONE!
CRASH!

WHAM
K.O.
ALRIGHT! I CAN'T LOSE WITH THIS COMBO!
HEY, NOT BAD!

PLING
NEW CHALLENGE
OH! SOMEONE'S CHALLENGING ME!

I LOVE THESE SIT-DOWN FIGHTING GAMES 'CAUSE YOU NEVER KNOW WHO YOU'RE FIGHTING AGAINST!

30'00
WHOA!
READY
HE'S USING BRUCE RYU TOO!!

AWRIGHT! I CAN'T LOSE!
READY!!

SMAK
AH-TAAH!
RACK
GO!
POWM
BAMM
SMAK

12'01
HAI-YAAH!
K.O.
AWRIGHT!! YOU GOT HIM WITH THE CLOSE-QUARTERS ATTACK, THE "ONE INCH PUNCH"!

"NEW CHALLENGER!"
OH, IT'S THE SAME GUY! HE CONTINUED!

I WIN!

I WIN AGAIN!

WHA... HE'S CHALLENGE ME AGAIN !!
IS THIS THE SAME GUY?!
NEW CHALLENGER
THIS IS LIKE THE 30TH TIME!
WEAK GUYS NEVER GIVE UP...
WANT SOMETHING TO DRINK, YUGI?
THANKS! I'LL HAVE A COLA!
IT'S ON ME!
WHAM POW

OK!
I WIN AGAIN!
OH... LOOKS LIKE HE'S NOT CONTINUING ...
HEE HEE... I WONDER IF HE GAVE UP.....
RRMMBB

GRR GRR GRR
THM THM

DOOOM
HEY KID!
HUH ...?!
TURN AROUND !
KABLAM
HAIIYAAA
YOU BRAT! DON'T ACT SO TOUGH JUST BECAUSE YOU WON AT A VIDEO GAME!
I'LL SHOW YOU WHAT A REAL FIGHT IS! HOYAAH!!

AH-TAH-TAH-TAH-TAH-TAH-TAH-TAH-TAH-TAH!
WHOK
WHOK
WHOK
WHOK
...!!!
HAI YAA!
THOK
HOYAAH!!
WOK
CRNCH
~~~
UGGH...
HA HA! WHERE'S YOUR ARROGANT GRIN NOW!
LET ME SEE YOU LAUGH AGAIN! HEY!!
SL
AM
HEY! THAT'S A COOL PENDANT YOU GOT THERE...
...
I ALWAYS TAKE A ***PRIZE*** FROM THE OPPONENTS I BEAT IN MY STREET FIGHTS!
HEH HEH ...
~~~

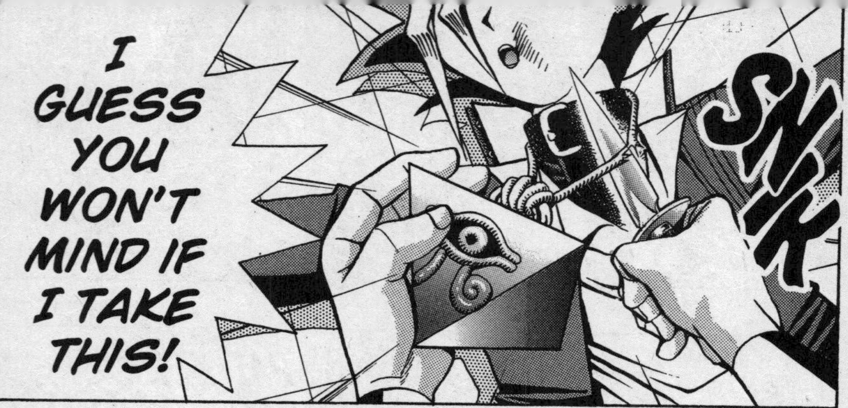
I GUESS YOU WON'T MIND IF I TAKE THIS!
SNIK

HA HA HA... FIGHTING GAMES REALLY DO HELP YOU BURN OFF STRESS!

HEY! HEY!
ARE YOU OKAY ?!
URK ...

!!
MY PUZZLE ...
MY PUZZLE IS ...

HOT HOT HOT ...
JEEZ, THIS CANNED COFFEE IS HOT...

WHA ...!

CLANK

YUG !!

YUGI! ARE YOU ALL RIGHT!?
Y-YEAH ...
I'M OKAY ....

GGRR ...
ROOAAR

HEH HEH... I LIKE THIS PENDANT! IT ALMOST LOOKS LIKE REAL GOLD...

HOLD IT RIGHT THERE!

EH ...?

HOW DARE YOU HURT MY BUDDY ...
I'M NOT GONNA LET YOU LIVE !!

HEH HEH ...

YOU GOT GUTS TO CHALLENGE ME TO A STREET FIGHT!
IT'S NOT A FIGHT! IT'S GONNA BE A SLAUGHTER! AND THEN I'M GONNA TAKE BACK THAT PENDANT.

WELL, GET THIS! I'VE NEVER LOST IN A FIGHT!
I KNOW KARATE AND BOXING !
YOU'RE THE ONE WHO'S GONNA DIE!

QUIT FLAPPING YOUR JAWS AND MAKE YOUR MOVE!

DON'T BE IN SUCH A HURRY... HEH HEH...

I MAY NOT LOOK LIKE IT, BUT I'M A BIG FAN OF BRUCE LEE...

BRUCE LEE WASN'T JUST AN ACTION STAR, HE WAS A *REAL* FIGHTER!

HE SHOWED HIS TRUE STRENGTH TO THE WORLD IN THE ED PORTER INTERNATIONAL KARATE TOURNAMENT T LONG BEACH! THAT'S WHERE HE USED HIS "ONE INCH PUNCH!"

THE RECORDS SHOW THAT WITH JUST ONE INCH, AND NO HANDICAP, HIS PUNCH BLEW HIS OPPONENT AWAY!

READ THIS WAY
A GAM ?!!
WHAT ?!
IF YOU DON'T LIKE IT, I CAN SMASH THIS PUZZLE RIGHT HERE!
LET ME TELL YO THE RULES!
YOU FIGHT WITH THIS KNIFE CLENCHED IN YOUR TEETH!!
GGGH ...!
SEE.. LIKE THIS ...
I'LL HAVE A KNIFE IN MY TEETH TOO. WE'LL BE EVENLY MATCHED!
OR SO YOU THINK... MINE IS A TRICK KNIFE WHERE THE BLADE SLIPS INTO THE HILT!
ALRIGHT! I'LL PLAY!
BUT FIRST ...
TAKE THAT KNIFE OUT OF YOUR MOUTH! I DON'T MIND DOING IT...
...BUT IF YOU HAD ONE, I'D HAVE TO HOLD BACK ON PUNCHING YOUR FACE!

BAM

BAM

HA HA HA...FINE, IT'S YOUR FUNERAL! BUT WHEN I PUNCH YOU IN THE FACE, THAT KNIFE WILL GO RIGHT INTO YOUR *THROAT!* ONE INCH IS ENOUGH TO KILL YOU!

THIS IS A "GAME OF DEATH" JUST LIKE THE FILM WITH BRUCE LEE!

WSSH

HAI-YAA!

URK...

WSH

WSH

HAI-YAA!
WSH WSH WSH
HAI-YAA!
SLSH
GGK …!
IT GETS WORSE! IN THIS NARROW ALLEY, I CAN'T DODGE THAT FAR TO EITHER SIDE!
HE'S GOT A DOUBLE ADVANTAGE!
WHAT …!?
WSSH
HEH… WHAT'S WRONG ?!
YOU PUNCH SO SLOW, I CAN SEE 'EM COMING THE DAY BEFORE!
Y-YOU !
ARE YOU MAKING FUN OF ME?! TAKE YOUR HANDS OUT OF YOUR POCKETS!
HFF
HFF
I HAVE PROMISES TO MY FRIEND IN BOTH THESE POCKETS …
YOU DON'T GET TO SEE 'EM 'TIL IT'S OVER!
HEH HEH …
YOUR LOSS, FOOL …

READ THIS WAY
YOUR TORSO IS WIDE OPEN!
GUK ...!
THIS IS IT!
WAM
GGHH ...
DIEEEE!!!
ALL RIGHT! THESE ARE MY PROMISES !!

PSSHT

AGH-
... PBBT ...
WHA ...?

HEH HEH ...
THIS IS THE PROMISE FROM MY LEFT POCKET ...
A COLA !

READ THIS WAY
THE PROMISE TO CLOBBER YOU!!
BA
DA
SPIT
HEH, NOT IN A MILLION YEARS, YOU JERK!
UH OH... BROKEN JAW... NOT MY PROBLEM...
YUG!
I'VE GOT YOUR PUZZLE BACK!
NOW ALL I'VE GOTTA DO...
...IS BUY ANOTHER COLA!

Duel 26: Russian Roulette

MASTER YUGI AND HIS FRIEND, I PRESUME?

MASTER SETO CORDIALLY REQUESTS YOUR PRESENCE AT HIS HOUSE!

Duel 26: Russian Roulette

VRRRRMMMMM

WHY IS KAIBA INVITING US TO HIS HOUSE?
HE HASN'T BEEN AT SCHOOL RECENTLY ....

YES... MASTER SETO HAS BEEN BUSY...
HE HAS BEEN WORKING ON AN IMPORTANT PROJECT ...
HE IS THE *PRESIDENT* OF KAIBA CORPORATION, AFTER ALL.

WHAT'S KAIBA CORP?
IT'S ONE OF THE TOP COMPANIES IN THE WORLD IN THE TOY AND GAME BUSINESS!

SO *THAT'S* WHY KAIBA IS SO PROUD OF BEING A GREAT GAMER...

WHAA?!! THE PRESIDENT OF KAIBA CORP ?!!
THE BIGGEST AMUSEMENT COMPANY IN THE BUSINESS ?!!
BUT HE'S STILL IN HIGH SCHOOL!

I HAD FUN THE OTHER DAY...
IT'S BEEN A WHILE, YUGI!
HEH HEH ...
BAM
AND I'M THE VICE PRESIDENT!
A GRADE SCHOOLER IS THE VICE PRESIDENT ...?!
YOU'RE KAIBA'S LITTLE BROTHER ...
IT'S MOKUBA. **MOKUBA KAIBA!**
HEH... I DIDN'T TELL YOU MY NAME LAST TIME.

WE HAVE ARRIVED AT THE KAIBA RESIDENCE.

TA-DA

WHOA! IT'S HUGE !!

DON'T HOLD BACK, COME ON IN!
WOW !

IT'S LIKE A EUROPEAN CASTLE!

WELCOME. WE HAVE BEEN WAITING FOR YOU!
HEH HEH ... THESE ARE OUR SERVANTS.
~~!

YOU ARE MASTER SETO'S SCHOOL FRIEND, MASTER YUGI, ARE YOU NOT?
MASTER SETO HAS ORDERED US TO MAKE YOUR STAY AS PLEASANT AS POSSIBLE.

HEY, WHERE'S MY BROTHER ?

YES... HE RETIRED TO HIS ROOMS A WHILE AGO...

WHAT'S HIS PROBLEM! ?
WHY ISN'T HE HERE FOR THE PRE-OPENING CELEBRATION?
MASTER MOKUBA, MASTER SETO HAS BEEN WORKING NONSTOP THESE LAST FEW DAYS...
I BELIEVE IT WOULD BE BEST NOT TO DISTURB HIS SLEEP...

SORRY 'BOUT THIS, YUGI...
LOOKS LIKE MY BIG BROTHER WON'T BE ABLE TO SEE YOU FOR A WHILE.
SO TONIGHT YOU'RE MY GUESTS! I'LL TAKE GOOD CARE OF YOU!

MASTER MOKUBA...
SHALL WE PREPARE A MEAL...?

YEAH! THAT SOUNDS GOOD!
I'M STARVING!

WHAT?! WHY DIDN'T YOU SAY SOMETHING?
I'LL TREAT YOU TO THE BEST FOOD IN THE WORLD!

WOW! THE BEST IN THE WORLD!
I WONDER IF IT'LL BE GOURMET FOOD?

YOU! PREPARE THE SPECIAL COURSE!
YES SIR!

WE WILL SERVE IT AT ONCE!
RMB

HEH HEH...
WE'RE BOTH GOING TO ENJOY THIS...
THIS IS GONNA BE GREAT!

DINNER IS SERVED!

TA DA

HUH ...?

!!

WHAT DO YOU THINK?! DOESN'T IT LOOK GOOD?!
DON'T HOLD BACK, DIG IN...

...THAT'S WHAT I'D LIKE TO SAY. BUT THAT WOULDN'T BE INTERESTING!
WHAT DO YOU THINK ABOUT PLAYING A LITTLE GAME?

A GAME?!

SEE THIS CIRCLE.
IT'S A TURNTABLE LIKE THEY USE AT CHINESE RESTAURANTS!
TURN
TURN

THE THREE OF US TAKE TURNS SPINNING THE TABLE!
THEN WE EAT THE FOOD THAT'S IN FRONT OF US!

THERE ISN'T ANY POISON IN THE FOOD, IS THERE?!

HA HA! THAT WOULD BE RUDE! I'D NEVER DO THAT TO A GUEST!
ACTUALLY, THERE'S A WONDERFUL TREASURE HIDDEN IN THESE DISHES!
THE PERSON WHO FINDS IT, WINS!

ALL RIGHT, LET'S DO IT!!

THEN YOU START, JONOUCHI!

AWRIGHT, LET'S GO!

SPIN!
WHIRR

KIDDIE LUNCH
PANCAKES
SPAGHETTI
CHOCOLATE PARFAIT
HAMBURGER
PIZZA

STOP

ACK! THE KIDDIE LUNCH ?!

YOU HAVE TO CLEAN YOUR PLATE, JONOUCHI!
THAT'S THE RULES OF THE GAME!
AND YOU MIGHT FIND THE TREASURE !

READ THIS WAY

AWRIGHT! I GET IT!

HEY, THIS ISN'T BAD!
MUNCH
MUNCH

UM ...

URGH ...

GWAAA ...
!!

JONOUCHI, WHAT'S WRONG?!
IT CAN'T BE... !!

JONOUCHI !!
URRGH ...

BINGO
!
LOOKS LIKE YOU GOT THE PRIZE, JONOUCHI! BWA HA HA HAHA!!

Y-YOU MEAN ...
URR-GGGH ...
MWA HA HA! HE WAS RIGHT ALL ALONG! IT WAS POISONED!

I CALL THIS GAME "RUSSIAN ROULETTE DINNER!"
'CAUSE IF YOU EAT THE WRONG THING, YOU'LL DIE OF POISON IN 30 MINUTES!

RUSSIAN ROULETTE !?
HE'S TRYING TO KILL US!
YOU WANT TO SAVE JONOUCHI?
THEN YOU'VE GOT TO WIN AND GET THIS ANTIDOTE!

RMB RMB RMB !!

HA HA... HE'S CHANGING LIKE BEFORE!
TODAY I'LL FINALLY DEFEAT THE OTHER YUGI!

READ THIS WAY

AFTER YOU EAT, YOU THINK "BOY, I'M GLAD I DIDN'T DIE!"
THIS MEAL MAKES YOU EXPERIENCE THE JOY OF LIVING. THAT MAKES IT "THE BEST MEAL IN THE WORLD!"
YUGI! HOW WAS THAT! WAS IT TASTY?
A MEAL WHERE YOU COULD LIVE OR DIE!

YOU'RE SAFE!
I GUESS THE POISON WASN'T IN THE SPAGHETTI!

NOW, NEXT IS MY TURN.

URK...
I ONLY HAVE HALF AN HOUR TO SAVE JONOUCHI...

YUM YUM!
MMM-GOOD!
MMM! YUMMY!
SLURP SLURP
CH-CH CHOMP CHOMP

STOP
YAHOO!
CHOCOLATE PARFAIT! MY FAVORITE!

SPIN
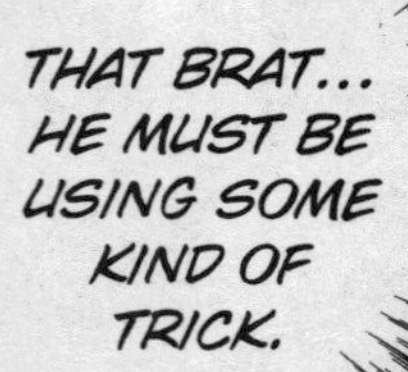
THAT BRAT... HE MUST BE USING SOME KIND OF TRICK.
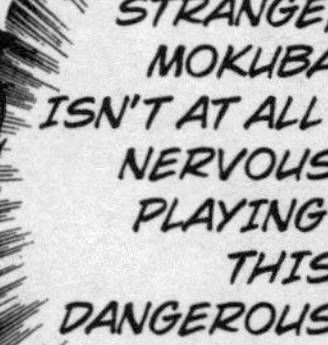
...STRANGE, MOKUBA ISN'T AT ALL NERVOUS PLAYING THIS DANGEROUS GAME...

I THINK HE TOUCHED THAT BOTTLE BEFORE SPINNING THE TURNTABLE...

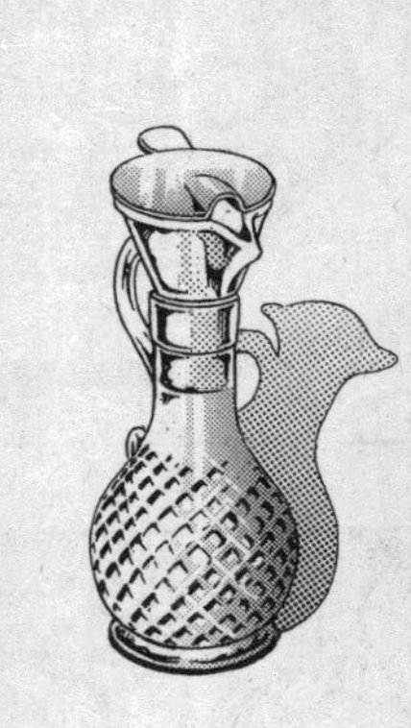

HEY, MOKUBA. WHAT'S IN THAT BOTTLE?
GULP

EHH ...
AHH, THIS IS...
IT'S A SYRUP BOTTLE!
THERE ARE PANCAKES, AREN'T THERE?

THEN WHY'S IT EMPTY?

HA HA ...
I'LL TELL YOU WHY...BECAUSE THIS BOTTLE WILL BE FILLED FOR THE FIRST TIME AS SOON AS YOU EAT THE POISON!
LIKE THEY SAY... "THE SUFFERING OF OTHERS MAKES THE SWEETEST SYRUP!"

NOW YUGI! IT'S YOUR TURN NEXT!

PHEW... I GOT A CHILL WHEN YUGI NOTICED THIS BOTTLE, BUT I BLUFFED THROUGH IT SOMEHOW...
IT'S ACTUALLY A SWITCH. IT LETS ME STOP THE TABLE WHEREVER I WANT...

THE GAME ENDS NEXT TURN!
I'LL GIVE YOU A TASTE OF THE POISON!

THE POISON IS IN THE HAMBURGER!
AND NEXT TIME, YUGI, I'LL STOP IT IN FRONT OF YOU! HA HA HA!

MOKUBA, LET'S FINISH THIS IN ONE GO!
ON THE NEXT TURN, LET'S BOTH EAT THE DISHES THAT END UP IN FRONT OF US!

ALL RIGHT!
LET'S GO!
SPIN
FOOL! YOU CAN SPIN THE TABLE AS HARD AS YOU LIKE, BUT THE POISONED HAMBURGER WILL ALWAYS STOP IN FRONT OF YOU!
AS LONG AS I HAVE THIS SWITCH!!
CRASH!

WHA ...?!
T-THE SWITCH IS BROKEN ?!!
HEH HEH... NOW THERE'S NO CHEATING. WIN OR LOSE, THE GAME IS UP TO LUCK!
SPIN SPIN
H... HOW ?!
THE POISONED HAMBURGER STOPPED IN FRONT OF ME!!
STOP
IMPOSSIBLE ...!!! WHY DID THE SWITCH BREAK?!!

BAM
!!
URK
...
W-WHEN DID HE...? HOW DID HE...? HE ATTACHED HIS PENDANT TO THE TURN-TABLE ...
I HATE YOU, YUGI !

MOKUBA, I'VE FINISHED THE PANCAKES ...
SINCE THERE'S NOTHING WRONG WITH ME, I MUST HAVE MISSED THE POISON!
NOW ...

BA DUM
!!

WEREN'T THE RULES TO CLEAN YOUR PLATE?

URRRR-GHHH .....!
CHOMP
OKAY! I'LL EAT IT! I'LL EAT IT !!
CHOMP
RR... RRRR ...

SO TOMORROW THE MYSTERIOUS PROJECT FINALLY STARTS... WHAT ARE YOU PLANNING, KAIBA?!

I'VE GOT THE ANTIDOTE FOR YOU, JONOUCHI!

AACK! HELP ME!
M-MASTER MOKUBA! WHAT IS IT!

DOOM
PENALTY GAME!!
I ACTUALLY LOST AT DUEL MONSTERS... ?!?!
Duel 27:
Project Start!!

AAAGGGHHHH!!
BA-DUMP
BA-DUMP
BA-DUMP
IS...IS THIS WHAT *DEATH* FEELS LIKE...?!!

Duel 27:
Project Start!

WSH
GASP ...
HFF

READ THIS WAY

YUGI... "DEATH-T" STARTS TODAY!

DO YOU FEEL BETTER, JONOUCHI?
YUP! ALL I NEEDED WAS A GOOD NIGHT'S SLEEP!

BUT I HATE STAYING AT KAIBA'S HOUSE! MAKES ME FEEL LIKE I OWE HIM A FAVOR!
I WONDER IF GRANDPA IS WORRIED ...
I WAS OUT ALL NIGHT WITHOUT CALLING HIM...

HEY YUGI!
WHAT'S WITH THIS "OPENING CEREMONY" THAT'S SUPPOSED TO BE TODAY?
DUNNO.
BUT I HAVE A BAD FEELING ABOUT IT!

I FEEL LIKE WE'RE IN JAIL ...
LIKE THEY'RE *GUARDING* US SO WE DON'T ESCAPE THE MANSION .....
AND THEY LOCKED US IN ...

SORRY TO KEEP YOU WAITING.
MASTER SETO WILL SEE YOU NOW.
!

TA DA
...!
GOOD TO SEE YOU, YUGI!
I'VE MISSED YOU SO MUCH!
GRIN

READ THIS WAY

CUT THE CRAP, KAIBA!
YOU FORCED US TO COME HERE! AND YOUR BROTHER ALMOST KILLED US!
AND YOU EXPECT US TO BE HAPPY TO SEE YOU?!

MOKUBA ...? THAT WAS BAD OF HIM ...
BUT BOYS WILL BE BOYS, YOU'LL HAVE TO FORGIVE HIS LITTLE GAMES.
YOU DON'T GET KILLED BY "LITTLE GAMES"!!

WHERE ARE YOU TAKING US, KAIBA?

HEH HEH ...
A PLACE YOU CAN ONLY DREAM OF!

WELL THEN ...
WE'RE WASTING TIME!
WE MUST LEAVE AT ONCE!

I CAN'T WAIT FOR YOU TO SEE THIS, YUGI!
HAVE A GOOD TRIP, MASTER SETO!

AS YOU KNOW, I OWN KAIBA CORPORATION ...
I HAD TO TAKE OVER WHEN MY FATHER, THE FOUNDER, PASSED AWAY SIX MONTHS AGO.

READ THIS WAY
BUT MY DREAM PROJECT IS FINALLY COMPLETE!
I'M SURE YOU'LL ENJOY IT AS MUCH AS I HAVE.
LOOK! YOU CAN SEE IT FROM HERE!
MY TOWER OF DREAMS THAT SOARS OVER DOMINO!!
TA-DUM
POP
POP
WOW! YOU BUILT THIS SKYSCRAPER, KAIBA?!!
!!
KAIBA LAND

THIS IS "KAIBA LAND"!

IT'S AN INDOOR AMUSEMENT PARK!!

WELL THEN, EVERYONE!

WE ARE OPEN!

WELCOME TO KAIBA LAND!!!

RUSH

YOU KILLED THE C.E.O.!

...!

YOU TOOK OVER KAIBA CORPORATION AND DROVE THE CEO, YOUR OWN FATHER, TO COMMIT SUICIDE...
YOU'RE THE DEVIL INCAR-NATE!

THROW HIM OUT!
YES SIR!
LET ME GO, DAMN IT!
HE'S THE DEVILLL!!

HE USED TO BE MY FATHER'S RIGHT-HAND MAN... BUT NOW HE'S A WORTHLESS HAS-BEEN.

THERE HAVE BEEN MANY RUMORS...
MY FATHER'S DEATH WAS A TRAGEDY, BUT I HAD NOTHING TO DO WITH IT.
I THINK MY FATHER WAS ABLE TO DIE IN PEACE KNOWING I WOULD TAKE OVER FOR HIM...

KAIBA LOOKS COMPLETELY DIFFERENT FROM BEFORE!
WHICH IS HIS TRUE FACE...?!

WELL THEN, YUGI!
LET ME SHOW YOU AROUND THE PARK!

THIS IS INTENSE! IT LOOKS JUST LIKE A REAL MONSTER!

RATTLE

AAAAGGGGH!!

THIS IS VIRTUAL REALITY?!

NO EXPENSE WAS SPARED ON KAIBA LAND. EVERYTHING IN THE PARK IS ON THE CUTTING EDGE OF TECHNOLOGY.

TRY OUR 3D SIMULATION RIDES!

YAAAAYYY
YEAHH! IT'S KAIBA!
WHAT THE... ?!
IT LOOKS LIKE AN ARENA!
DADADADA
THERE'S A CUBE IN THE MIDDLE...?!
DOO
KAI-BA!
KAI-BA!
THERE'S SOMEONE INSIDE IT!
AH...!!
THAT'S...!!
MY GRANDPA!!!

WHAT IN THE WORLD IS GRANDPA DOING HERE...?!

GRANDPA !!

!!

YUGI !

GRANDPA!

I CAN SEE YOUR LIPS MOVING, BUT I CAN'T HEAR ANYTHING!

...

...

NO ONE CAN BEAT KAIBA AT ANY GAME!
THAT'S WHAT MAKES HIM SO COOL!
YAAAYYY
YAAY KAIBA!
YYY
YUGI... ONCE YOU HUMILIATED ME BY DEFEATING ME AT DUEL MONSTERS! THE DAY HAS COME TO AVENGE THAT SHAME!
HWOOOOO RRRA
YOU WILL REPAY ME WITH YOUR DEATH!
GRANDPA!
I KNEW HE WAS A JERK! WHAT'S HE UP TO?!

FOR YOUR ENTERTAINMENT, YOU WILL NOW WITNESS A MATCH OF THE WORLD'S #1 COLLECTIBLE CARD GAME, "DUEL MONSTERS"!

MY CHALLENGER IS THIS GENTLEMAN, SUGOROKU MUTOU!

HE IS SAID TO BE A GAME MASTER WHO HAS NEVER LOST A DUEL!

DUEL MONSTERS ?!

GRANDPA AND KAIBA ?!

WA HA HA! THAT OLD GUY IS CHALLENGING KAIBA?!

RM RM

THERE'S NO WAY HE CAN WIN!

YUGI... I WILL WIN!

GRANDPA LOOKS SERIOUS !

B-BUMP B-BUMP

GAME START!!!
INCIDENTALLY, OLD MAN, THIS CUBE IS A HIGH-TECH PRODUCT MADE ESPECIALLY FOR THIS GAME...
IT MAY BE HARD ON SOMEONE OF YOUR ADVANCED AGE...
?
HEH HEH... WELL, LET ME JUST SHOW YOU. WHEN I PLACE THIS CARD ON THE FIELD.....
...A MICRO-CHIP IN THE CARD IS ACTI-VATED AND...
Hitotsu-Me Giant
ATK/1200
DEF/1000
LOOM
YIPE!!
...THE FOUR WALLS OF THE CUBE PROJECT THE CARD AS A THREE DIMENSIONAL IMAGE!
THIS IS A VIRTUAL SIMULA-TION BOX MADE JUST FOR DUELS!
A-AMAZING ...!!
IT'S LIKE A REAL CYCLOPS ATTACKING ME!

HOBBIT ATTACK !
YOU LOSE 500 LIFE POINTS, KAIBA.

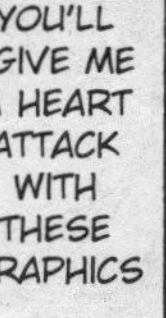
YOU'LL GIVE ME A HEART ATTACK WITH THESE GRAPHICS ...
IT'S MY TURN NOW ...

SPELL CARD!
DEFENSE !

MHEH HEH... I'VE RECREATED MY GAME WITH YUGI USING VIRTUAL REALITY! MY MONEY CAN BUY POWERS JUST LIKE HIS!

WOW, THAT OLD GUY'S PRETTY GOOD!
DOESN'T MATTER! HE CAN'T BEAT KAIBA!

I'M NOT OUT YET...

AND YOU LOSE 300 POINTS... OLD MAN.
NOW I'M AHEAD .....

B-BUMP
B-BUMP

ROOAAR
URG ...

THIS IS AN AMAZING GAME! THEY BOTH PLAY AT SUCH A HIGH LEVEL!

GOOD LUCK, GRANDPA !

HO HO...THIS YOUNG MAN IS PRETTY GOOD...EVEN IF HE DOESN'T KNOW HOW TO USE SPELL CARDS PROPERLY ...

...

IT'S OVER, KAIBA.
I WIN!

I'VE DRAWN THE BLUE-EYES WHITE DRAGON!
BAM
WHEN I PUT THIS CARD DOWN, IT'S GAME OVER!
ATK/3000
ATK/2500

!

HO HO ...

THEN I...
...CHOOSE TO PLAY THIS CARD.

...!!

AND ON THE NEXT TURN...

!!
IT CAN'T BE...

AND ON THE TURN AFTER THAT...
HEH HEH HEH ...
I... I LOSE !!
THREE BLUE-EYES WHITE DRAGON CARDS!!

I USED MY WEALTH TO FORCE THEM TO BANKRUPTCY, OR I MADE DEALS WITH THE MAFIA ...
OF COURSE, NONE OF THEM AGREED WHEN I TOLD THEM TO HAND IT OVER... SO I USED A BIT OF FORCE...
ONE OF THEM EVEN COMMITTED *SUICIDE!*

OF COURSE, THEY ARE IN THE HANDS OF FANATIC COLLECTORS AROUND THE WORLD. I SEARCHED THEM OUT...
MHEH HEH...ONLY FOUR COPIES OF THE "BLUE-EYES WHITE DRAGON" ARE KNOWN TO EXIST.
ONE IN AMERICA, ONE IN GERMANY, ONE IN HONG KONG...
AND *YOU,* OLD MAN!

TH-... THIS YOUNG MAN... HOW DID HE GET HIS HANDS ON THESE ULTRA RARE CARDS...

GRANDPA LOST...!!

NO WAY ...

WHAT A TERRIBLE YOUNG MAN!!
...!!

WA HA HA HA HA!! NOW I'M THE ONLY ONE WITH THIS CARD IN THE ENTIRE WORLD!

MY BLUE-EYES WHITE DRAGON ...!!

THIS IS YOUR PUNISHMENT FOR LOSING TO ME! AND TO YOUR CARD FOR BETRAYING ME LAST TIME!
RIP
RIP
RIP

AND NOW, OLD MAN! I'LL GIVE YOU A "PENALTY GAME"!
GG GG GG
YIEEEEEE!!
YOU'LL "KNOW DEATH" BY VIRTUAL REALITY!!!
BWA HA HA HA HA HA HA!

GWAAAGGGHHHH!
BBMP
BBB
GRANDPA!
GRANDPA!!
RRMMMBB
KAIBA'S AWESOME!
YAY KAIBA!
Y-IEEEEE!
KAIBA!! LET MY GRANDPA OUT OF THAT BOX!!
HEH HEH...
WE'VE DONE HUMAN EXPERIMENTS IN THAT SIMULATOR.
WE DISCOVERED THAT THE AVERAGE PERSON GOES INSANE IN ABOUT 10 MINUTES.
IF WE DON'T STOP IT SOON, YOUR GRANDFATHER WILL BE DESTROYED...

!!

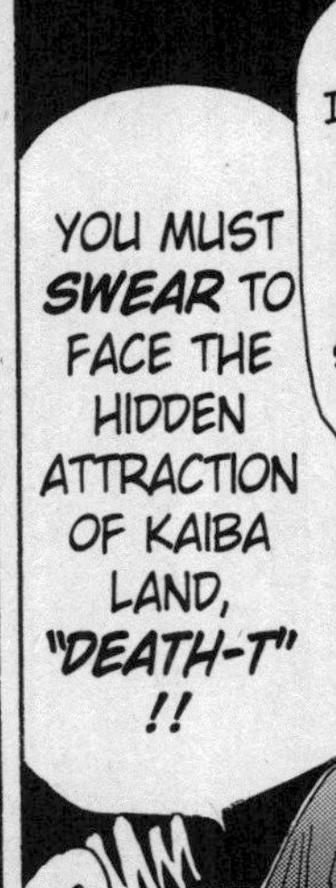
I HAVE ONE CONDITION FOR STOPPING THE SIMULATOR!
YOU MUST **SWEAR** TO FACE THE HIDDEN ATTRACTION OF KAIBA LAND, "DEATH-T"!!
RMM RMM
RMM

THE THEME PARK OF DEATH THAT I BUILT TO EXACT MY REVENGE ON YOU!!

DA DA DOOM
THEME PARK OF DEATH!!!

Duel 28: Arena #1

GGRRRM
YIIEEEE!!!
B-BMP
B-BMP
B-BMP
B-BMP
B-BMP
B-BMP
GYAAAGHHH!
GRANDPA!
GRANDPA!!

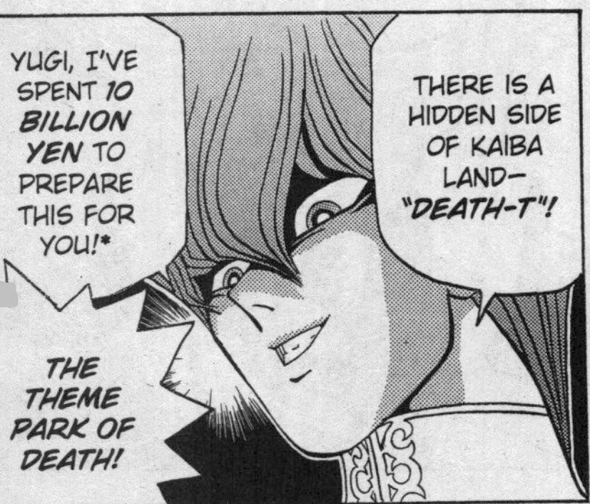

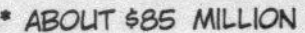
* ABOUT $85 MILLION

YUGI!

I'LL STOP THAT SIMULATOR IF YOU SWEAR TO FACE "DEATH-T"!

GWOOO

!!

I UNDER-
STAND!!
I'LL FACE
"DEATH-
T"!!

HEH
HEH
...

STOP
THE
SIMULATOR
!!
YESSIR
!

RMMMB

WHEEZE
GASP

GRANDPA!
GRANDPA,
ARE YOU
ALL
RIGHT?!
GASP
GASP

GASP
...
WHEEZE
...
GRANDPA!

Y-... YUGI ...

I'M SORRY... I LOST...

GRANDPA !!

HE... HE'S A TERRIBLE YOUNG MAN ...

HE'LL DO ANYTHING TO WIN A GAME... EVEN... TAKING A PERSON'S LIFE.....

GRANDPA, DON'T TALK ...!

GASP

YUGI ...

TH-... THESE ARE THE CARDS I USED IN MY DUEL ...

I LOST, BUT TO ME, THESE CARDS ARE MY *SOUL*...

... TAKE THEM ...

GRANDPA ...!

YUGI ...

I KNOW YOU CAN DEFEAT THAT YOUNG MAN!!

!!

GASP GASP

YUGI!
I CALLED THE AMBULANCE!
QUICK, GET YOUR GRANDPA...!

I'M SORRY, GRANDPA... I CAN'T GO WITH YOU...

GRANDPA!!
CLENCH

I GOT IT, GRANDPA!
I'LL BEAT HIM!

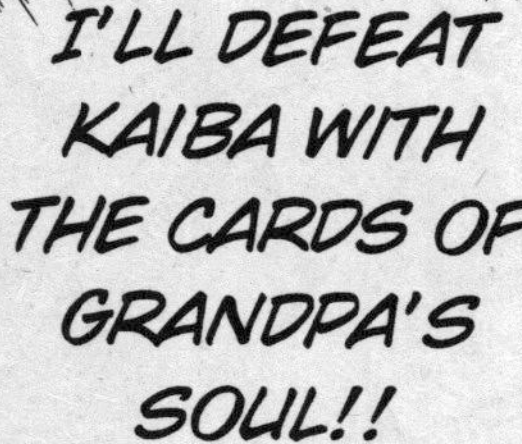
I'LL DEFEAT KAIBA WITH THE CARDS OF GRANDPA'S SOUL!!

HA HA HA HA HA....YUGI! I SEE YOU HOLDING YOUR LOSER GRANDFATHER'S CARDS. YOU THINK YOU CAN DEFEAT ME WITH THOSE?!
DOOM

I PROMISED MY GRANDPA!
I'LL BEAT YOU WITH THESE CARDS!

OH, YOU WILL, WILL YOU?
I HAVE THREE OF THE MOST POWERFUL CARDS ON EARTH, THE BLUE-EYES WHITE DRAGON!
TAKE A GOOD LOOK!
NOW YOU DON'T EVEN HAVE ONE BLUE-EYES IN YOUR DECK!!

I KNOW! YOU TORE UP GRANDPA'S BLUE-EYES WHITE DRAGON, YOU COWARD!
THE CARD HE LOVED THE MOST...THE CARD OF GRANDPA'S HEART!

HEH HEH... DON'T WORRY.
A REMATCH WITH YOU IS WHAT I'VE WANTED FROM THE BEGINNING.
MHEH HEH... AND THIS TIME, THE PROBABILITY OF MY WINNING IS OVER 99%.....

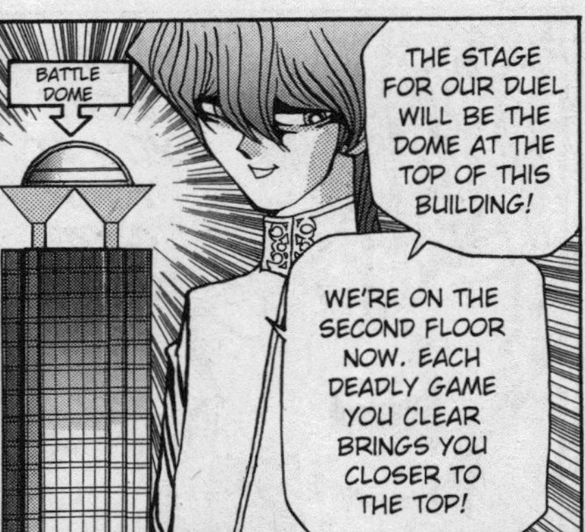
THE STAGE FOR OUR DUEL WILL BE THE DOME AT THE TOP OF THIS BUILDING!
BATTLE DOME
WE'RE ON THE SECOND FLOOR NOW. EACH DEADLY GAME YOU CLEAR BRINGS YOU CLOSER TO THE TOP!

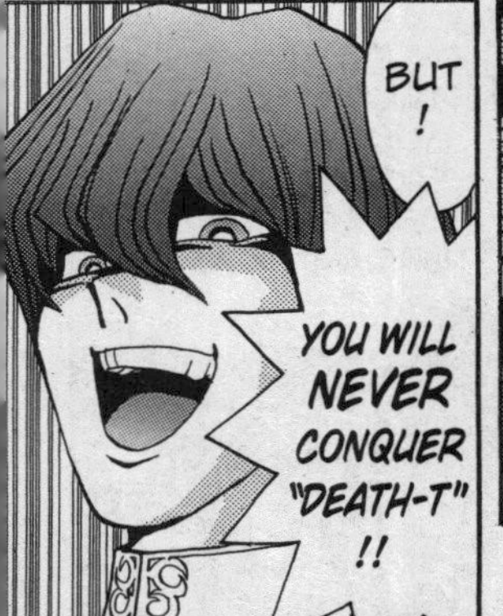
BUT!
YOU WILL NEVER CONQUER "DEATH-T"!!

KAIBA! COUNT ME IN TOO! I'M NOT LETTING YUGI GO ALONE!

YUGI! JONOUCHI !!

HONDA !!

COUNT ME IN, YUGI! YOU'RE NOT GOING IN THERE WITHOUT ME!

WE WERE IN THE AUDIENCE WHEN THINGS STARTED GETTING WEIRD AND YOU GUYS SHOWED UP!
GOOD THING I WAS HERE—YOU LOOK LIKE YOU NEED A HAND!

HONDA! WHAT'S WITH THE KID ON YOUR BACK?!
AH, THIS THING?
MY SISTER MADE ME BABYSIT HER KID.
HE KEPT WHINING TO GO TO KAIBA LAND...
GAAA ...

YAAY KAIBA! KAIBA'S GONNA WIN!
GOO
GAAH
!!

HONDA, YOU'RE SO...

HONDA ... JONOUCHI ...
YOU'RE DOING ALL THIS FOR ME... THANKS GUYS ...

HEY, DON'T MAKE HIM CRY, HONDA!
BAP
SHADDUP YA LITTLE BRAT!
WAAH! WAAH! WAA-AAA-AAAH!

JUST SHUT UP!
I'LL TELL MOMMY!
THAT HURT, HIROTO!

HMPH.

TA-DA

SO LET'S START THE GAME ALREADY !!

MHEH HEH HEH ...

FINE THEN... I'LL BURY YOU ALL IN THE SAME GRAVE!

RRRMMMBBB
PSSHT
DEATH T
DANGER

RRRMMM
BBMP
BBMP
WHAT HORRIBLE THINGS ARE WAITING FOR ME BEHIND THOSE DOORS...?

STEP THROUGH THE GATE, YUGI!
WE'RE ALL WAITING FOR YOU!

WHOA! WHAT'S GOING ON?!
THAT MUST GO TO A WHOLE OTHER THEME PARK THAT ONLY SPECIAL GUESTS CAN GET INTO!
THEY'RE SO LUCKY!
YAAY KAIBA! LET US GO TOO!

...

YUGI! I'LL BE WAITING FOR YOU AT THE TOP!
HA HA HA HA HA!

GA
SHUNK

...!
THERE'S NO TURNING BACK...

HEY... THIS FEELS CREEPY ...
AND IT'S DARK ....
YOU'RE NOT *SCARED*, ARE YOU, JONOUCHI?
WNGWN GWNG
WNG

HOW FAR DOES THIS DAMN TUNNEL GO...
WHERE'S THE STUPID GAME!?

IS THIS THE FIRST GAME?!
"DEATH-T ONE" ...!!

DRRNNNNBB
CAUTION!
DEATH T-1

CLANK
THE DOOR OPENED!

EMERGENCY!
BZZT
EMERGENCY!
BZZT
WHAT'S GOING ON?!

PLEASE HELP ME!!
HUH ?!

!!

ANZU!?!

WHAAA?!

WHAT ARE *YOU* DOING HERE?!
THAT'S *MY* LINE!

I STARTED WORKING AT THIS AMUSEMENT PARK TODAY!
I LOST MY JOB AT BURGER WORLD WHEN I PUNCHED OUT THIS CUSTOMER WHO TOUCHED MY BUTT.
.....
SO I APPLIED AT KAIBA LAND! THEY PUT ME IN THIS COSTUME AND MADE ME THE GUIDE FOR THIS GAME.

YOU GUYS SURPRISED ME!
SO, WHY DID YOU YELL "HELP"?

IT'S AN *ACT!* PART OF THIS GAME!
AFTER THAT, I SAY THIS LINE TO THE CUSTOMERS ...!

"THE ENEMY IS ABOUT TO BLOW UP THIS SPACE STATION"!
"YOU ARE THE ONLY ONES WHO CAN SAVE IT!"
"PUT ON YOUR CYBER-VESTS AND DEFEAT THE INTRUDERS WITH YOUR LASER GUNS!"

TA DA

YEAH! LOOKING GOOD!

OKAY! THE GAME IS A SHOOTING MATCH, THREE AGAINST THREE!

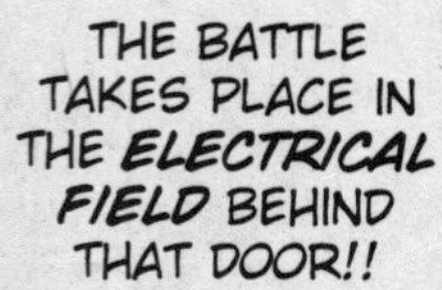

READ THIS WAY

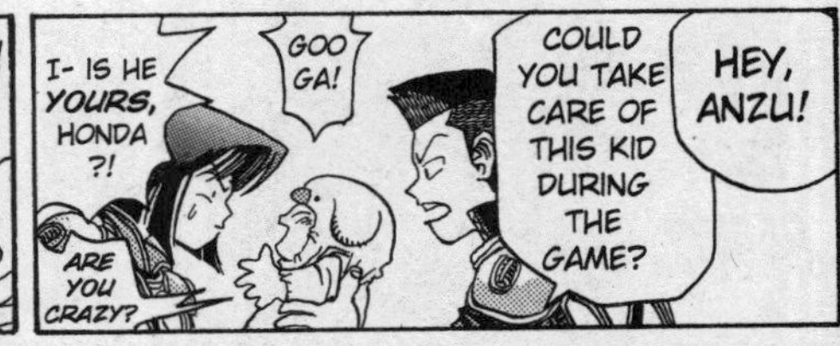

WHO THE HELL HIRED THAT GIRL!?
SHE'S ONE OF THEIR FRIENDS!
MY APOLOGIES, SIR.

AH, WELL ...

DEATH T-1, STARDUST SHOOTOUT! THEY'VE ENTERED THE ELECTRICAL FIELD!
IS OUR TEAM READY?

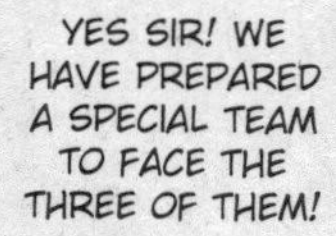
YES SIR! WE HAVE PREPARED A SPECIAL TEAM TO FACE THE THREE OF THEM!

EACH ONE IS A PRO IN HIS FIELD!

HEH HEH ...

• NAME UNKNOWN
• NATIONALITY: UNKNOWN
• ASSASSIN
• TARGETS STILL LIVING: 0%

• BOB MCGUIRE
• NATIONALITY: AMERICAN
• FORMER SWAT TEAM LEADER
• LONG DISTANCE SNIPER

• JOHNNY GAYLE
• NATIONALITY: AMERICAN
• FORMER GREEN BERET COMMANDER
• SPECIALTY: GUERRILLA WARFARE

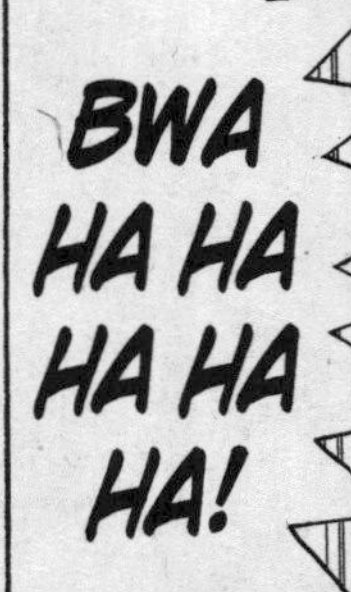

GOGOGOHHHHH

I'M GONNA ENJOY THIS GAME!

HEH HEH ...

HEH HEH ...SURE WAS NICE OF KAIBA BOY TO PUT A BOUNTY ON THEIR HEADS!

$10,000 EACH! PIECE OF CAKE!

OF COURSE, I'LL FINISH ALL THREE ON MY OWN...

DOOM

AWRIGHT! LET'S DO IT!

RPP

RMM

RMM

GAME START !!

Duel 29:
Shooting Stardust

BADUM

BADUM

DADA

STARDUST SHOOTOUT RULES

- THIS SHOOTING GAME IS FOR TWO TEAMS OF THREE PEOPLE.
- PLAYERS AIM FOR THE SENSOR ON THE LEFT SIDE OF THEIR OPPONENTS' CYBER-VEST (THE HEART). IF THE SENSOR IS HIT, THAT PERSON LOSES AND MUST LEAVE THE GAME.
- THE FIRST TEAM TO DEFEAT ALL THE MEMBERS OF THE OPPOSING TEAM WINS.

DOOM

• NAME & NATIONALITY UNKNOWN

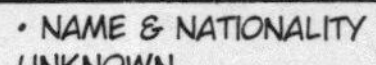

WELCOME TO DEATH T-1, THE FIRST GAME OF THE THEME PARK!
HELLO AGAIN, YUGI!

BING!
KAIBA!

VMMMM
KAIBA
INFORMATIO
WELCOME TO KAIBA INFORMATION!

IF YOU'RE LUCKY, YOU'LL DIE IN A BLAZE OF GLORY LIKE A *SHOOTING STAR* ACROSS THE SKY!

THE THREE ENEMIES YOU ARE ABOUT TO FACE ARE *MERCENARIES* I'VE HIRED ESPECIALLY FOR THIS GAME!

MMEH HEH HEH...
THE GUNS YOU'VE BEEN GIVEN ARE MERE *TOYS*, YUGI...
BUT WHAT YOU DON'T KNOW IS, THE MERCENARIES HAVE *REAL LASERS!* WHEN THEY HIT THE SENSOR ON YOUR CYBER-VEST, YOU'LL BE SHOCKED TO DEATH WITH A MILLION VOLTS...

BZZN
ENJOY YOUR LAST GAME.

YOUR GAMES SUCK! WE'RE GONNA MAKE IT TO THE TOP!

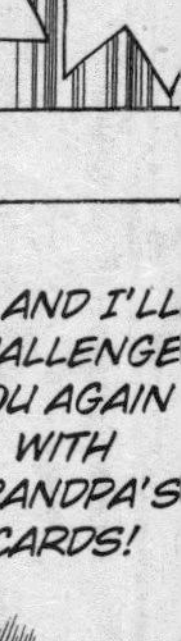
LISTEN UP, BOWL HEAD!

I PROMISE, KAIBA!
...AND I'LL CHALLENGE YOU AGAIN WITH GRANDPA'S CARDS!

AWRIGHT! CONCENTRATE, EVERYONE!
KAIBA WILL DO *ANYTHING* TO WIN! THE ENEMY WILL BE TOUGH!
NO PROBLEM! I'M AN ACE WITH MODEL GUNS!
WHEN I WAS A LITTLE KID, I COULD HIT A 100-YEN PIECE WITH A BB GUN AT 50 FEET!
GAME START!
DASH

SHF

BA DUM

BRRMM
HOW SHOULD WE DEAL WITH THOSE KIDS?!

I'M THE EXPERT AT GUERRILLA WARFARE! LEAVE IT TO ME!
I'LL PULL A *SURPRISE ATTACK* AND FINISH THEM IN AN INSTANT!

THEY'RE AMATEURS. THEY'LL BE SCARED STIFF WHEN I JUMP RIGHT OUT IN FRONT OF THEM.
A GAME LIKE THIS IS NOTHING TO SOMEONE WITH *REAL COMBAT* EXPERIENCE!

SHF

SHEE-OOT... SHOW-OFF WANTS THE BOUNTY ALL TO HISSELF!
HEH HEH ...

SULK

STAY STILL! LET *THEM* MAKE THE FIRST MOVE!
IDIOT!
WHISPER
WHISPER
WHISPER

HEY! WHAT ARE WE WAITING AROUND HERE FOR?
WHISPER
WHISPER

JUMP

YEAH! NOW I'VE GOT ROOM TO FIGHT!

TMP TMP TMP

HERE I COME!!!

JONOUCHI!??!

THAT MORON!

TMP TMP TMP

HUH...?!

FOUND ONE!
WHAT!!??
BAM
HE THOUGHT UP AN ATTACK EVEN MORE SURPRISING THAN MINE!!!
HA HA HA!
BUT I'M THE ONE WITH WEAPONS TRAINING!
I CAN DRAW A BEAD FIRST!
DIE!!!
THWOK
URGH!

... THAT IDIOT ...
HE DID IT!
HE GOT ONE OF THEM...
MY WAY IS FASTER!
NO WAY! THEY GOT JOHNNY!
!!
K-KAMI-KAZE BOY...

I'LL FINISH THEM OFF!

ZAPOW

HE'S IN MY SIGHTS...

NOW!

BING

HUH...?!

THAT'S WEIRD...I HIT HIM DEAD ON...

ZAP ZAP

NO PROBLEMO!

JONOUCHI, ARE YOU OKAY?

I'LL HELP TOO!

ZAPOW

ZAPOW

OW
...
FZZ
WH-WHAT THE?! I GOT SHOCKED!

ZAP
ZAP ZAP
TMP TMP TMP

MAN, THIS IS BAD!
IF THEY COME ANY CLOSER, I WON'T BE ABLE TO KEEP COVERING THE SENSOR ON MY CHEST!

@#%&!!!
ZADOW
ZADOW
AARGH! I KEEP MISSING!

YUGI!
JONOUCHI!
WE HAVE TO PULL BACK!
WHAT?! RUN AWAY?!
THERE'S SOMETHING WRONG WITH THIS GAME!!

WOW! THE GUYS GOT ONE OF THE ENEMY, SO THEY'RE AHEAD!

UMFF UMM ...

READ THIS WAY

HEY, ANZU, BABY!
LET'S DITCH THOSE GUYS AND GO FOR A DATE IN THE PARK!
WHAAAA?!!

MY NAME?
I'M JOHJI! GOOD TO MEET YOU!
Y'KNOW, THERE'S THIS COOL MILK STAND IN THE PARK...
WHATCHA THINK...?

YOU ACT AWFULLY MATURE FOR A BABY.
WHAT WAS YOUR NAME AGAIN?

BANG
HEY, HONDA! WHY ARE WE RUNNING AWAY?! IT'S NOT COOL TO SHOW YOUR BACK TO THE ENEMY!
WAH!

YOU GUYS, YOU CAN'T LEAVE IN THE MIDDLE OF THE GAME!
WHAT'S WRONG, HONDA?

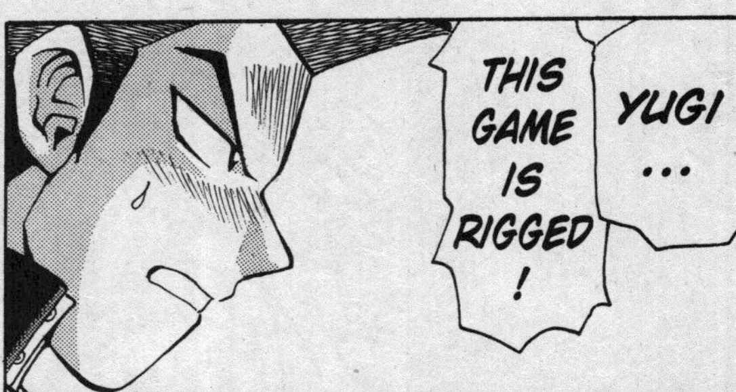
YUGI...
THIS GAME IS RIGGED!

WHAT...?!

OUR GUNS ARE USELESS!

THERE'S NO WAY WE CAN WIN!

WHAT?!

WHAT A LOUSY TRICK... AND IT'S ALL BECAUSE OF KAIBA! THAT SONOVA-

GRRR...

YOU BIG BULLY! NOT ONLY DO YOU INTERRUPT MY TIME ALONE WITH ANZU--

--NOW YOU'RE TALKING BAD ABOUT KAIBA!

I WON'T LET YOU GET AWAY WITH IT!!

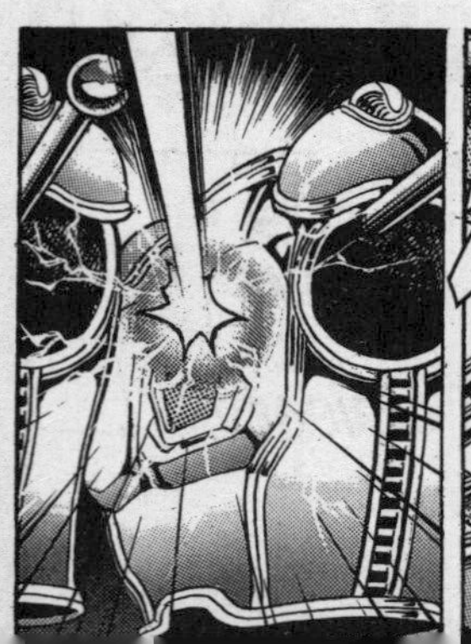

WHAT THE ...?!!
THERE WAS AN ELECTRIC SHOCK WHEN THE LASER HIT THE SENSOR ON THAT SPARE VEST!
GIMME THAT GUN, JOHJI!
WAH!
I KNEW IT!
BRRRR
IF THAT HAD BEEN ONE OF US...
ANZU'S GUN AND OUR GUNS LOOK THE SAME, BUT THEY'RE BUILT COMPLETELY DIFFERENT!
TA

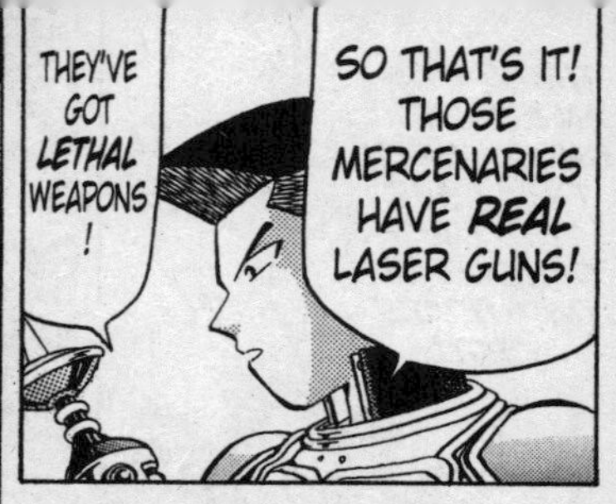
SO THAT'S IT! THOSE MERCENARIES HAVE **REAL** LASER GUNS!
THEY'VE GOT **LETHAL** WEAPONS!

CURSE YOU,
KAIBA!
IS THIS COWARDLY KILLING GAME PART OF YOUR THEME PARK OF DEATH??

KAIBA DIDN'T KNOW ANZU WAS OUR FRIEND WHEN HE HIRED HER AND GAVE HER THAT GUN.
BDRRR

THAT'S IT! I QUIT!

KAIBA DIDN'T PREDICT THIS!
BUT NOW WE HAVE AT LEAST **ONE** GUN WE CAN FACE THEM WITH!

THERE ARE ONLY TWO ENEMIES LEFT, BUT THEY'RE BOTH PROS.
WHAT CAN WE DO WITH ONE GUN.....?
I'LL DO ANOTHER SURPRISE ATTACK!
IDIOT! THAT TRICK WON'T WORK AGAIN!
FIRST TIME WAS A MIRACLE!

SHUT UP! KAIBA'S THE GREATEST! YOU GUYS BETTER STOP SAYING BAD THINGS ABOUT HIM!
I'D LIKE TO SHOOT **YOU** WITH THE GUN!
!
SULK

LEAVE THIS TO ME!

...'CAUSE IT'S ***TWO 'GAINST ONE!*** YEW DON'T STAND A CHANCE ON YER OWN!

EH?

CLANK

YEAH. WHUT HE MEANS IS, OL' KAIBA BOY TOLD US TO KILL YEW!
SO SAY YER PRAYERS! HEH HEH HEH...

BUT I'M AFRAID IT'S NO USE.

SO YEW CHICKENED OUT?! YEW GONNA SURRENDER?!
WA HA HA HA HA HA HA!!!

IT'S EXECUTION TIME!
TADA
NYEE HEE HEE ...
NOW !!

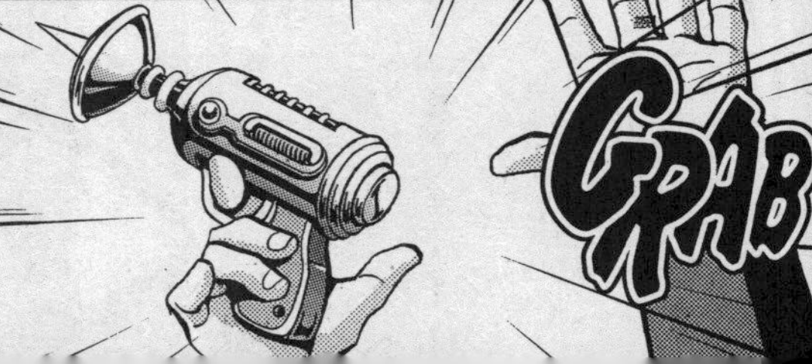

ZAP

ZAPP

HAVEN'T YOU EVER WATCHED ANY ***WESTERNS?*** THE ***HERO*** IS ALWAYS THE ONE WHO SAYS THE ***LEAST!***

GWAAAGGGHH!

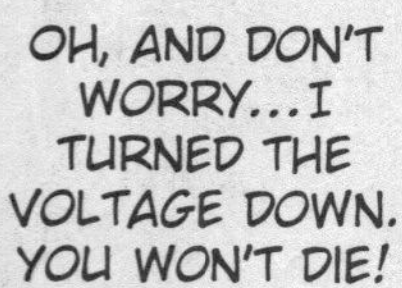

HE DID IT!
YAY HONDA!!

HEY, HIROTO!
I HELPED YOU OUT, SO DON'T FORGET YOUR PROMISE!
......

WHAAAT?! YOU WANT ME TO TAKE A BATH WITH THAT LITTLE PERV!?
PLEASE, ANZU! I'M BEGGING YOU!
GRIN GRIN
GOO GA! WHEE!

AWRIGHT! LET'S GET OUT OF HERE!
NO WAY!
YOU'VE GOT TO!
YUP!

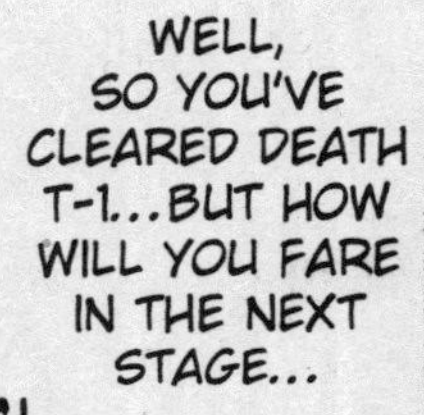
WELL, SO YOU'VE CLEARED DEATH T-1...BUT HOW WILL YOU FARE IN THE NEXT STAGE...

YUGI?

Duel 30:
Don't Make a Sound!

YEAH! WE- ARE- THE- CHAMPIONS!
BAM
BA
BRING ON STAGE TWO!

HOLD ON A MINUTE!
WHY AM I CARRYING THIS BRAT?!

SORRY, ANZU!
JOHJI CRIES IF HE'S HELD BY ANYONE ELSE!
THIS IS YOUR FAULT, SO SHUT UP!

UMMM MMMM MMMM ...
MMM, ANZU ...♡
....

GRRR

ANYWAY!
NO MATTER WHAT IT IS, WE CAN BEAT IT!!

YUP!
YOU GOT IT!

LET'S GO!

MMEH HEH...TH FOOLS!
ACTING SO *PROUD* BECAUSE THEY CLEARED DEATH T-1!
THEY HAVE NO *IDEA* HOW HARD THE NEXT GAME IS...

BUT THEY'RE STARTING TO LOOK LIKE A WORTHY ENEMY.
I SPENT A LOT TO BUILD THIS THEME PARK FOR YUGI...MY MONUMENT TO MY REVENGE...
I NEED TO GET MY MONEY'S WORTH OUT OF HIM.

YUGI AND HIS FRIENDS ARE LEAVING THE "SPACE ZONE," DEATH T-1.
ESTI-MATED TIME OF ARRIVAL IN ZONE TWO: FIVE SECONDS.

MM HMM ...
I WONDER ...

...HOW WILL THEY DO IN DEATH T-2, THE "*HORROR ZONE*"?
MMEH HEH HEH...

!!

IS THIS IT... ?
GWOOOOOO
DEATH-T 2
"DEATH T-2" !?!?

READ THIS WAY

ANYWAY, LET'S KEEP MOVING!
YUP!

ANZU! YOU GO FIRST!
WHAT HAPPENED TO ALL THAT COURAGE YOU JUST HAD?

I... UH...
I JUST HATE THIS SORT OF THING, ALRIGHT?

WELCOME TO THE HORROR ZONE...
BA DUM
YEEP!

CACKLE CACKLE CACKLE CACKLE...
OOOOOOOOO
GYAAAHHHH!

WELL WELL...
IF THIS SCARES YOU, YOU WON'T SURVIVE THE NEXT RIDE... CACKLE CACKLE...
I W-WASN'T SCARED, JERK!
YOU JUST STAR-TLED ME!

I WILL BE YOUR GUIDE FOR THE NEXT ATTRACTION...
PLEASE FOLLOW ME...

HEY, HE'S THE BUTLER FROM KAIBA'S MANSION!
WHOA, YOU'RE RIGHT!
JERK

WHAT'S THIS WEIRD CAR ?!!!

THIS SEAT IS HARD ....
MY SEAT IS NICE AND SOFT!
MOMMY ...

IS EVERYONE SEATED?

YEEK !
POP
WHAT THE-- ?!!

KACHAK
HUH ?!

CACKLE CACKLE ...

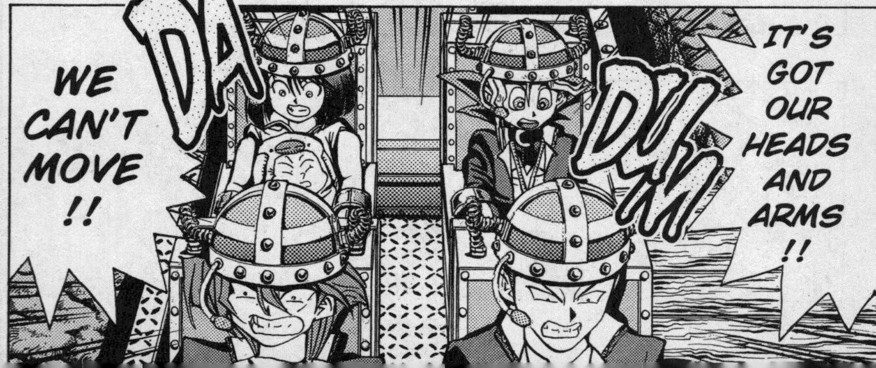
WE CAN'T MOVE !!
DA
DUM
IT'S GOT OUR HEADS AND ARMS !!

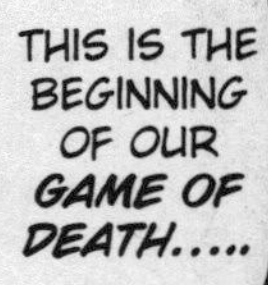
THIS IS THE BEGINNING OF OUR GAME OF DEATH.....

CACKLE CACKLE ...

HEY YOU !!
WHAT ARE YOU PLANNING TO DO WITH US?!

A GAME OF DEATH !!?
RUMBLE

FIRST LET ME TELL YOU WHERE THIS RIDE LEADS...
IT LEADS TO THE MURDERER'S MANSION ...
ONLY IN A THEME PARK OF DEATH CAN AN ATTRACTION OF SUCH REFINED TERROR BE POSSIBLE!

THE MURDERER'S MANSION ?!!
BADUM

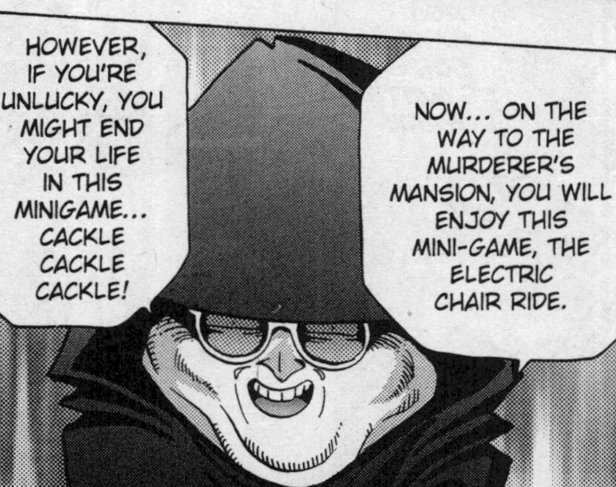
NOW... ON THE WAY TO THE MURDERER'S MANSION, YOU WILL ENJOY THIS MINI-GAME, THE ELECTRIC CHAIR RIDE.
HOWEVER, IF YOU'RE UNLUCKY, YOU MIGHT END YOUR LIFE IN THIS MINIGAME... CACKLE CACKLE CACKLE!

THE ELECTRIC CHAIR RIDE?!!

LET ME EXPLAIN THE RULES OF THIS GAME...

AS YOU'VE GUESSED, THE CHAIRS YOU ARE SITTING IN ARE ELECTRIC CHAIRS...

THOSE ARE CERTIFIED WORKING ELECTRIC CHAIRS. THEY HAVE SENT MANY CRIMINALS TO THE NEXT WORLD!

RUMBLE

SOON WE WILL ENTER THE DARKNESS OF THE ELECTRIC CHAIR RIDE...

DURING THIS RIDE, NO MATTER WHAT YOU ENCOUNTER, YOU MUSTN'T MAKE A SOUND!

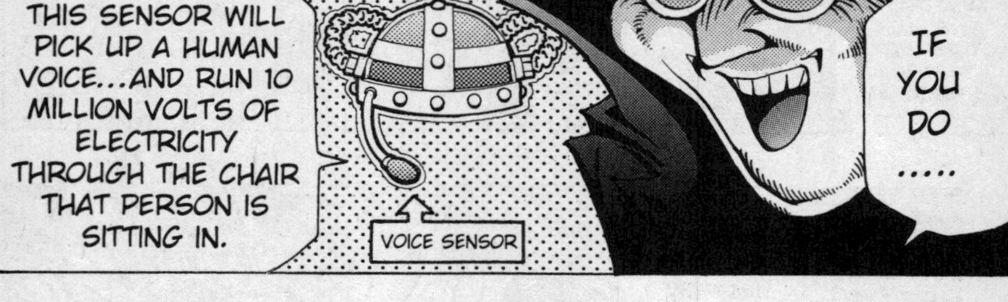

WH... WHAT ?!

BADUM

10 MILLION VOLTS !!?

THE ELECTRIC CHAIR RIDE OF "DEATH"?!

KAIBA! HOW CAN YOU BUILD SUCH A TERRIBLE RIDE!?

HEY, EVERYONE! DON'T MAKE A SOUND, NO MATTER WHAT!

IT'S MY FAULT. I GOT YOU INTO THIS ...
I'M SORRY, ANZU...
YUGI ...

WAAAAH! I WANNA GO HOME!!
ANZU ...

JONOUCHI, YOU'RE THE ONE MOST LIKELY TO SCREAM!
OH, YEAH ... RIGHT ...

NOW, HAVE YOU PREPARED YOUR-SELVES?!
~~~

AS THE GUIDE, I WILL PARTICIPATE IN THIS GAME AS WELL!!
KA CHIK
TO MAKE THINGS FAIR, I AM BOUND BY THE SAME RULES.
IF I MAKE A SOUND, THE ELECTRICITY WILL FLOW!

WOMEN FALL IN LOVE WITH THE GUYS WHO PROTECT THEM ON RIDES LIKE THIS!

GRAB
DON'T WORRY ANZU.
I'LL PROTECT YOU!

HEE HEE ...
GRR ...
~~~

HO HO HO... I'M NOT ONLY KAIBA'S BUTLER, I'M ALSO AN EXPERT IN ALL FORMS OF TORTURE.....
I KNOW THE BEST WAYS TO MAKE MY PRISONERS WRITHE IN PAIN..... THERE ARE MANY WAYS TO MAKE A VICTIM RAISE THEIR VOICE.
HO HO HO .....

CLATTER CLATTER CLATTER
DON'T MAKE A SOUND, EVERYONE!

GAME START !!
CREEEEE

IN CONTRAST, A GOOD TORTURER KNOWS HOW TO KEEP SILENT NO MATTER WHAT HAPPENS TO HIM. AND I DESIGNED THIS GAME! IT DOESN'T SCARE ME!

HEH HEH HEH... IN OTHER WORDS, THIS GAME IS MINE.....
I'LL DESTROY YOU FOUR IN THIS ROUND! HO HO HO...

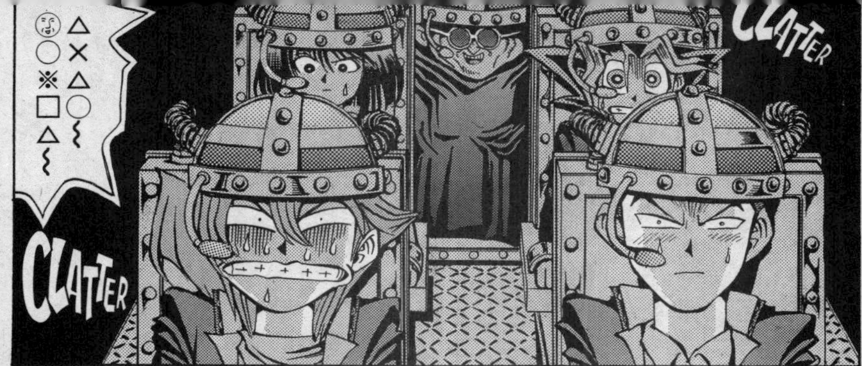
CLATTER
CLATTER

CLATTER

CLATTER

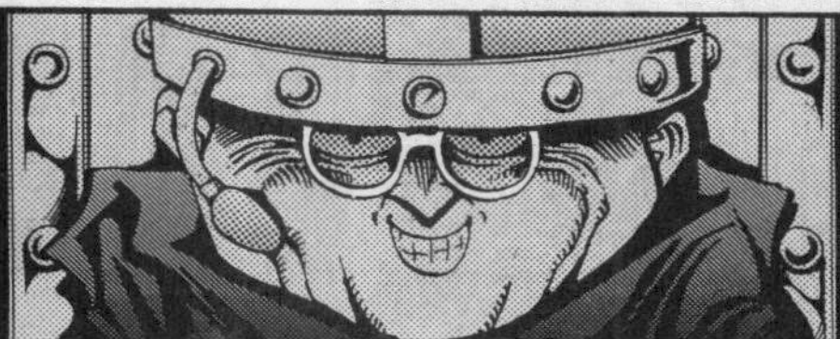
NOW WITNESS THE FIRST TERROR...
HO HO HO...

DO
OM
※×○△~
△×☺○△

CLATTER
CLATTER

IMPRESSIVE.... SO THIS LEVEL OF TERROR WON'T MAKE YOU SCREAM...
THEN HOW ABOUT THIS ....

PSSH

BEEP

KACHAK

AND THIS!!
BEEP
BOING
BA DUM
~~!!
TOUCH
FEELY
NOOO! STOP!

URK.....

AND HOW ABOUT...
BEEP
BEEP
THIS! HEE HEE HEE...
BEEP
SCREAM!

NNNN
HUFF
PSHH
TOUCH
NYAAAH
TOUCH
IT'S NO GOOD... I'M GONNA SCREAM...

ANZU!!
YOU CAN'T MAKE A SOUND!!

IT'S NO GOOD ......
AAHH ...

ANZU !!

CRUD! I DON'T CARE IF THE OTHER THREE ARE FRIED TO A CRISP...
BUT I HAVE TO SAVE ANZU!!

TADA
I'LL SHOW HER MY MANLINESS !!

JOHJI !!
I FORGOT! HE CAN MOVE AROUND!

WE'LL HAVE TO DEPEND ON HIM!

I'LL TORTURE YOU EVEN MORE!
I'LL MAKE YOU SCREAM !

BWA HA HA!

I'LL USE MY SPECIAL ATTACK !!

THIS IS THE END!!
BEEP

DOOM
GA GA
WHA ...!!
WHEN DID THIS KID GET ON MY LAP...?!

EH ...?

WH-WHAT THE... ?!

GO TO HELL... BABY!

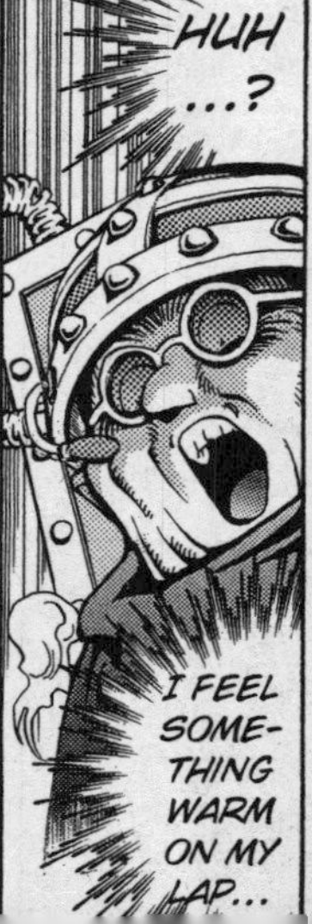
HUH ...?
I FEEL SOME-THING WARM ON MY LAP...

TH... THIS SMELL .....!
HE DIDN'T ...!!
STINK

ZZZZT
ZZT
UURRGGHHHH!!!
BAM
UCK
...

WOW! HE DEFEATED THE BUTLER BY HIMSELF ...!
JOHJI'S AWESOME!

YOU'LL BE ALL RIGHT NOW, ANZU!
EH HEH HEH ...

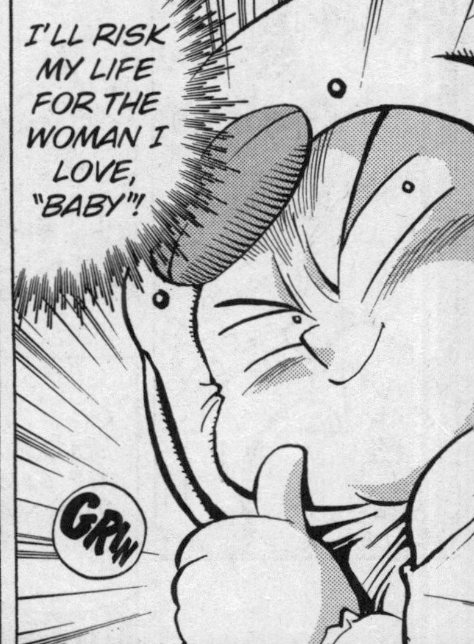
I'LL RISK MY LIFE FOR THE WOMAN I LOVE, "BABY"!
GRW

READ THIS WAY

HUH ?!

WE'RE HERE!

THIS IS THE NEXT GAME!

GNOOOO

I CAN'T *STAND* IT...

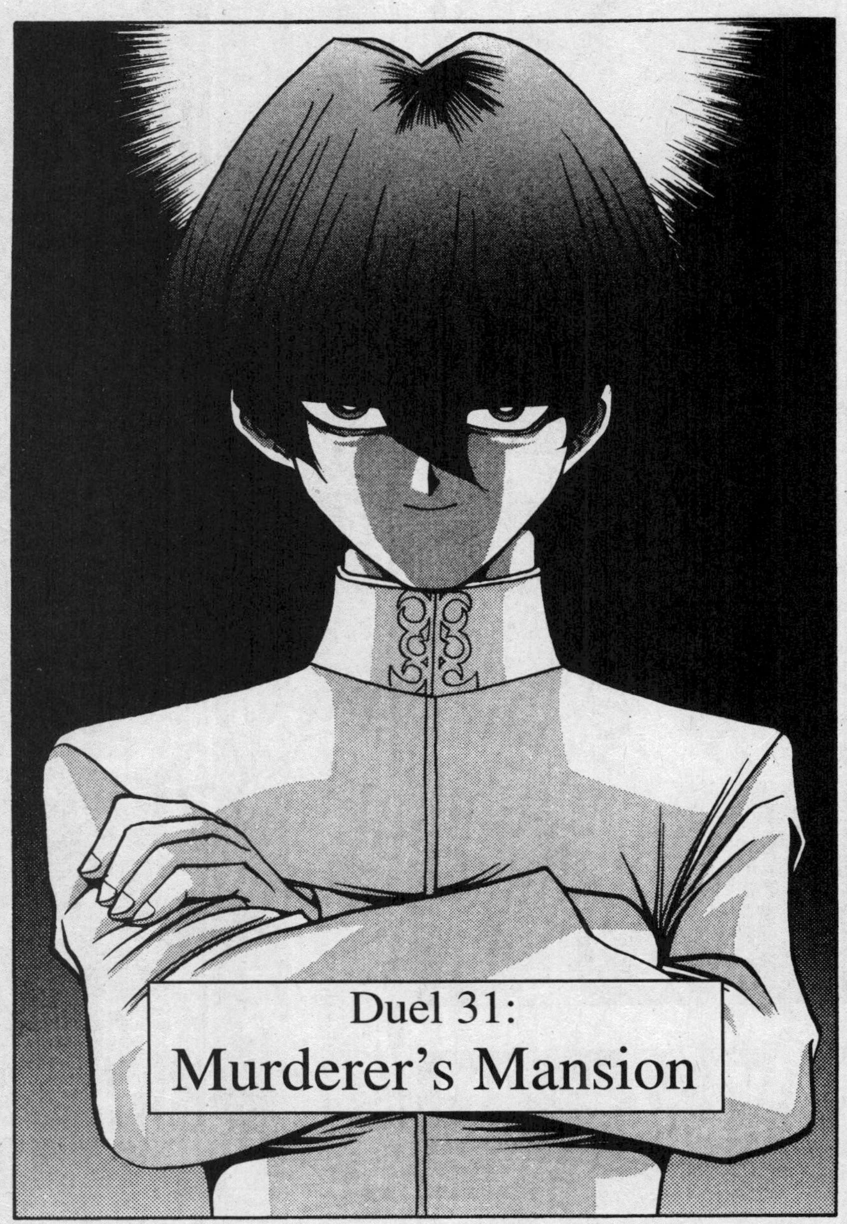
Duel 31:
Murderer's Mansion

HWOOOOO

THIS IS THE MURDERER'S MANSION?!!
YECH! CREEPY!

THIS IS THE NEXT GAME!!
KAIBA... WHAT KIND OF TRAPS HAVE YOU SET FOR US HERE?!

BADUM
!

BADUM
GASP!
BADUM

SOMETHING'S VIBRATING IN MY POCKET ...!!
BADUM

WHAT'S THIS ...?!
BADUM
BADUM
BADUM!!

I FEEL A HEARTBEAT FROM GRANDPA'S CARDS!!
BADUM
GASP!

BADUM
GRANDP...

WHAT'S UP, YUGI?!
IS SOMETHING WRONG?

THESE CARDS ARE TELLING ME...!
GRANDPA IS IN CRITICAL CONDITION!
!!
WH-WHAT DO YOU MEAN?!

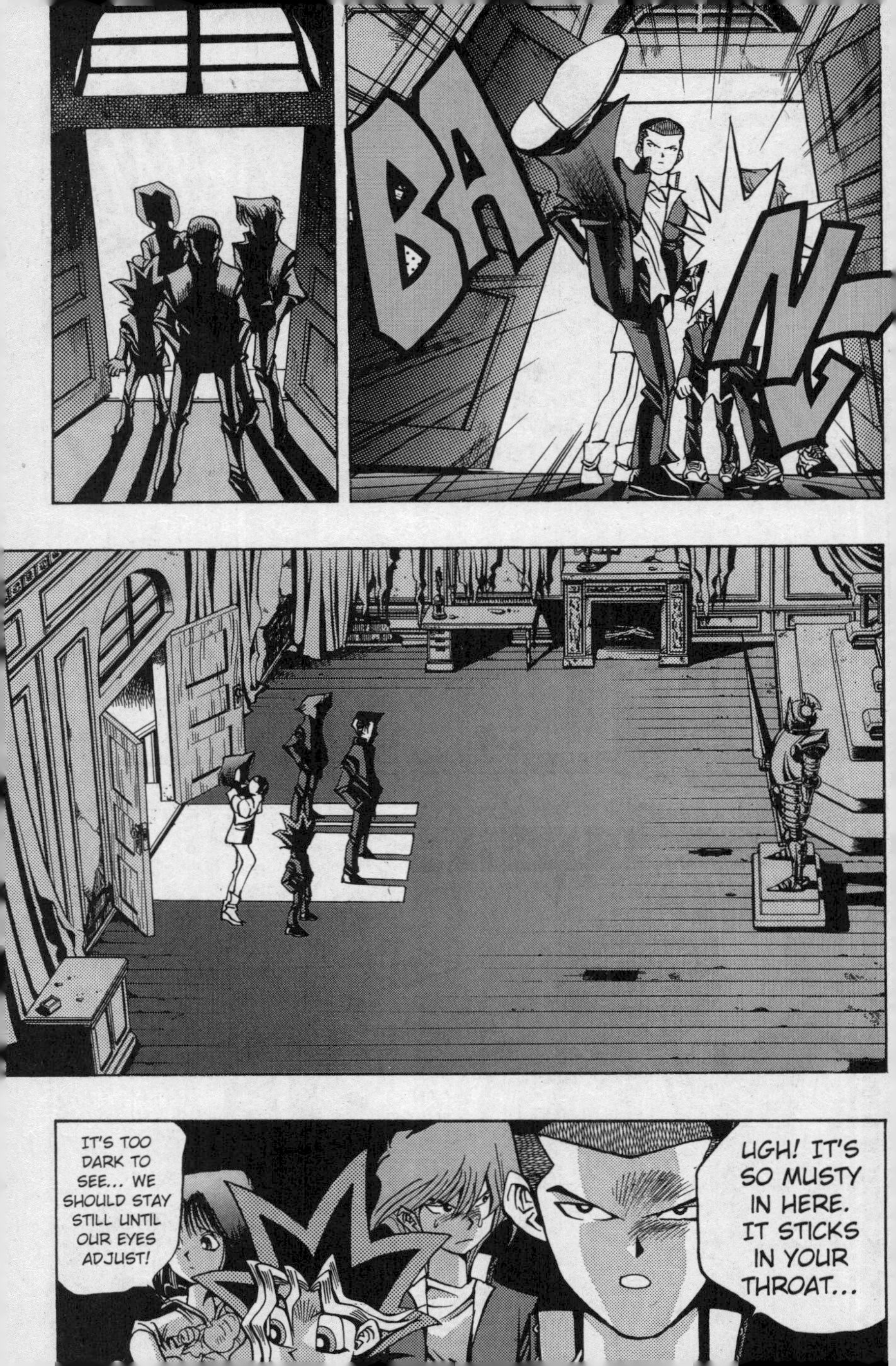

BA
NG

UGH! IT'S SO MUSTY IN HERE. IT STICKS IN YOUR THROAT...
IT'S TOO DARK TO SEE... WE SHOULD STAY STILL UNTIL OUR EYES ADJUST!

READ THIS WAY

blood
...HUH?

blood

WHAT'S THIS SCRAP OF PAPER...
THERE'S SOMETHING WRITTEN ON IT...

blood
BLOOD ...?!

WHAT ON EARTH COULD IT MEAN ...?
THAT'S A BAD OMEN ...

HEY, THIS IS STRANGE! THERE'S NO WAY OUT!
I'LL CHECK THE SECOND FLOOR!

HUH!
WHAT THE-! THE STAIRS ARE BLOCKED OFF!
THERE ISN'T A SECOND FLOOR !!

VM MM

HEH HEH HEH...

KAIBA !!

WELCOME TO THE MURDERER'S MANSION!
HE'S FLOATING IN THIN AIR!

IT'S NOT REALLY HIM! IT'S A HOLO-GRAM!
!!

I SEE YOU'RE SEARCHING FOR THE EXIT TO THIS MANSION. HAVE YOU FOUND IT YET?
LET ME GIVE YOU A WORD OF WARNING...IF YOU DON'T ESCAPE SOON, SOMETHING TERRIBLE WILL HAPPEN!

READ THIS WAY

SO! WILL YOU BE ABLE TO ESCAPE THIS MANSION WITHOUT RUNNING INTO THE CHOPMAN?!

HA HA HA HA!

GGK ...

HOWEVER, I COULDN'T HAVE YOU CALL THIS GAME *UNFAIR*...

SO I'LL GIVE YOU A *HINT* TO FIND THE WAY OUT OF THE MANSION!

00 01 10 11

WHAT THE?!?! FOUR HOLES IN THE WALL!!

THERE ARE NUMBERS WRITTEN ABOVE EACH OF THE HOLES!
00 - 01 - 10 - 11 ...... ?!?!?!

THERE ARE SWITCHES ON THE OTHER SIDE OF THAT WALL.
IF YOU PRESS THE RIGHT SWITCH, THE LOCATION OF THE EXIT WILL BE REVEALED!
NOW, GATHER YOUR COURAGE AND PUT YOUR HANDS IN THOSE HOLES!

GUH ...
THIS IS A TRAP!! THERE HAS TO BE SOME KIND OF TRICK!

WHAT IS IT, YUGI? YOU LOOK SUSPICIOUS .....
YOU'LL NEVER GET OUT UNLESS YOU PRESS THE RIGHT SWITCH!
CRIPES ...
YEAH... WE SEARCHED EVERYWHERE AND COULDN'T FIND A THING...
THERE'S NO CHOICE. WE HAVE TO STICK OUR HANDS IN...

KACHAN☆
WHA...?!
OUR HANDS ARE TRAPPED!!
PANG
TH-THAT'S A...!!!
YEEK!

RR

RR

...A GUILLOTINE !!

RRRM

HA HA HA! NOW THE GAME BEGINS!

ONLY ONE OF THE SWITCHES IS THE REAL ONE! IF YOU PRESS THE WRONG SWITCH, THE BLADE WILL FALL AND CUT OFF YOUR HANDS!

YOU HAVE FIVE MINUTES BEFORE THE BLADE DROPS!

DON'T FORGET! YOU CAN ONLY PRESS ONE SWITCH!

KAIBA !!!

THIS IS IMPOSSIBLE ...!
WHICH IS THE RIGHT SWITCH ...?
I CAN'T STAND THIS! WHAT'S *WITH* ALL THESE GAMES?
00
01
10

THESE NUMBERS MUST MEAN SOMETHING!
00 - 01 - 10 - 11 ...
10

THEY'RE ALL ONES AND ZEROS ...
THAT'S LIKE... WHAT'S IT CALLED... THAT COMPUTER CODE.......
11

ARGH, I DON'T GET IT!
THAT FRIGGIN' KAIBA SAID THERE WAS A HINT SOMEWHERE IN THIS ROOM...

AH ...!
THAT SCRAP OF PAPER!

BLOOD ...
blood

READ THIS WAY

....
"BLOOD ..."?!
WHAT'S THIS?!
CREEPY LETTERS ...
I FOUND THAT SCRAP OF PAPER IN THIS ROOM.
THAT HAS TO BE IT!

@#%&*! I DON'T GET IT. NUMBERS AND LETTERS... I HATE THIS KIND OF PUZZLE!

YUGI CAN SOLVE IT!
YOU SOLVED THE MILLENNIUM PUZZLE! YOU CAN DO IT!

OKAY ...

blood
"BLOOD ..."
"BL ..."

HUH ...?!

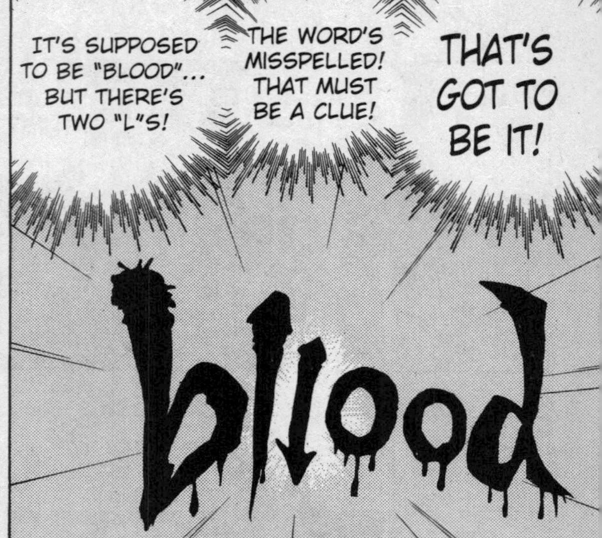
THAT'S GOT TO BE IT!
THE WORD'S MISSPELLED! THAT MUST BE A CLUE!
IT'S SUPPOSED TO BE "BLOOD"... BUT THERE'S TWO "L"S!
bllood

HEY, WE ONLY HAVE TWO MINUTES LEFT!

....

YAAAWN ...

C'MON YUGI!
ABOUT ONE MINUTE LEFT!

TIME IS UP!!

ROAAR

THE GUILLOTINE BLADE !!!

ROA

IT'S ANZU'S 11!!

PUSH YOUR SWITCH, ANZU!!

HUH ?!

RR

....

OKAY !

CLICK☆

.....

THE BLADE STOPPED!
I WAS RIGHT!

CLICK

YOU DID IT!!
AWRIGHT! GO, YUGI!

PHEW!
HOW DID YOU GET THE ANSWER?

AT FIRST, I KEPT THINKING ABOUT THE *MEANING* OF THE WORD BLOOD!

BUT THE SHAPE OF THE LETTERS WAS WHAT MATTERED!

SEE... THEY MADE THE WORD BLOOD WITH JUST ZEROS AND ONES!

bllood

↓

|0||000|

↓

10 11 00 01

AND WHEN YOU LOOK CLOSELY AT THIS "L" IN THIS WORD BLOOD...

SEE ...

bllood

THERE'S AN ARROW POINTING DOWN!

THAT MUST MEAN THAT THE EXIT IS IN THE BASEMENT!

SO THE RIGHT ANSWER WAS THE 11 THAT THE ARROW IS DRAWN ON!! ANZU'S SWITCH!

GOOD WORK, YUGI!

EXIT

YOU WERE RIGHT, THERE'S AN EXIT IN THE FLOOR!!

CREAK
EXIT
HOW BORING ...
EXIT
HMPH!
TADA
AWRIGHT! NOW WE CAN GET OUTTA HERE!
BRMM MM MBB

CREAK
NO ONE ASKED ME FOR MY HELP...
HMPH...
EXIT
THIS IS BORING! I WANNA GO HOME!
WE DID IT! WE FOUND THE EXIT!
EXIT

Duel 32: Chainsaw Deathmatch!!

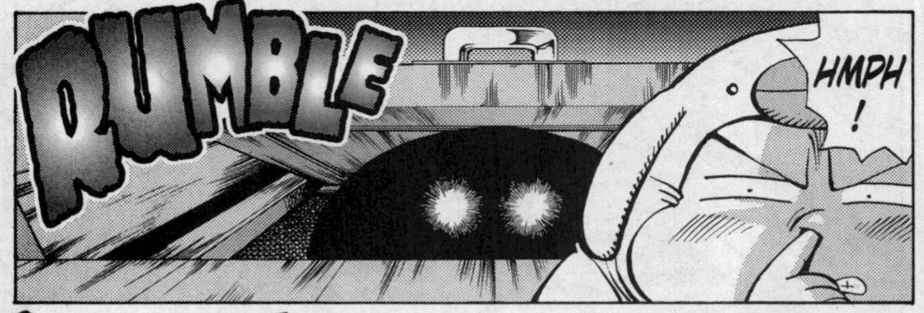

SOMEONE PULLED HIM THROUGH THAT TRAP DOOR!!
JOHJI!!
DA
DOOM
EXIT
Duel 32: Chainsaw Deathmatch!!

IT MIGHT BE THAT "CHOPMAN" KAIBA WAS TALKING ABOUT!!

AWW, NO WAY!
WE THOUGHT IT WAS THE EXIT, BUT IT'S REALLY THE ENTRANCE TO A SERIAL KILLER'S HIDEOUT!?!
EXIT

JEEZ... I CAN'T STAND THAT LITTLE BRAT...
...BUT WE CAN'T LEAVE HIM THERE WITH THAT NUTCASE!

LET'S GO!
EXIT

KREE EEEK

HEEY! HELP ME!
!

IT'S JOHJI'S VOICE!
AWRIGHT! LET'S GO DOWN!

BE CAREFUL EVERY-ONE!
KAIBA SAID THE MURDERER WAS ON HIS SIDE! THIS COULD BE A TRAP!

AH
...

HEY! OVER HERE!
IT'S JOHJI!
HE'S IN THAT ROOM!!

THERE HE IS!

HEY GUYS!
I'M IN HERE! COME AND GET ME!
COME ON BABY!

NNNN ...
THIS HAS GOTTA BE A TRICK.
I THINK YOU'RE RIGHT!

JOHJI! TELL THE TRUTH!
IS ANYONE IN THERE WITH YOU?

HUH? NO, NO ONE!
IT'S JUST SWEET LITTLE ME!

I DON'T TRUST THAT BRAT AS FAR AS I CAN THROW HIM!
THAT'S GOTTA BE A TRAP!

OHH, PLEASE HELP ME! PRETTY PLEASE! ♡

NOW HE'S ACTING CUTE!
IF YOU DIDN'T BELIEVE HIM BEFORE ...!
I JUST KNOW IT! THAT BRAT WOULD BETRAY US IN AN INSTANT!

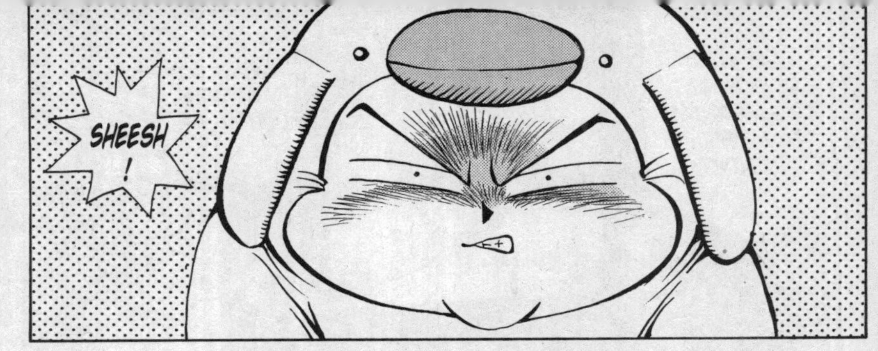
SHEESH !

THEY AREN'T COMING IN, SIR!
HURGHHH

H-HE'S TALKING TO SOMEONE !!!
THAT BRAT... HE'S ALREADY SWITCHED SIDES...

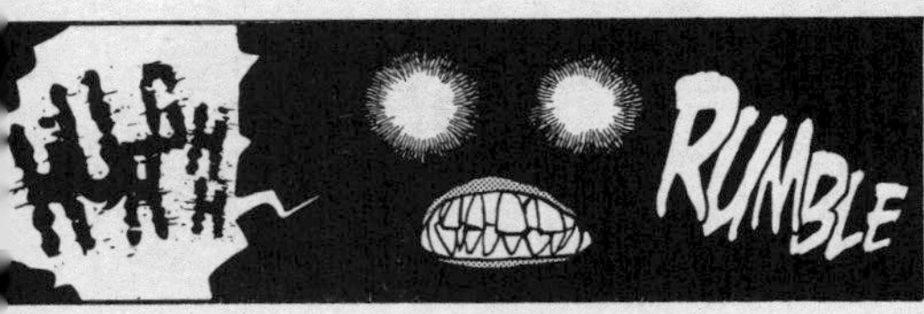
RUMBLE
HUGHHH

TCH ... NOW WHAT ?
THE CHOPMAN MUST BE IN THAT ROOM!

BZZT
AH!

IT'S KAIBA !!
A TV SCREEN! WITH KAIBA'S HEAD!

WHAT DO YOU THINK, EVERYONE?
ARE YOU ENJOYING KAIBA LAND'S GAMES OF DEATH?
WOW! KAIBA! ♡

MMEH HEH... OF ALL GAMES, I LIKE CARD GAMES THE BEST...
BUT CHESS IS MY SECOND FAVORITE ...

KAIBA! I DON'T KNOW WHERE YOU'RE HIDING--
--BUT IF YOU HAVE ANY GUTS, COME OUT AND TALK TO US IN PERSON!

RIGHT NOW, YOU ARE LIVING CHESS PIECES ON THE GIANT BOARD THAT IS KAIBA LAND!
I WATCH AS EACH MOVE BRINGS ME CLOSER TO CHECKMATE ...
AND I'M ENJOYING IT IMMENSELY.

!

NOW ABOUT THE NEXT GAME ...

YOU WILL PLAY IT *IN HERE* WITH THE *CHOPMAN!*
SELECT ONE PERSON TO ENTER THIS ROOM!

!!
A GAME WITH THE CHOPMAN !!

YOU CAN'T AVOID THIS GAME!
YOU DON'T WANT TO SEE THIS CHILD'S *HEAD* CUT OFF, DO YOU?

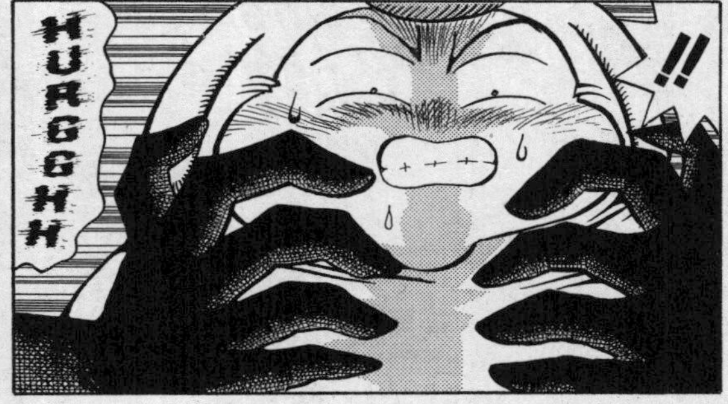
HURGGHH
!!

THE CHOPMAN OBEYS ONLY MY ORDERS!
IF I SAY THE WORD, THE BOY DIES!

M-MISTER KAIBA, YOU'RE KIDDING, RIGHT?
YOU DON'T NEED TO DO THAT TO BEAT THEM! YOU WOULDN'T REALLY HURT ME, WOULD YOU?

KAIBA, DON'T YOU DARE TOUCH THAT KID !

WHO WILL STEP UP TO PLAY THIS GAME?

HELLLL-PPP !!

@#%*! I'LL ...
WAIT, HONDA!
LET ME GO!

JONOUCHI!

THAT WEIRD-LOOKING DIAPER-BAG SAVED OUR LIVES MORE THAN ONCE!
I HATE HIS GUTS, BUT I PAY WHAT I OWE!

HURR HURRGH

MMEH HEH...

WITH THIS MOVE, I CAPTURE JONOUCHI, THE KNIGHT!

JONOUCHI!
THE DOOR'S LOCKED!

SLAM
!!

JONOUCHI!
I KNEW YOU'D COME FOR ME!
QUICK, SAVE ME!
YEAH, YEAH, I'M COMIN'. JUST STAY PUT!

WHAT THE HELL ...?
SCHLK
OIL ...?
THERE'S OIL ON THE FLOOR ...!

KACHAK

DON'T GET MAD AT ME!
KAIBA MADE ME DO IT!
I'M TOO CUTE TO DIE!

WHY YOU ...!
YOU LITTLE TRAITOR!

NOW, THE GAME IS SET!!
HURRRGH
AARGGH! HE CHAINED ME TO THE MONSTER!!
HEH HEH ... ALLOW ME TO INTRODUCE YOU!
THIS IS THE CHOPMAN!
MASTER KAIBA! CAD I CUD HIM UB?
ID'S BEEN SOO LONG...!
NOT UNTIL I GIVE THE SIGNAL.
HMPH...
CRUD, HE LOOKS TOUGH!!

THE RULES OF THE GAME ARE SIMPLE!
AFTER THE SIGNAL TO BEGIN, YOU EACH PICK A WEAPON AND FIGHT TO THE DEATH!

YOUR CHOICES ARE HUNG FROM THE CEILING.
STAND ON THE PODIUM IN THE MIDDLE TO REACH THEM!
BE CAREFUL NOT TO SLIP ON THE OIL ON THE FLOOR!

GGGK ...
JONOUCHI! I'M HERE FOR YOU, MAN!

JONOUCHI!

HURRRGH
GUH HUH HUH... I CUD YOU UB!

THIS CAN'T BE REAL!
I HAVE TO GET THIS HANDCUFF OFF....
I NEED SOME KIND OF PIN OR WIRE TO PICK THE LOCK!

GAME START!!

GUH HUH HUH HUH...
WHAD TO CUD YOU UB WID...?
I DON'T HAVE A CHANCE AGAINST THAT!
HEY! ANY OF YOU HAVE SOME KIND OF WIRE!?
WE'LL FIND YOU SOMETHING, JONOUCHI!

I CUD YOU UB WID DIS!

BRRRM

AAACK!

RUN, JONOUCHI!

SLIP

AAAGGH! CAN'T KEEP MY FEET ON THIS OIL!

I SLICE YOU IN TWO!

ONOUCHI !!

RMMGRMMGRM

MMM

CH ...

ID'S STILL STUGK!
GRM GRM GRM
I HAVE TO GET THIS HANDCUFF OFF...!
GRRG ...!

THERE HAS TO BE SOME-THING!
JONOUCHI!
SOME-THING WITH A POINT!

JONOUCHI ...

AT THIS RATE, JONOUCHI WILL DIE.....!

JONOUCHI! OVER THERE!!

BA
BAM

HUH ...?

A CANDLE-STICK ...?!

I GET IT...
IT HAS A POINT TO STICK THE CANDLE ON!

I CAN USE IT TO PICK THE CUFF!!
KACHA
KA CHA
HURRY, JONOUCHI!

BUT... EVEN IF I GET IT OFF...
THE DOOR'S LOCKED! AND IT'S TOO HEAVY TO BUST THROUGH!

I'VE GOT AN IDEA, JONOUCHI !!
RMMB RMMB
OKAY !

GRMMM
BWUH HUH HUH HUH HUH ...
I GOD THE CHAIN-SAW FREE!!

!
YOU CAN'D HIDE OBER DERE!
GUH HUH HUH HUH ...

COBE HERE !
I CUD YOU UB!
YANK

CLANK
WUH ...?!
WHAT... HE GOT THE HANDCUFF OFF...!!
...AND ATTACHED IT TO THE DOOR!
ALONG WITH THE CANDLE ...!!
I JUST USED THAT MONSTER STRENGTH OF YOURS!
THANKS FOR OPENING THE DOOR FOR ME!

KAIBA ...
WHEN YOU TEAMED UP WITH THE CHOPMAN ...
IT WAS A DEMON'S MIND WITH A MONSTER'S POWER!
THAT WAS A COMBO MADE IN HELL! TOO BAD IT'S OVER NOW!
BOFF
YEEP ...
C'MON... LET'S HIT THE NEXT ONE!
YOU LITTLE ...
THANKS, JONOUCHI. I MEAN IT. REALLY.
ROARRR
AAAGGHHH!!

BA-DUM
YUGI ...
BA-DUM
Duel 33: Terror Cubed!!!
CLATTER
PATIENT IS IN RESPIRATORY DISTRESS FOLLOWING AN ACUTE BOUT OF ANGINA SECONDARY TO PSYCHO-GENIC SHOCK!
PATIENT'S HEART RATE AND BLOOD PRESSURE ARE ELEVATED!
HE IS IN EXTREMELY CRITICAL CONDITION!
YUGI ...
HUFF
HUFF
YUGI ...
BA-DUM
BA-DUM

Duel 33: Terror Cubed!!!

GRANDPA ...
THE HEARTBEAT I FEEL THROUGH GRANDPA'S CARDS IS GETTING FASTER...!!
BA-DUM

HANG IN THERE, GRANDPA!
BA-DUM
BA-DUM

TO SAVE GRANDPA, I HAVE TO DEFEAT KAIBA WITH THE HEART OF THE CARDS!!

YUGI! LOOK!
THERE'S THE ENTRANCE TO THE NEXT GAME!

WE'RE GETTING CLOSER TO THAT JERK KAIBA, ONE STEP AT A TIME!
YUP!
C'MON! HURRY!

READ
THIS
WAY

SO THEY'VE MADE IT TO "DEATH T-3"...

NOT OUTSIDE THE REALM OF CHANCE, BUT...
LOOKING OVER THEIR PROGRESS, I SEE SOME FACTORS I UNDERESTIMATED...
THEY'RE A GOOD TEAM... THEIR CLOSE FRIENDSHIP HAS BEEN THE REAL KEY TO BEATING THE GAMES...

I NEED TO BREAK UP THAT UNION...

AFTER ALL, FRIENDSHIP IS JUST AN ILLUSION... EVERYONE CARES THE MOST ABOUT HIMSELF...
WHEN THEY FIND THEMSELVES IN REAL TROUBLE, THEY'LL SOON BETRAY THEIR FRIENDS TO SAVE THEIR OWN HIDES!

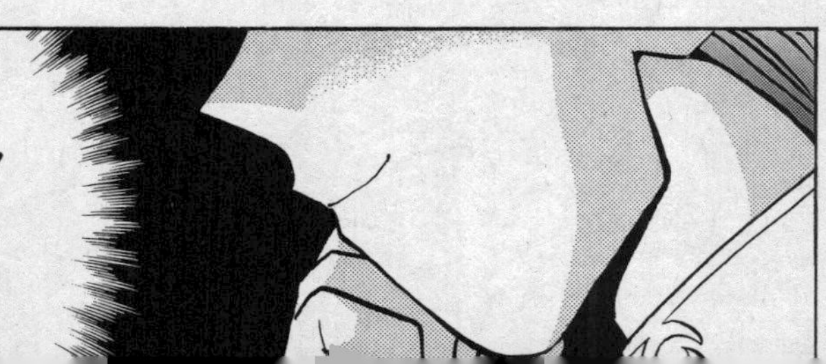
THAT'S WHERE "DEATH T-3" COMES IN... MMEH HEH HEH...

TMP

DOON!!
DEATH T-3
ZZZ

THIS IS THE ENTRANCE TO "DEATH T-3"!

WHAT COULD COME AFTER THE HORROR ZONE?!
KAIBA DESIGNED THIS THEME PARK. YOU KNOW IT'S GOTTA BE SOMETHING EVEN MORE CHEAP AND SADISTIC!
LET'S GO!!

!!
WH-WHAT THE--?!

BAN

DEATH T-3

THE DOOR!!

YEAH, YEAH, JUST LIKE ALWAYS.

IT'S AN EMPTY ROOM!!

THERE'S NOTHING HERE!

LET'S LOOK FOR THE WAY OUT!

ALL RIGHT...

THE CEILING'S PRETTY HIGH!
IT'S TOO DARK TO TELL, BUT MAYBE IT'S OPEN AT THE TOP...
OH ...!

THERE'S A *HOLE* IN THE WALL UP THERE ...!
IT'S ABOUT 10 METERS ABOVE THE FLOOR!
THEY CAN'T EXPECT US TO CLIMB UP THERE!
THAT'S IMPOS-SIBLE!

CRAP!
THERE'S NOTHING WE CAN DO! WE'RE STUCK!

MAYBE ...
......

MAYBE... MAYBE WE'RE TRAPPED HERE...
...AND THIS WAS KAIBA'S PLAN ALL ALONG...

YUGI! DON'T GIVE UP, OKAY?!
......!

OKAY ...

WE'LL JUST HAVE TO WAIT AND SEE WHAT HAPPENS ......

JOHJI'S SOUND ASLEEP. H MUST BE EXHAUSTE ...
THIS WHOLE THING MUST BE HARD ON A LITTLE, TALKING, PERVY KID LIKE HIM.
ZZZ

WE'VE BEEN HERE AGES... NOTHING HAS CHANGED...
MAYBE ...
~~ ...
MAYBE IT DOES END HERE...

GRANDPA ...
EVERYONE ...

I'M SORRY! I'M SORRY EVERYONE! IT'S MY FAULT...!
GLARE
IF I WEREN'T HERE, THIS WOULDN'T HAVE HAPPENED...
THAT'S ENOUGH, YUGI! DON'T YOU DARE SAY THAT AGAIN!!
GRAB
...!
STOP, JONOUCHI! WHAT'S THE MATTER WITH YOU?!
J-JO...
YUGI...
DON'T SAY THINGS LIKE THAT!
DON'T YOU UNDERSTAND WHY WE CAME WITH YOU?!
IT'S BECAUSE WE'RE FRIENDS!

!!
ANYWAY ... JONOUCHI ...
LET GO OF HIS COLLAR ...
YOU'RE NOT THE SAME JONOUCHI WHO USED TO BEAT HIM UP, REMEMBER!
YEAH ...
WE WERE STUPID PUNKS, ALL RIGHT...
HONDA !
WE'VE BEEN SUCH STUPID PUNKS...

BUT... I WASN'T REALLY MAD AT YOU, YUGI...
I WAS MAD AT *MYSELF* ...

I KNOW HOW YOU FEEL...
I WAS THE SAME.

I WOULD GET SO WOUND UP ...
I JUST NEEDED TO PICK A FIGHT... IT DIDN'T MATTER WHO...
SOME LOCAL PUNKS... EVEN A TELEPHONE POLE ...
I'D HIT THEM WITH EVERY-THING I HAD...

THEN I'D REALIZE, THE PERSON I REALLY WANTED TO HIT...
WAS ME ...

!

YUGI ...
YOU REMEMBER WHEN I STOLE PART OF YOUR PUZZLE?
......

WHEN I GAVE THAT BACK...YOU CAN LAUGH, BUT THAT TOOK MORE COURAGE THAN ANYTHING ...

......!

BUT, JUST THEN ...
I STARTED TO LIKE MYSELF A LITTLE BIT...
FOR THE FIRST TIME IN MY LIFE...

GRAB
LISTEN TO ME, YUGI!
YOU KNOW WHAT FRIENDS ARE?! THEY'RE SOMEONE YOU LIKE!
AND BECAUSE OF THEM YOU LEARN TO LIKE YOURSELF!
THAT'S WHY I HANG OUT WITH YOU, YUGI!
SO IF IT HURTS, OR WHAT-EVER--
LET ME SHARE IT!
THAT'S WHAT FRIENDS ARE FOR!
JONOUCHI ...I ...

I'M NOT GIVING UP YET ...
SO DON'T YOU GIVE UP EITHER!
'KAY, YUGI ...?
O-OKAY ...

NO ONE LEARNS TO LIKE THEMSELVES ON THEIR OWN...
IT'S A BIG GAME YOU PLAY THROUGHOUT YOUR LIFE...
HEY! LOOK AT THIS WHITE ROOM!
DOESN'T IT REMIND YOU OF A BLANK CANVAS?

I ALWAYS THOUGHT IF I WENT SOMEWHERE SPECIAL WITH MY FRIENDS, I'D LEAVE MY NAME THERE TO REMEMBER IT BY!
ARE YOU A TAGGER, ANZU?!

HEH HEH ...
I'VE GOT A MAGIC MARKER !

...?!
PUT YOUR HANDS OUT, EVERY-ONE!

WHAT ARE YOU UP TO, ANZU ?!
JUST GIMME YOUR HANDS !

SEE! SMILEY FACE!
WHAT THE-?!

HWOOO
LOOK OUT!!
WHAM
!!
!
ZZZ
WH-WHAT THE-?!
A GIANT CUBE DROPPED FROM ABOVE?!

NOW THEN! LET'S SEE HOW MANY MAKE IT OUT OF THAT ROOM WITHOUT BEING FLATTENED...
URK ...!!
!!
WHAM☆
MMEH HEH HEH ...
WHAM☆

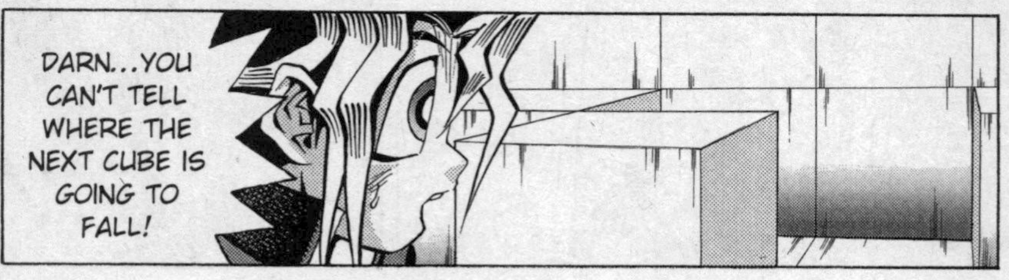

DARN...YOU CAN'T TELL WHERE THE NEXT CUBE IS GOING TO FALL!

IN THIS GAME, YOUR NUMBERS ARE A LIABILITY! STOP TO WORRY ABOUT SOMEONE ELSE, AND YOU'LL BE SQUASHED BY A CUBE!
MMM HEH HEH... THAT'S RIGHT, RUN...
YOU CAN'T WIN THIS GAME WITHOUT SACRIFICING YOUR FRIENDS!
ALL WE CAN DO IS RUN AROUND DODGING !!
WHAM☆

THIS IS LIKE DANCING WITH DEATH!
THERE'S NO PLACE LEFT TO RUN!
WHAM
EVERYONE CLIMB ON TOP OF THE CUBES!
THE POINT OF THE GAME IS TO GET OUT OF THE ROOM!!
I GET IT! WE DODGE THE FALLING CUBES AND CLIMB UP UNTIL THEY GET TO THAT EXIT!!
WHAM
GUYS! KEEP AWAY FROM THE EDGES OF THE ROOM!
IF YOU GET BOXED IN, YOU'RE DEAD!
GGK ...!
WHAM
CRAP... AT THIS RATE WE'RE GOING TO BE FLATTENED!
HOW DO WE GET OUT OF THIS ?!!

HEY, HONDA! THROW JOHJI TO ME!
ZZZ ZZZ
WHAM
CATCH!
HOW CAN HE SLEEP AT A TIME LIKE THIS?!
ZZZ ZZZ
!
HOLD ON!
THERE'S A RHYTHM TO THE TIMING OF THE FALLING CUBES!
MAYBE THERE'S SOME RULE TO WHERE THEY FALL AS WELL......
I GET IT! YOU'RE TRAINED AS A DANCER!
YOU'VE GOT A TALENT FOR READING RHYTHMS!
ONE... TWO...
THREE...
THERE!!
WHAM
THAT'S AWESOME!
YOU KNEW WHERE THE NEXT CUBE WOULD FALL!

IF THE TIMING OF THE FALLING CUBES IS RHYTHM AND THE PLACES WHERE THEY FALL ARE THE STEPS OF A DANCE...
I GET IT! THE MECHANISM OF THIS GAME IS TOO BIG FOR THE COMPUTER PROGRAM CONTROLLING IT TO BE TOO COMPLEX! THEY HAD TO KEEP IT SIMPLE!!
SO THE CUBES ONLY KNOW EASY DANCES!
THEN IT'S LIKE THE CUBES ARE FOLLOWING A SIMPLE DANCE!!
ALL RIGHT! ALL WE HAVE TO DO IS STAY LIGHT ON OUR FEET...LIKE DANCERS...AND MAKE IT TO THE EXIT!!
THIS GAME'S EASY IF YOU KNOW WHERE THE CUBES ARE GOING TO FALL!!
HANG IN THERE GUYS!
WE'RE ALMOST TO THE EXIT!
HURRY, YUGI!
!!
HUH...?!
THE RHYTHM CHANGED...?!
HONDA, LOOK OUT!!
!!
AAAH

HONDA! ARE YOU ALL RIGHT?!
PHEW ... THAT WAS CLOSE...
BE CAREFUL, THE RHYTHM IS GETTING FASTER!
ALL RIGHT, LET'S MOVE!!
!!
ANZU AND I ARE OUT!
YUGI! HONDA! GET UP HERE!
YUGI! GIVE ME YOUR HAND, QUICK!
YOU GO FIRST, HONDA!
JUST GIVE ME YOUR HAND, BEFORE THE CUBES BLOCK THE EXIT!
GRAB
JONOUCHI! TAKE YUGI!
GOT 'IM!

C'MON, HONDA
!
WHAT'RE YOU WAITING FOR?
THIS IS AS FAR AS I GO...
!!
H--
HONDA'S JACKET... CAUGHT UNDER THE CUBE...!!
GOODBYE, GUYS
...
HONDA
...!
WHAM
HONDAAA
!!

SPECIAL BONUS! THRILLING BOARD GAME!

Number of Players: 1-5
What You Need:

- A 6-sided die
- Something to use as game pieces (coins, pebbles, etc.)

How to Play:

- Place your game pieces on the "Start" space on page 203!
- Roll the die to see who goes first. The players take turns rolling the die and moving according to the rules below!

☆ ⚀ • When you roll a 1, you can move one or two spaces (your choice) *in a straight line* in any direction you want. (But not diagonally!)

☆ ⚁ ⚂ ⚃ ⚄
• When you roll a 2, 3, 4 or 5, you must move one space according to the chart below!

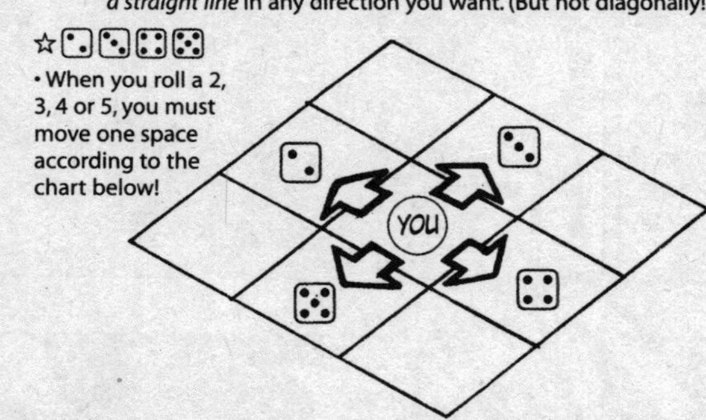

☆ ⚅ • When you roll a 6, you can move one or two spaces (your choice) in any direction you want. You can even change direction, like going up and then right. (You still can't move diagonally, though.)

- If the dice says to go into a rock wall (like the top of page 203), just stop at the edge. You cannot go into a rock wall.
- If the dice says to go over the edge (like the bottom of page 203), *you fall off and you have to return to "Start" on page 203!* If you're playing alone, the game is over.
- You can also push other players off the edge! (See figure 1.)

FIGURE 1

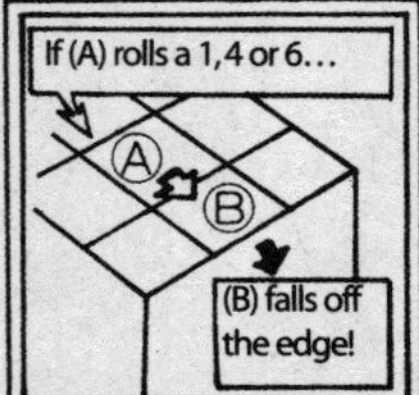

THE FIRST ONE TO MAKE IT TO THE GOAL (ON PAGE 207) WINS!

WARP TO C
WARP TO A
START
WARP TO B
WARP TO A
WARP TO C
WARP TO D
WARP TO F

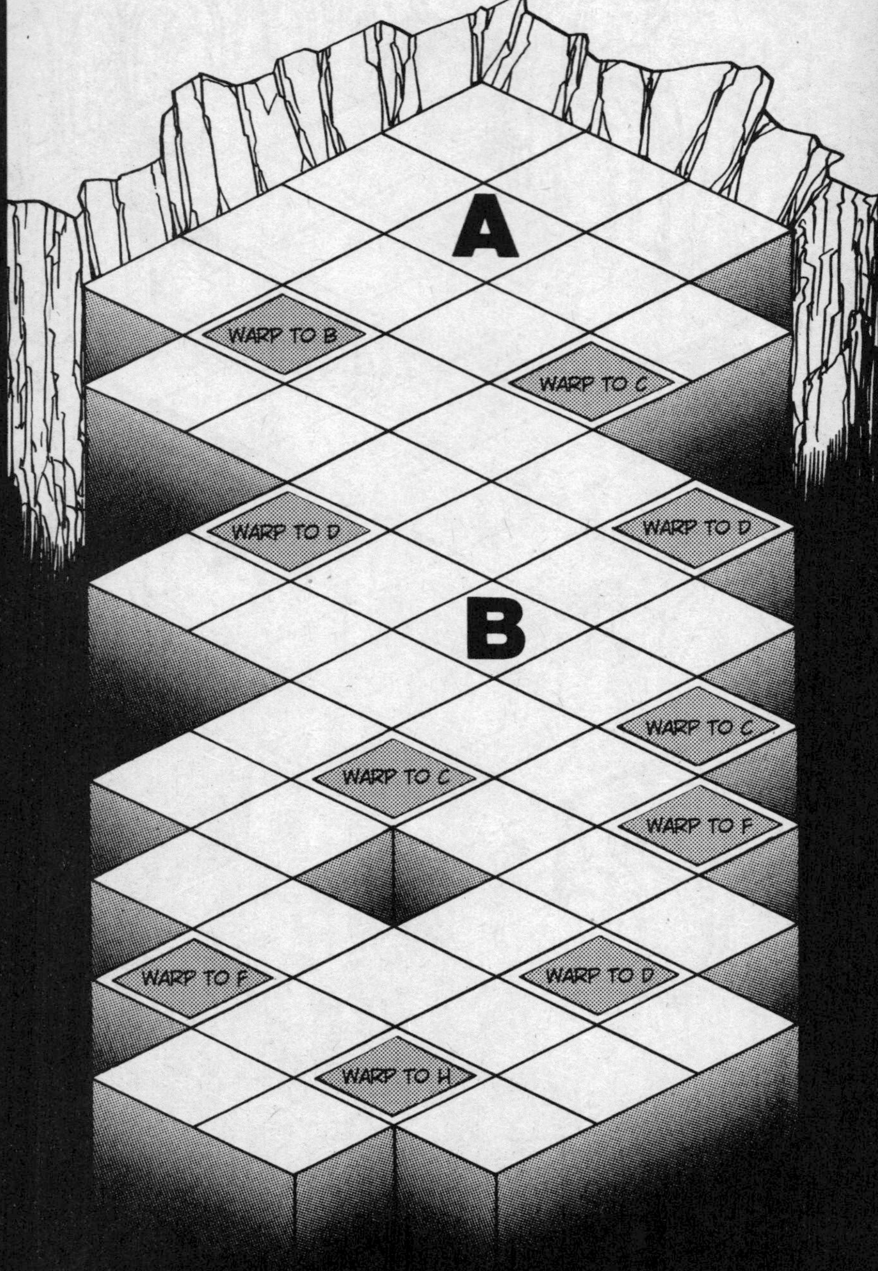
A
WARP TO B
WARP TO C
WARP TO D
WARP TO D
B
WARP TO C
WARP TO C
WARP TO F
WARP TO F
WARP TO D
WARP TO H

If you roll a 1 or 3, you're monster bait! Game over!
C
WARP TO F
WARP TO H
WARP TO E
WARP TO B
WARP TO H
WARP TO C
WARP TO F
D
WARP TO G
WARP TO E

WARP TO H
WARP TO G
WARP TO G
WARP TO H
F
WARP TO D
WARP TO G
WARP TO H
E

LOSE A TURN

G

WARP TO C

GOAL

WARP TO D

WARP TO F

LOSE A TURN

H

WARP TO B

WARP TO A

WARP TO G

WARP TO G

MASTER OF THE CARDS

Collectible card games first appeared in **Yu-Gi-Oh!** in Duels 9 and 10, "The Cards with Teeth" (see **Yu-Gi-Oh!** volume 2). As **Yu-Gi-Oh!** fans know, the manga and anime version of the "Duel Monsters" card game has simpler rules than the real-world version. Also, many of the card names are different between the English and Japanese versions. Here's a rundown of the cards in this graphic novel.

1. Blue-Eyes White Dragon
In the manga, this card is extremely rare—only a few are supposed to exist.

2. Hitotsu-me Giant
Known as "Cyclops" in the original Japanese. "Hitotsu-me" is Japanese for "one-eyed."

OH, HE CAME FROM THE SANDS OF TIME
HE'S THE KING OF GAMES, LEGENDS COME ALIVE
EVILDOERS WILL HIDE IN SHAME
WHEN THEY TASTE JUSTICE
IN A SHADOW GAME
(SHADOW!)
OH, BUT EVEN A KING HAS A HEART
AND THE DOOR TO THAT HEART, IT OPENS, IT PARTS
THERE IS ALWAYS A FRIEND IN YOUR HEART!
YUGI! YUGI! YU-GI-OH!

THIS IS A ***YU-GI-OH!*** THEME SONG I WROTE AND COMPOSED MYSELF (IN A SAMBA RHYTHM).

KAZUKI TAKAHASHI, 1997

SHONEN JUMP MANGA

Vol. 5
THE HEART OF THE CARDS

STORY AND ART BY
KAZUKI TAKAHASHI

THE STORY SO FAR...

When Yugi beat his classmate Seto Kaiba at the collectible card game "Duel Monsters," he didn't know the lengths to which Kaiba would go to get revenge! The insane super-genius Kaiba spent $85 million to build a *Theme Park of Death* to torture Yugi and his friends, with death traps, chainsaw-wielding maniacs, and hitmen for play partners! Now, Yugi, Jonouchi and Anzu have made it almost to the end of the line—but their friend Honda, trapped in the "room of falling blocks," wasn't so lucky...

DARK YUGI

武藤遊戯

YUGI MUTOU

The main character. When he solved the ancient Egyptian Millennium Puzzle, he developed an alter ego, the King of Games, which emerges in times of stress. Afterwards, the regular Yugi doesn't remember what happened.

城之内克也

KATSUYA JONOUCHI

Yugi's classmate, a tough guy who gets in lots of fights. He used to think Yugi was a wimp, but now they are good friends. In the English anime he's known as "Joey Wheeler."

真崎杏子

ANZU MAZAKI

Yugi's classmate and childhood friend. She fell in love with the charismatic voice of Yugi's alter ego, but doesn't know that they're the same person. Her first name means "Peach." In the English anime she's known as "Téa Gardner."

海馬モクバ

MOKUBA KAIBA

Seto's little brother. He's lost to Yugi twice at different games. His favorite game is the collectible miniatures game "Capsule Monster Chess."

海馬瀬人

SETO KAIBA

Heir to Japan's biggest gaming empire, Kaiba is an expert at the American collectible card game "Duel Monsters." After losing to Yugi, he kidnapped Yugi's grandfather and forced him to play a duel in a prototype "Virtual Reality Simulation Box," which was so realistic it gave Yugi's grandfather a heart attack.

本田ヒロト

HIROTO HONDA

Yugi's classmate, a friend of Jonouchi. He was babysitting his nephew Johji, a talking baby, when he got caught up in the Theme Park of Death. In the English anime he's known as "Tristan Taylor."

武藤双六

SUGOROKU MUTOU

Yugi's grandfather, the owner of the Kame ("Turtle") game store. Currently in the hospital undergoing heart surgery.

Vol. 5

CONTENTS

READ THIS WAY

WHAM

THIS IS AS FAR AS I GO......

HONDA!

HONDAAAA!!

....
....
HONDA IS ....
HONDA IS ......
I WON'T BELIEVE IT!!
HONDA CAN'T BE GONE !!
YOU CAN'T GET RID OF THAT IDIOT SO EASILY...

YUGI
...
RRM
RRM
RR
HONDA'S ALL RIGHT!
I'M SURE HE'S ALIVE!
RRM
RRM
HONDA
!
LISTEN UP!
WE'RE GONNA GO ON AHEAD--
--BUT YOU USE THAT HARD HEAD OF YOURS TO GET OUTTA THAT FIX
!!
WE'LL BE WAITING FOR YOU...!
YOU IDIOT
!
C'MON! LET'S GO, YUGI, ANZU!
WAIT
...
RRM
RRM
YUGI'S ACTING STRANGE
...
SOMETHING'S WRONG...
RRM
RRMM
RRMM
!

IF THIS IS CHESS ...
YUGI IS THE KING ...
JONOUCHI IS THE KNIGHT ...
AND HONDA MUST BE THE ROOK...

TOPPLE
THE ROOK HAS BEEN CAPTURED.

THE COUNTDOWN TO CHECKMATE HAS BEGUN ...

THEY DON'T GIVE UP EASY ...
DO THEY, BIG BROTHER?

MOKUBA ...?

THEY'RE ALMOST AT THE FINAL STAGE!
AND YOU KNOW WHAT THAT MEANS!

DO YOU REMEMBER YOUR BET WITH ME?
THE ONE WE MADE BEFORE YOU STARTED THE "DEATH T" PLAN!?

WE BET ON ***WHICH STAGE*** OF THE THEME PARK YUGI WOULD DIE IN!
YES ...

AND YOU BET ON "DEATH T-5"!
ISN'T THAT RIGHT, BIG BROTHER ?!!

YOU BET ON "DEATH T-4," DIDN'T YOU...?

OF COURSE I DID, YOU JERK!
"DEATH T-4" IS THE STAGE WHERE I FIGHT YUGI!

YES, I KNOW, MOKUBA ...
I BET ON THE FINAL STAGE OF THE THEME PARK, "DEATH T-5" ...
THE FINAL GAME OF "DUEL MONSTERS"!

YOU KNOW WHAT I MEAN! YOU BET ON ***YUGI*** INSTEAD OF ***ME, YOUR OWN BROTHER!***
HOW DO YOU THINK THAT FEELS ?!

I OPPOSED YOUR PARTICIPATION FROM THE BEGINNING.
AND I STILL FEEL THE SAME.
YOU CAN'T BEAT YUGI.

GRR ...!

MOKUBA... YOU TRIED TO SHOW ME UP BY CHALLENGING YUGI TO A GAME BEFORE, DIDN'T YOU...?
DO YOU THINK I DON'T KNOW THE ***OUTCOME*** OF THAT GAME?

....
TH-THAT'S NOT...

I...
I JUST ...
I JUST THOUGHT YOU'D LIKE ME IF I BEAT HIM...

GLARE
KNOW THIS! THERE IS NO SUCH THING AS BROTHERLY LOVE IN THE GAMING WORLD!
UNTIL YOU FIGURE THAT OUT, YOU WILL ALWAYS BE A LOSER, MOKUBA!!
GULP ...
I'LL SHOW YOU! I'LL BEAT YUGI MYSELF!
BOOM

YOU! ARE THE PREPARATIONS FOR DEATH T-4 READY ?!!
YES SIR!
YES, MASTER MOKUBA !

THEN LET'S GO !!
VSH
TODAY I'LL FINALLY SHOW MY BROTHER THAT I **AM** A GAMER!
JUST YOU WATCH !
GW
DDD

RRMMB

READ THIS WAY

YUGI !
ARE YOU OKAY, YUGI? DO YOU NEED YOUR INSULIN OR SOME-THING?
RRRMMMB

GASP
....!
I...

I CAN'T HOLD IT BACK...
RMB RMB
SOME-THING INSIDE OF ME ...

YUGI...YOU'RE JUST TIRED FROM ALL THE STRESS...
IT'S OKAY ...
RMBB
NO ...
I...

THERE'S SOMETHING I'VE KEPT SECRET FROM YOU ...

...?!

I THINK THERE'S ANOTHER "ME" INSIDE MYSELF THAT I DON'T KNOW ABOUT...
!!

ANOTHER YUGI ?!
...!
EVER SINCE I SOLVED THE MILLEN-NIUM PUZZLE...
THERE'S BEEN TIMES WHEN I BLACK OUT...
I THINK I'M *CHANGING* INTO SOMEONE THAT I DON'T KNOW ABOUT...
I'M SCARED...
I'VE FINALLY BECOME FRIENDS WITH YOU GUYS...
I WAS AFRAID THAT IF YOU KNEW ABOUT THE OTHER ME...
YOU MIGHT *LEAVE* ME!
YUGI...
I SWEAR TO YOU!
EVEN IF THERE *IS* ANOTHER PERSON INSIDE OF YOU...
WE'LL ALWAYS BE FRIENDS!!

...!
JONOUCHI!
HE'S RIGHT!
WE'LL ALWAYS BE FRIENDS!
ANZU...
GUYS...
...
THANK YOU...
OKAY, LET'S KEEP GOIN'!
TMP
YUGI!
OKAY!
HONDA...
I PROMISE TO COME BACK FOR YOU...
R RRAAA
HUH...?
!!
AAA
I CAN HEAR CHEERING!
FROM BEHIND THAT DOOR!
RR R AAA
RR AAA

RRR
AAAA
TH-
THIS
IS...

... THE SECOND ARENA!
WELCOME TO MY STAGE!
"DEATH T-4"!
YUGI !!

LEAVE YOUR FRIENDS WHERE THEY ARE AND COME TO THE DUEL BOX ALONE!

YUGI! THIS IS A BATTLE BETWEEN YOU AND ME!

MOKUBA !!

RRMMMB

...

YUGI! IT'S TOO DANGEROUS FOR YOU ALONE!

I'LL GO TOO!

NO!

LET ME GO ALONE!

RRMM

RM

YUGI ...!

IT'S OKAY! I'M NOT A ***WEAKLING*** ANYMORE!

I'M NOT ALONE!

I HAVE MY FRIENDS!

I HAVE YOU GUYS NO MATTER WHERE YOU ARE!

OKAY!

YOU TAUGHT ME WHAT REAL COURAGE IS!

IT'S THANKS TO YOU, JONOUCHI ...YOU AND HONDA.

I'M GLAD ...

I WON'T BE AFRAID ANYMORE... OF THE OTHER ME...

AND I...

!!
YU ...

SHOOOOM

JONOUCHI!!
ANZU!
I WILL WIN!!
BAM

RRRAAAA

HEY! THAT'S THE LOSER WHO'S GONNA GO UP AGAINST MOKUBA!

THERE'S NO WAY HE CAN WIN!

RRAAA

YOU'RE GONNA DIE AT THIS STAGE!
LIKE YOU HAVE A CHANCE!
ALONG WITH YOUR FRIENDS!
SO I'VE GOT TO BEAT YOU TO GET TO IT...
THE LAST STAGE YOU'RE TRYING TO GET TO... THE FINAL ARENA WITH MY BIG BROTHER... IS ON THE FLOOR ABOVE THIS ONE...
YUGI! I'LL LET YOU IN ON SOME-THING!
RAAA
SEE! THAT ELEVATOR TAKES YOU THERE!

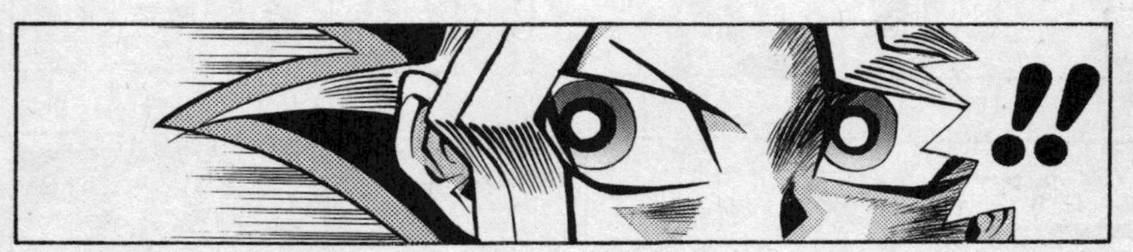

JONOUCHI!
ANZU...
MOKUBA...
YOU LITTLE...
HEH HEH HEH...
YUGI!
DON'T WORRY ABOUT US!
JUST KICK HIS BUTT AT HIS OWN GAME!
JONOUCHI!
RUMBLE
NOW! LET THE GAME BEGIN!
GLEAM
"DEATH T-4"!
THE COMPETITION THIS TIME IS...
DADADADA

CAPSULE MONSTER CHESS!
THE VIRTUAL REALITY VERSION!
CAPSULE MONSTER CHESS!
D DA DOOM

WE WILL PLAY CAPSULE MONSTER CHESS ON THIS BOARD...
BUT THE BATTLE WILL BE DISPLAYED BY VIRTUAL REALITY ON THE GIANT FIELD BELOW US!
!!
GWOOOOOO
THIS STRONG PIECE IS LIKE ME!
IT WILL DO BATTLE WITH THIS PATHETIC, LOW-LEVEL PIECE LIKE YOU!
LET ME GIVE YOU A DEMON-STRATION!
WATCH CLOSELY, YUGI!

OM
THE VIRTUAL MONSTERS APPEAR ON THE FIELD BELOW!
CHAK
AAAAH
ARMORSAURUS LEVEL 5
GYAAAAH
peep!
HYUMOKO LEVEL 1
THUD
A
R

OF COURSE, THE LOSER WILL PLAY A PENALTY GAME—
"THE EXPERIENCE OF DEATH"!!
NOW FIGHT !
DO
"THE EXPERIENCE OF DEATH ...!!"
NOW, THE GAME BEGINS!
I'LL TAKE YOU ON, MOKUBA !!
WAIT FOR ME, GRANDPA !!
BWA HA HA HA! I'LL DESTROY YOU JUST LIKE I DESTROY THIS WEAK LITTLE MONSTER!!
I WILL DEFEAT YUGI!!
PEEP!
I'LL BE THE ONE TO DESTROY HIM! I'LL SHOW MY BROTHER! HEH HEH HEH HEH!
I HAVE TO WIN TO MAKE IT TO THE FINAL STAGE... AND KAIBA!!
RO

Duel 35: Board Game Deathmatch

BAM

MEGATON
LEVEL 5
<ABILITIES>
* FLATTEN
* NOSE BREATH HURRICANE

NAMA HARGEN
LEVEL 4
<ABILITIES>
* CHOMP
* GLARE

BIG FOOT
LEVEL 5
<ABILITIES>
* MUSCLE PUNCH
* BEAR HUG
* GIANT SWING

ZOID "M"
LEVEL 5
<ABILITIES>
* ZOID GAS
* HEAD BUTT

ARMORSAURUS
LEVEL 5
<ABILITIES>
* FLAME
* ARMOR ATTACK

MOKUBA'S CAPSULE MONSTER TEAM

BWA HA HA HA HA! THERE'S NO WAY I CAN LOSE, YUGI!

Duel 35: Board Game Deathmatch

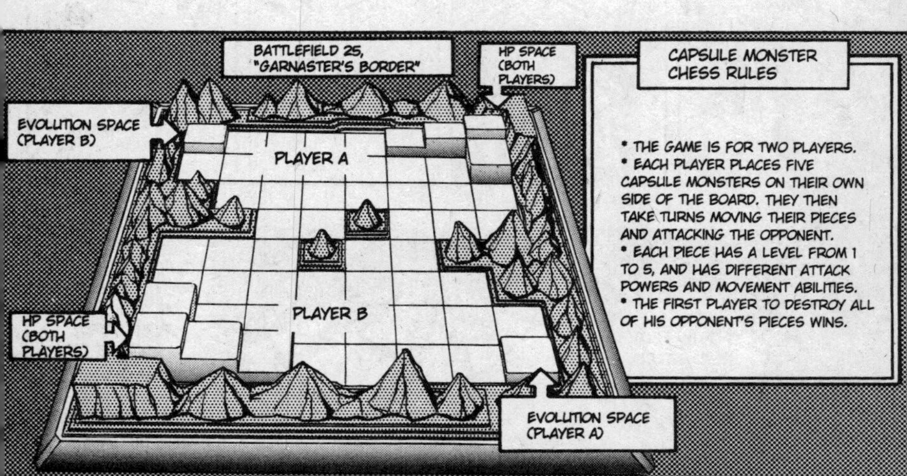

BA
!!
YUGI'S CAPSULE MONSTER TEAM
MOGLEY LEVEL 1
<ABILITIES> • DIG • CHEER OTHERS
NINJA SQUID LEVEL 2
<ABILITIES> • WATER-FU • SELF DESTRUCT
BEETON LEVEL 2
<ABILITIES> • CURL UP • ENDURE
BRAIN SLIME LEVEL 1
<ABILITIES> • THINK • POISON ATTACK
TOPPO LEVEL 1
<ABILITIES> • FLY • NOSE BALLOON
TCH ...
THE MACHINE MUST HAVE BEEN RIGGED! THERE'S TOO MUCH DIFFERENCE IN THE MONSTERS' LEVELS!
MOKUBA! YOU PLANNED THIS ALL ALONG...!
PLACE YOUR CAPSULES IN YOUR TERRITORY !!
HEH HEH HEH! SEE IF YOU CAN THINK UP A GOOD FORMATION FOR THOSE MONSTERS!
NOW..... HOW TO FIGHT...
THIS BOARD HAS ONE PATH ON EACH SIDE...
BUT YOU CAN'T GET BY IF THE ENEMY IS WAITING FOR YOU...
I HAVE IT!

IF YOU'RE DONE, THEN CAPSULES OUT!
DON'T WET YOURSELF WHEN YOU SEE MY MONSTERS, YUGI!
HUH?!
UGH! WHAT'S THAT SETUP SUPPOSED TO BE?
ALL THE WEAKLINGS CLUMPED TOGETHER!! WHAT A WUSS!
YUGI, YOU SUCK! BWA HA HA HA!

WHOOOOO

THE VIRTUAL MONSTERS ARE ON THE BIG FIELD!

WHOA! YOU CAN SEE WHERE ARMOR-SAURUS CAN MOVE!

ARMORSAURUS MOVEMENT CAPABILITIES (NOT INCLUDING MOUNTAINS OR OTHER STEEP AREAS)

THM

YOUR MOVE, YUGI!

THM
THM
THAT POINTY HAIRED KID HASN'T MADE A SINGLE MOVE!
MOKUBA'S MONSTERS ARE CLOSING IN ON HIM!
YUGI ...
WHAT ARE YOU DOING ...?!
THM
GO!! INVADE THE ENEMY TERRITORY!
LOOK! MOKUBA'S GOT HIM SURROUNDED!
DA
DOOM
THIS DUEL IS MINE, YUGI!

SNK
!
CLAK
WOW! HE MADE HIS FIRST MOVE!
OOOH
I THOUGHT HE GAVE UP!
YOU'RE TOO LATE, YUGI!!
I'LL ATTACK WITH ARMOR-SAURUS!
ROAR
HE BURNS UP YOUR WEAKLING MONSTER IN ONE BLAST!!
RR
ARMORSAURUS LEVEL 5
BRAIN SLIME LEVEL 1
ZGGGK!
URK...
HA! I'M NOT DONE YET...
ARMOR-SAURUS' TURN ISN'T OVER!

WIR
WHIR!
HE ATTACKS ONE MORE MONSTER!
ARMORSAURUS LEVEL 5
SPECIAL ABILITY
• ARMOR ATTACK: BY CURLING UP INTO A BALL AND ROLLING, ARMORSAURUS CAN DESTROY THE NEAREST MONSTER IN A STRAIGHT LINE.
YIPE!
WHAM
TOPPO LEVEL 1
BWA HA HA HA! YUGI, YOU'VE ALREADY LOST TWO MONSTERS!
BOOM
BA BA
RMMB
...
IT'S NOT OVER YET... ...I WON'T GIVE UP UNTIL THE END!
I'M GOING TO HAVE SOME FUN AND DESTROY ALL YOUR MONSTERS WITH JUST ARMORSAURUS!
BWA HA HA HA HA HA!
GO, ARMOR-SAURUS!
FLATTEN THAT WIMP!
WHOO
OOOM

WHIR WHIR

!

SHUK SHUK

GRIN

MOGLEY
LEVEL 1

SPECIAL ABILITY
* DIG

W-
WHAT
!?

NO WAY
...

I FORGOT
HE CAN
BURROW!

KA-BANNG

ONE OF
MY
MONSTERS
!!

MEGATON
LEVEL 5

WHIR

!

HE'S
HEADING
TOWARD
...

ARMOR-
SAURUS
CAN'T
STOP
MOVING
!!

WHIR

THWAM
THEY DESTROYED EACH OTHER ...!!!
GGKK ...
GULP
THIS IS WHAT HE WAS UP TO...
YUGI ...
HIGH LEVEL MONSTERS HAVE UNRIVALED POWER, BUT YOU NEED TO LEARN TO CONTROL IT!
NOW YOU'VE LOST TWO MONSTERS, MOKUBA!
BA
BA
NOW THEY'RE EVEN !!
MOKUBA LOST TWO MONSTERS !
AWRIGHT! YUGI'S FIGHTING BACK!
AND NOW, I'LL MOVE THIS PIECE TO ATTACK ZOID "M"....
A LEVEL 2 MONSTER CAN'T HOPE TO MATCH IT, BUT...
NINJA SQUID LEVEL 2
THERE IS ONE WAY IT CAN DEFEAT A LEVEL 5 ENEMY...
FORGIVE ME ...

AND NOW ...
UH ... UH ...
I-IT TOOK OUT MY MONSTER IN A **SUICIDE** ATTACK!!
...A PATH HAS BEEN OPENED!
YUGI, YOU JERK!
NINJA SQUID LEVEL 2
SPECIAL ABILITY * SELF DESTRUCT
HUH ...?!
!!
EVOLUTION SPACE
YUGIIIIII!! HE **SACRIFICED** THE OTHER PIECES TO LET **ONE** WEAK MONSTER REACH THE EVOLUTION SPACE!!
THE EVOLUTION SPACE IS UNGUARDED!

EVOLUTION SPACE
MY MONSTERS ARE TOO FAR AWAY! I CAN'T STOP BEETON FROM EVOLVING!!

CLAK
BEETON LEVEL 2

MONSTERS THAT REACH THE EVOLUTION SPACE AUTOMATICALLY EVOLVE THREE LEVELS!!
WHICH MEANS THIS USELESS LEVEL 2...

CLAK

BA DUM
...WILL TRANSFORM INTO A POWERFUL MONSTER!

CLAK

CLAK
I'VE REACHED THE EVOLUTION SPACE!

GSH
NOW EVOLVE!
LOOK!
THE BEETON'S TRANS-FORMING!
OOSH
OOSH
OOSH
....!!
FOM
DO
NO MATTER HOW WEAK A MONSTER IS, IF YOU BELIEVE IN EACH STEP IT TAKES, IT WILL GROW STRONG!!
BEETON LEVEL 2
EVOLVES TO
HYPER BEETLE LEVEL 5

!!
HYPER BEETLE LEVEL 5
SPECIAL ABILITIES
* FLY
* HORN ATTACK
LET'S GO!
FLAP
WEEEE
R DAR
ENGAGE!
NAMA HARGEN LEVEL 4
SLASH
HORN ATTACK!
ARGH ...!
URGH ......
HE GOT ME ....
WHOA!
YAAY
THIS IS *CRAZY!* MOKUBA HAS ONLY ONE MONSTER LEFT!!

YUGI... THIS BATTLE WILL DECIDE THE GAME!!
HEH HEH... HYPER BEETLE'S LONG RANGE ATTACKS ARE POWERFUL ...
BUT IN CLOSE QUARTERS, BIG FOOT IS STRONGER !!

YAA
AHH
BIG FOOT LEVEL 5
HYPER BEETLE LEVEL 5

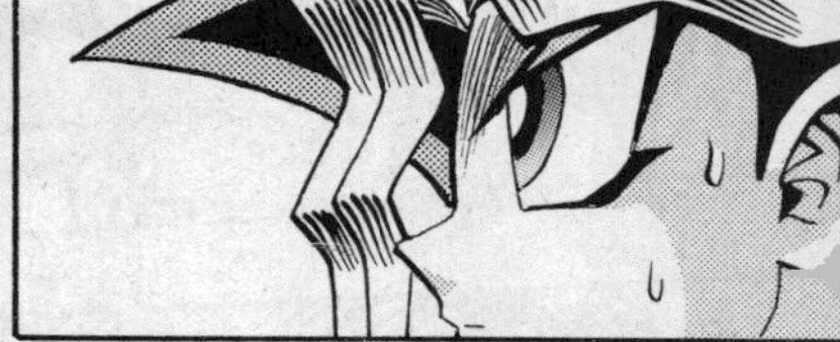

GGGG

SH
FIGHT
!!!
SLA
THUD
HEHN

HA HA HA! HYPER BEETLE IS DEAD!
YUGI! YOU'RE DONE FOR!!
URK ...!!

MWA HA HA ... YUGI ...
YOU HAD ANOTHER MONSTER HIDING ON THE BOARD, DIDN'T YOU?
DO YOU THINK I'LL LET IT GET AWAY?
!!

PEEK
!?

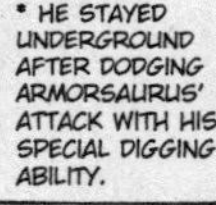
MOGLEY
LEVEL 1
* HE STAYED UNDERGROUND AFTER DODGING ARMORSAURUS' ATTACK WITH HIS SPECIAL DIGGING ABILITY.

THIS IS IT! THE LAST MONSTER!

THM

HA HA HA! BIG FOOT! STOMP THAT COWARD FLAT!!

I DID IT! I WIN!

GRRAAAAGGGH!
GOOD-BYE, CRUEL WORLD!

CRACK★
!!
!
BIG FOOT'S BODY IS...!!
IT CAN'T BE... HYPER BEETLE'S ATTACK WAS A CRITICAL HIT...?!
YOU KNOW THE SAYING "IT'S NOT OVER 'TILL IT'S OVER"?
HUH ...?!
WELL, NOW IT'S OVER!
I WIN, MOKUBA!

CRUMBLE

SLAM

BAM

BAM

...!

I WIN THIS GAME...

...MOKUBA.

Duel 36: Battle Beyond Hope

Duel 36:
Battle Beyond Hope

WHOO-HOO! YOU DID IT, YUGI!
AY
YAA
M-MASTER MOKUBA...

NO WAY! MOKUBA LOST AT CAPSULE MONSTERS?!
!
WHAAA
WHO IS THAT POINTY HAIRED KID...!!

MORONS! HE'S NOT "THAT POINTY HAIRED KID"!
HIS NAME IS YUGI!
HE'S MY BUD!

OKAY, YUGI... YOUR CARD GAME WITH KAIBA IS NEXT!

RAAAAA

GGH ......
NO WAY ...
NO WAY ...
NO WAY ...
NO WAY ...

I'M GOING.

TO THE FINAL STAGE WHERE KAIBA IS WAITING ...!
WAIT! YUGI ...!!

I ...
I WON'T BELIEVE IT!
THERE'S NO WAY I COULD LOSE!

ALL OF MY CAPSULE MONSTERS WERE HIGHER LEVEL AND STRONGER THAN YOURS!
THERE WAS NO WAY I COULD LOSE TO YOU!!

BAM☆

KAIBA !!

YAAAYY

KAIBA !!

YOU'LL GET YOUR GAME ALL RIGHT, KAIBA!
I WILL! DON'T YOU GO ANYWHERE!
DOOM

B-BIG BROTHER!
......!!

STARING AT MY BACK FOR YEARS...
I'VE FELT YOUR PATHETIC, CLINGING, LOSER'S GAZE....
I KEPT TELLING YOU OVER AND OVER, MOKUBA... IF YOU PLAY WITH FIRE YOU'LL GET BURNED...

S-SETO...
AH... I...

GLARE

THAT IS THE LAW OF "DEATH T"!!
A PENALTY GAME AWAITS THE LOSER!!
YOU UNDERSTAND, DON'T YOU? ONLY THE WINNER IS ALLOWED OUT OF THAT DUEL BOX!
CLICK

HUH ...?!
MY BROTHER WOULDN'T DO IT TO ME...NOT THAT...
HE WOULDN'T ...
FSSHH
NOT "THE EXPERIENCE OF DEATH" !!!
FSSHH
GYAAAAHHH !!
AAAAAGGHHH ?!
!
MOKUBA !!
IMPOSSIBLE! KAIBA'S PUTTING HIS OWN BROTHER THROUGH A PENALTY GAME!!!

YIIIEEEEEE!!
FSSSHH
BA DUM
GRAAAHHH!!
AAAAGGGH!
S-SAVE ME, BIG BROTHER!
AAAAGGHHH
SHDOOO
MOKUBA!!
SHDOOO
MOKUBA... TAKE MY HAND!!
......
SHDOOO
GRAB

CH
OM
P
...!
GASP
!
WIP
WH
...
WHY
...?!
WHY
DID
YOU
SAVE
ME...
?!
MOKUBA
...
I WOULDN'T HAVE WON THIS GAME IF I DIDN'T HAVE *FRIENDS* WHO REACHED OUT TO ME.
...

FRIENDS ...?!

!

MOKUBA!

UH ......

UNTIL YOU REALIZE THAT THERE IS NO SUCH THING AS BROTHERLY LOVE, YOU WILL ALWAYS BE A **LOSER!**

NOOOOO!

GRIP

YUGI ...
MAYBE WHEN YOU FACE MY BROTHER ...
NNN
BA
BAM
I'M HEADING TO THE FINAL STAGE, "DEATH T-5"!
MY REVENGE WILL END THERE!!

READ THIS WAY

SHOOT! KAIBA AND YUGI'S FIGHT IS IN THE DUEL RING UPSTAIRS!
STOP PUSHING!
WE'VE GOTTA HURRY IF WE WANT TO GET GOOD SEATS!

YOU'RE GOING UPSTAIRS AS WELL!

GRR...
ONE MORE THING...
LET ME BORROW YOUR CELL PHONE!

IT'S JUST ...
THE SURGEON SAYS... THERE ISN'T MUCH HOPE ......

!!
PLEASE HANG IN THERE, GRANDPA MUTOU...

...I SEE ...
HANASAKI ... STAY THERE AND KEEP WATCH.
YES! I GOT IT!
CLICK

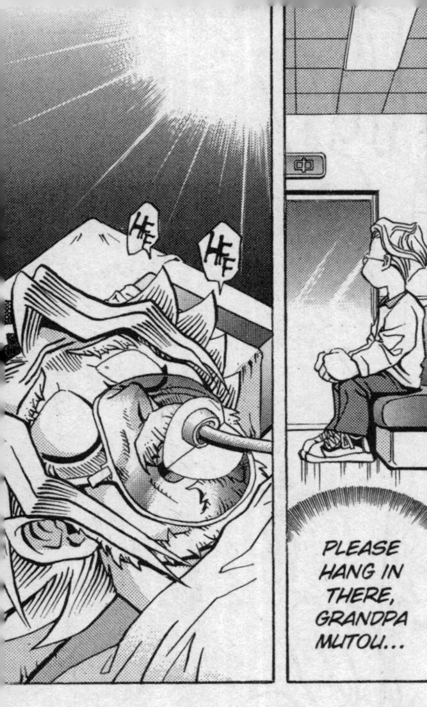
HEF
HEF

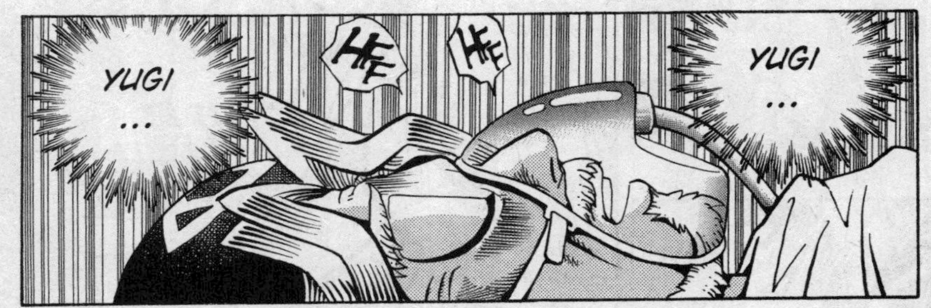
YUGI ...
HEF
HEF
YUGI ...

HOW IS HE ...?
IT SOUNDS BAD...

...!

CRAP ...
HONDA ISN'T ANSWERING HIS CELL EITHER...
IT CAN'T GET MUCH WORSE ...
...!

ANYWAY, RIGHT NOW...ALL WE CAN DO IS WATCH OVER YUGI IN HIS BATTLE...!

KAIBA ...
YOU'VE HURT MY FRIENDS AND MY FAMILY...
I'LL NEVER FORGIVE YOU, EVEN IF YOU BEG FOR MERCY!
"DEATH T-5," THE DOME DUEL ARENA !!
HM ...!

RRAAAAAA
RRMMM
YAAAYYYY
HEY! LOOK!
IT'S GAME MASTER KAIBA!
UNNNN

WELCOME TO THE FINAL STAGE, YUGI!

KAIBA !!

HEH HEH ..... WORDS MEAN NOTHING TO US ANY-MORE...
WHAT WILL DECIDE OUR FATES ...
...ARE THE CARDS !!
BAM
DA
ALL RIGHT !
GRANDPA'S DECK AND THE HEART OF THE CARDS!!
DUM

MMEH HEH HEH...
I CONGRATULATE YOU ON GETTING THIS FAR...
IT'S ALMOST A SHAME THAT THIS IS WHERE YOU'LL PROBABLY DIE...
I HAVE IN MY DECK THREE OF THE STRONGEST CARDS IN THE WORLD, THE UNFATHOMABLY RARE BLUE-EYES WHITE DRAGON!
NO CARD EXISTS THAT CAN DEFEAT THEM!!
BEFORE STARTING THE GAME...
WE WILL SHUFFLE AND CUT EACH OTHER'S DECKS!!
DUEL MONSTERS--
YUGI • LIFE POINTS 2000
I BELIEVE IN MY GRANDPA'S DECK...

THEY'RE ABOUT TO START!
WHOAAA
YUGI ...
BANG
...DUEL!!
KAIBA • LIFE POINTS 2000
I WILL WIN!!
MMEH HEH HEH...

WINGED DRAGON, GUARDIAN OF THE FORTRESS!
Winged Dragon, Guardian of the Fortress
ATK/1400
DEF/1200
ATTACK MODE!
I'LL TAKE YOU ON!!
MY CARD IS...
FIRE BALL!!!

HITOTSU-ME GIANT*!

RRMM

RR

Hitotsu-me Giant

ATK/1200
DEF/1000

* JAPANESE FOR "ONE-EYED GIANT"

FIREBALL ATTACK! YUGI'S WINGED DRAGON ANNIHILATES KAIBA'S HITOTSU-ME GIANT!

ATK/1200
DEF/1000

WINGED DRAGON, GUARDIAN OF THE FORTRESS ★★★★

ATK/1400
DEF/1200

HEH

KAIBA • LIFE POINTS 1800

YUGI • LIFE POINTS 2000

Duel 37: To the Death!

Duel 37: To The Death!

DUEL MONSTERS BASIC RULES

• EACH PLAYER STARTS WITH 2000 LIFE POINTS AND A DECK OF 40 CARDS. AT THE BEGINNING OF THE GAME, EACH PLAYER DRAWS 5 CARDS FROM THEIR DECK.

• PLAYERS TAKE TURNS DRAWING CARDS FROM THEIR DECK, AND PLAYING MONSTER CARDS IN EITHER ATTACK OR DEFENSE MODE. PLAYERS MAY ALSO USE SPELL CARDS FOR VARIOUS EFFECTS.

• THE FIRST PLAYER TO RUN OUT OF LIFE POINTS LOSES.

BATTLE SYSTEM

1) ATTACK VS. ATTACK

• THE MONSTER WITH THE HIGHER ATTACK POINTS WINS. THE LOSING CARD GOES TO THE "GRAVEYARD" AND THE DIFFERENCE IN POINTS IS SUBTRACTED FROM THE LIFE POINTS OF THE OWNER.

2) ATTACK VS. DEFENSE

• IF THE ATTACKER'S ATTACK POINTS ARE HIGHER THAN THE DEFENDER'S DEFENSE, THE DEFENDING CARD GOES TO THE "GRAVEYARD." HOWEVER, THE OWNER'S LIFE POINTS ARE UNAFFECTED.

• IF THE DEFENDER'S DEFENSE IS HIGHER THAN THE ATTACKER'S ATTACK POINTS, THE DIFFERENCE IN POINTS IS SUBTRACTED FROM THE ATTACKING PLAYER'S LIFE POINTS. BOTH CARDS STAY PUT.

MMEH HEH... YUGI ...
I CAN FEEL YOUR PUNY HEART *POUNDING* EVERY TIME I DRAW A CARD.
THAT'S BECAUSE YOU KNOW THE MOMENT I DRAW MY BLUE-EYES WHITE DRAGON, YOU *WILL DIE*...
THE CARD I DRAW IS...
THE WICKED WORM BEAST
ATK/1400
DEF/700
DA DOOM
THE WICKED WORM BEAST !!
IT EQUALS THE WINGED DRAGON IN BOTH LEVEL AND ATTACK POINTS!!
WORM BEAST, KILL HIM!
ZGG ZGG
I'LL TAKE YOU ON!
NOOOSH

WORM BEAST ATTACK! POISON SOUL!

ITS ACID SPRAY ATTACKS THE DRAGON!

!

BUT THE WINGED DRAGON HAS THE POWER OF FLIGHT!

GYAAAHHH!
SH
SH
POF
POF
FIRE-BALL!!!
BOOM☆
BOOM☆
BOOM☆
THE WINGED DRAGON DESTROYS THE WORM BEAST!!
HMPH...
SINCE THEIR ATTACK POINTS WERE THE SAME, MY LIFE POINTS AREN'T AFFECTED...
BIG DEAL. ROUND THREE...
RRMMB
KAIBA • LIFE POINTS 1800
MY TURN IS OVER, BUT I DON'T HAVE ANY MONSTERS ON THE FIELD...
ACCORDING TO THE FIRST EDITION RULES, THIS MEANS I CAN PUT OUT A FREE MONSTER IN DEFENSE MODE USING ONE OF THE CARDS IN MY HAND.
NOW, WHICH ONE SHOULD I USE...
THIS ONE HAS GOOD DEFENSE. I'LL MAKE IT MY BARRIER MONSTER!
AWRIGHT!
K-KAIBA LOST AGAIN...
YAAAA
WAY TO GO, YUGI!

MY TURN!
I DRAW A CARD FROM MY DECK!
I'M NOT FAMILIAR WITH THE CARD KAIBA JUST PLAYED...
IF I ATTACK HIM AND HIS DEFENSE IS HIGHER THAN MY ATTACK POINTS, I WOULD BE THE ONE DAMAGED...
I'LL PLAY *MY* CARD IN DEFENSE MODE AS WELL.
TURN OVER!
MMEH HEH... I GET IT...
YOU PLAN TO BUILD UP A STRONG DEFENSE BEFORE I DRAW A BLUE-EYES WHITE DRAGON...
BUT...
...*THAT WON'T WORK!*
I WAS A CHAMPION *BEFORE* I OWNED A BLUE-EYES, AND EVEN *WITHOUT* ONE, I CAN DEFEAT YOU!
I'LL PROVE THAT RIGHT NOW!
I CHANGE MY BARRIER MONSTER FROM DEFENSE TO ATTACK MODE!!
RMMB

READ THIS WAY
!!
THAT'S ...
MMEH HEH ...
SAGGI COULD NEVER DEFEAT THE WINGED DRAGON AT HIS CURRENT ATTACK POWER.
THAT'S WHY ...
SAGGI THE DARK CLOWN !!
SAGGI THE DARK CLOWN
ATK/600
DEF/1500
TA-DAA
I USE THE SPELL CARD "DARK ENERGY" TO TRIPLE HIS ATTACK POWER!!
DARK EN
(Spell Card)
A Fiend-type monster equipped with this card has 3x its original ATK.
BRRMM
RRMM
ATK/600 --> ATK/1800
!!
NOW! KILL THE DRAGON!

DARK GLIDE !
WINGED DRAGON, GUARDIAN OF THE FORTRESS ATK/1400 DEF/1200
WNNNGG
SAGGI THE DARK CLOWN ATK/1800 DEF/1500
GRNNG
!!
HE GOT ME!
YUGI • LIFE POINTS 1600
MMM HEH HEH HEH HEH ...
"WINGED DRAGON, GUARDIAN OF THE FORTRESS" IS DESTROYED !!

WHAT DO YOU THINK? JUST YOUR BASIC COMBO... THE POWER OF SAGGI THE DARK CLOWN ENHANCED BY THE SPELL CARD "DARK ENERGY"!
GRR ...
STRONG CARDS ALONE AREN'T ENOUGH TO WIN IN THIS GAME!
USING MONSTERS TOGETHER WITH SPELLS IS THE KEY TO VICTORY!
KAIBA KNOWS THIS GAME INSIDE AND OUT!!
BUT GRANDPA BUILT THIS DECK! HE'S A GAME MASTER!
THERE MUST BE A TRUMP TO DEFEAT KAIBA IN HERE!!
!
RRRG ...
USELESS !
RIGHT LEG OF THE FORBIDDEN ONE
ATK/200
DEF/300
THIS CARD CAN'T DEFEAT SAGGI THE DARK CLOWN!
I'LL PLAY ANOTHER MONSTER IN DEFENSE MODE AND WAIT HIM OUT!
SANGAN
ATK/1000
DEF/600
LET'S START FROM THE LEFT !!

DARK GLIDE!!

GAAHH

BOOOOM

BAM

YUGI • LIFE POINTS 1400

NO GOOD! NOW THAT SAGGI'S BEEN POWERED-UP, THE CARDS IN MY HAND ARE NO MATCH FOR HIM

MMHEH HEH HEH...

CURSES ...

!!

WHSHH

YUGI!
YUGI!

HANG IN THERE ...
FOR YOUR GRANDPA'S SAKE..

YUGI! YOU HAVE TO WIN!!

BA BOOM
DARK GLIDE !!

YUGI ...
YOU DISAPPOINT ME!
I DON'T EVEN NEED MY BLUE-EYES FOR THIS DUEL!!

...

I CAN HEAR THE GASPS OF HIS LAST BREATHS ECHOING FROM THE CARDS!
BUT WHAT DO YOU EXPECT WITH THE DECK THAT FAILURE OF AN OLD MAN LEFT BEHIND!
HA HA HA HA!
!!
YUGI ...
YOU MUST DEFEAT KAIBA...
GRANDPA ...
I CAN HEAR IT, GRANDPA!
GRANDPA TRUSTED ME WITH HIS DECK! I'VE GOT TO HAVE FAITH IN HIM!
BA DUM
BA DUM
I HEAR YOUR HEART BEATING IN THESE CARDS!
FWP
I BELIEVE IN THESE CARDS!!
KAIBA ...
DO YOUR CARDS HAVE THE POWER OF YOUR TRUST?!
...!
WHAT DO YOU MEAN?

GAIA THE FIERCE KNIGHT !!
BRM
BRM
ATK/2300
DEF/2100
!!
GAIA THE FIERCE KNIGHT! THE MOST POWERFUL CARD IN THE WARRIOR CLASS!
GO, DARK KNIGHT! VANQUISH SAGGI!
C-CLOP

SPIRAL SABER!
UR...
GA...
KIIINNN
GAAH...
BAM
ONE DOWN!

YAAAHH

NOW THEY'RE *EVEN* AGAIN!

WHAT A GREAT DUEL!

ALRIGHT, YUGI! YOU KNOW YOUR GRANDPA WOULDN'T GIVE YOU SUCKY CARDS!

WELL, WELL ...

I SUPPOSE THE DECK OF A GAME STORE OWNER WOULD HAVE TO HAVE A DECENT CARD OR TWO...

KAIBA • LIFE POINTS 1300

YOU CAN'T PREDICT THIS DUEL...

NOT UNTIL THE VERY END...

YUGI • LIFE POINTS 1400

I'VE DRAWN THE BLUE-EYES WHITE DRAGON !!
!
THE BLUE-EYES WHITE DRAGON !!
BAM
RUMBBLE
BLUE-EYES WHITE DRAGON
ATK/3000
DEF/2500
WA HA HA HA!
TOO BAD! JUST AFTER YOU'D DRAWN YOUR TRUMP CARD!!

UH ...!
BADUM
RRRUMMBLE
HE FINALLY GOT THE BLUE-EYES WHITE DRAGON!
YAAY! KAIBA WON!
YUGI!

BLUE-EYES WHITE DRAGON, ATTACK!

BURST STREAM OF DESTRUCTION!

OOO

BLUE-EYES WHITE DRAGON
ATK/3000
DEF/2500

M

DIE, GAIA— AND PREPARE A PLACE IN HELL FOR YOUR MASTER!

Z-BOO

GHH..

GW
GAIA THE FIERCE KNIGHT ATK/2300 DEF/2100
WA HA HA HA! WELL, YUGI?
ZUM ZUM ZUM
GYAAAAA!!!
AND REMEMBER, I STILL HAVE TWO MORE BLUE-EYES WHITE DRAGONS IN THIS DECK!
YOU'RE FINISHED!
YUGI, NO!
!!
GRANDPA... WHAT SHOULD I DO...?
YUGI • LIFE POINTS 700

MMMM MEH HEH HEH... I'VE DRAWN THE BLUE-EYES WHITE DRAGON!

IT'S OVER FOR YOU, YUGI!!

DADADOOM

Duel 38: The Terror of Blue-Eyes!!

READ THIS WAY
!!
DA
NOW, YUGI... DRAW!
KAIBA • LIFE POINTS 1300
IMP
ATK/1300 DEF/1000
YAAAHHH
NO CARD CAN BEAT THE BLUE-EYES!
THIS DUEL IS OVER !!
YUGI !!
NO MATTER WHAT MONSTER YOU BRING OUT, THE BLUE-EYES WHITE DRAGON WILL BLOW IT AWAY!
MHEH HEH HEH!
NO GOOD... THIS CARD WON'T LAST MORE THAN AN INSTANT!
DEFENSE MODE!!

URK ...
ZBOOM
ATTACK!
KILL!
SLAUGHTER!
DESTROY!
YOU'RE ONLY DRAWING OUT YOUR INEVITABLE DEMISE!
BUT!
AS LONG AS YOU PLAY YOUR MONSTERS IN DEFENSE MODE, YOUR LIFE POINTS DON'T CHANGE... NO MATTER HOW MANY MONSTERS I SLAUGHTER!
IT'S PAINFUL TO WATCH!
DEFENSE MODE!
IT'S NO GOOD! MY CARDS' ATTACK SCORES JUST AREN'T HIGH ENOUGH...
GGH ...!
NOW! PLAY YOUR NEXT MONSTER!
EVENTUALLY, YOU'LL RUN OUT OF CARDS! THEN YOU LOSE!
...!
KAIBA'S RIGHT!
BUT IF I PLAY A MONSTER IN ATTACK MODE, I LOSE...!

ATTACK ...!
GULP ...!

...IS THAT WHAT YOU EXPECT ME TO DO?
I WON'T... NOT THIS TIME!
RATHER THAN PUT YOUR "BEAVER WARRIOR" OUT OF ITS MISERY, I'LL DRAW ANOTHER CARD. I'LL INCREASE THE SIZE OF MY ARMY!

HMM ...
I KNEW THIS WAS COMING ...!
RRRMM

EACH MONSTER CAN ONLY DEFEND AGAINST THE ATTACK OF ONE ENEMY MONSTER...
IF HE BRINGS OUT MORE MONSTERS, I WON'T HAVE ENOUGH DEFENDERS TO STOP THEM! I'LL LOSE IN THE NEXT TURN!

IT LOOKS LIKE THE GODDESS OF VICTORY IS ON MY SIDE...
MY NEXT CARD IS...

WHA ...!
RRRRRMMM

BLUE-EYES WHITE DRAGON !!!
TWO BLUE-EYES WHITE DRAGONS !!
HSSSSST
MMEH HEH HEH... ON MY NEXT TURN, THESE TWO WILL ATTACK AT THE SAME TIME!
ULP ...
BADUM
I COULD PLAY ANOTHER MONSTER THIS TURN, BUT NEXT TURN I'D BE DEFENSELESS! HIS DRAGONS CAN KILL TWO OF MY MONSTERS EACH TURN, BUT I CAN ONLY DRAW ONE NEW CARD!
I WIN !!
KAIBA WINS! (OF COURSE!)
YAAHHHH
THERE'S NOTHING YUGI CAN DO!
YOUR LIFE IS OVER, YUGI!!
I'VE LOST ...
YUGI ...
DON'T GIVE UP UNTIL THE END ...

GRANDPA
!

I
...

FSH
I WON'T GIVE UP!
I'M NOT FIGHTING THIS DUEL ALONE!!

FWP
EVERY-THING RIDES ON THIS CARD!

SWORDS OF REVEALING LIGHT (SPELL CARD)
Counting from your opponent's turn, none of your opponent's monsters can attack for 3 turns of his/her own.
I'VE DRAWN THE SPELL CARD, "SWORDS OF REVEALING LIGHT"!
THE SWORDS OF LIGHT *BIND* YOUR BLUE-EYES WHITE DRAGONS!
!!
WHAT ?!!

READ THIS WAY
SHREE
SHREEE...
NOW I'M SAFE... EVEN IF JUST FOR THREE TURNS!
FEH...
YOU'RE BEGIN-NING TO ANNOY ME...
YOU STILL HAVEN'T GIVEN UP?
THE DUEL ISN'T OVER YET!
WAY TO GO, YUGI!!

VOOOOO

WELL... YOU'VE USED UP THE ***LAST*** OF YOUR LUCK, ANYWAY...
YOU CAN ONLY BIND THE BLUE-EYES FOR THREE TURNS!
WHAT CAN YOU DO IN THAT SHORT TIME ?

.....
HE'S RIGHT... I'VE ONLY EXTENDED MY LIFE THREE TURNS... THERE'S NOTHING I CAN DO...

NOW... IT'S ***MY*** TURN TO DRAW A CARD...

I'LL PUT THIS MONSTER IN ***DEFENSE*** MODE.
THAT WAY THE ***BLUE-EYES WHITE DRAGONS*** WILL HAVE THE HONOR OF FINISHING YOU OFF.
THAT'S HOW I ENVISIONED THIS FINALE FROM THE START.

NOW LET'S BEGIN THE ***COUNTDOWN*** TO YOUR DEATH.
DRAW YOUR CARD! YOU HAVE THREE TURNS!

SHREEE

I HAVE FOUR CARDS IN MY HAND ...
ONLY ONE IS A MONSTER CARD I CAN USE IN BATTLE ...

THE OTHER THREE ARE USELESS. I DON'T EVEN KNOW WHAT THEY MEAN...
LEFT LEG OF THE FORBIDDEN ONE ★★
ATK/200 DEF/300
LEFT ARM OF THE FORBIDDEN ONE ★★
RIGHT LEG OF THE FORBIDDEN ONE ★★
ATK/200 DEF/300
THESE ARE JUNK CARDS... THERE'S NO WAY TO DEFEAT KAIBA...
THE SPELL CARD THAT I MANAGED TO DRAW—THE SWORDS OF REVEALING LIGHT—IS ONLY A PLOY FOR TIME...

I REALLY LOSE ...

!

GRANDPA ....
HO HO...
YOU LOOK DOWN, YUGI...

YUGI ...
HAVE YOU GIVEN UP? THAT'S NOT LIKE YOU...
BUT... WHAT CAN I DO...?

YUGI ...
NOT TOO LONG AGO YOU WERE SUFFERING. REMEMBER HOW YOU GOT OVER IT THAT TIME...

HUH ...?!
...

THE MILLENNIUM PUZZLE ...
I COMPLETED THE MILLENNIUM PUZZLE!

MM-HM ...
YOU PUT EACH PIECE OF THAT PUZZLE IN ITS PLACE...
YOU DIDN'T GIVE UP... YOU BELIEVED IN YOURSELF AND COMPLETED THE PUZZLE, EVEN THOUGH IT TOOK YOU EIGHT YEARS!
YUP!

YUGI !
THERE IS NOTHING MEANINGLESS IN THIS WORLD!
LIKE PIECES OF A PUZZLE.
THE CARDS AS WELL ...

HUH ...?!
SHH
AH ...

GRANDPA ...
AAAA

THE MILLENNIUM PUZZLE ...
AND THE CARDS ?
AA AA

RRAAAAA
GASP
EXODIA!!
CAN IT BE...
RRAA
AAA
THIS DECK OF CARDS ...?
CAN IT REALLY HAVE EXODIA?!
DM
DMDMDM
YUGI!
WHAT ARE YOU WAITING FOR! DRAW YOUR CARD!!

!
THERE ARE NO MEANINGLESS CARDS!
FWIP
!!
THAT'S IT!

THAT'S ENOUGH, YUGI! YOU'RE JUST STALLING TO EXTEND YOUR MISERABLE EXISTENCE! DRAW YOUR CARD!

YES! I'LL DRAW NOW!

FWIP

!

RIGHT ARM OF THE FORBIDDEN ONE

ATK/200

DOOM

LEFT LEG OF THE FORBIDDEN ONE

ATK/200
DEF/300

I'VE COLLECTED FOUR OF THE CARDS!!

READ THIS WAY
MY TURN ...
JUDGEMAN
ATK/2200
DEF/1500
WELL, IT'S DULL JUST SITTING HERE SO...
THE STRESS WILL DO YOU GOOD...
I'LL USE THE JUDGEMAN TO DESTROY YOUR DEFENSIVE MONSTER...
CRACK
...!
JUDGEMAN ATK/2200 DEF/1500
BEAVER WARRIOR ATK/1200 DEF/1500
MMEH HEH HEH...
TWO TURNS LEFT!
DARK MAGICIAN
ATK/2500
DEF/2100
THE DARK MAGICIAN!
I COULD PLAY IT IN DEFENSE MODE, BUT IT WON'T MATTER AGAINST TWO BLUE-EYES WHITE DRAGONS ...

RUMBLE
I PLAY THIS CARD IN ATTACK MODE! JUDGEMAN, DIE!
DARK MAGICIAN ATK/2500 DEF/2100
FEH...
THE FUTILE STRUGGLES OF THE CONDEMNED!
BLACK MAGIC!!
JUDGEMAN IS DESTROYED!
KAIBA! I WON'T GIVE UP ON THIS DUEL UNTIL THE END!
I'LL TAKE EVERY CHANCE I GET TO CHIP AWAY AT YOUR LIFE POINTS!
YOU LOST 300 POINTS WITH THAT MOVE!
MMEH HEH HEH...
IS THAT SO...
IT'S THE LAST TURN!
YOU HAVE NO CHANCE LEFT...
KAIBA · LIFE POINTS 1000

READ THIS WAY
AND THE LAST CARD I DRAW IS...
THE THIRD BLUE-EYES WHITE DRAGON !!!
!!
BURST STREAM OF DESTRUCTION!! DESTROY THE DARK MAGICIAN!!
!

RAAARRRRR
HA HA HA HA HA HA!
NOW! DRAW YOUR LAST CARD, YUGI!
GULP ...
YUGI • LIFE POINTS 200
NO MATTER WHAT CARD YOU DRAW, YOU WILL DIE!
YUGI! NO!

NOW, THE BLUE-EYES WHITE DRAGONS HAVE BEEN RELEASED !!
ON THE NEXT TURN, THE THREE BLUE-EYES WILL ATTACK TOGETHER AND YOU'LL GO TO NEGATIVE 8800 LIFE POINTS!
ROARR
ROARR
WA HA HA HA HA HA !!

Duel 39: Endgame

BADUM
......

AND ON MY NEXT TURN, MY *THREE* BLUE-EYES WHITE DRAGONS WILL ATTACK TOGETHER, AND THAT WILL BE THE *END* OF *YOU!* *MMEH HEH HA HA HA HA HA HA!*

BADO

Duel 39: Endgame

BADUM

IN MY HAND I HAVE FOUR PIECES OF THE FORBIDDEN ONE...BOTH LEGS...BOTH ARMS...

IF THESE ARE THE CARDS GRANDPA WAS TALKING ABOUT ...THE CARDS THAT SUMMON THE FORGOTTEN GOD EXODIA...
IF I CAN GET ALL FIVE, I'LL BE ABLE TO SUMMON EXODIA!
ALL I NEED TO DO IS DRAW THE LAST CARD!

BUT......

40 CARDS IN MY DECK...5 CARDS IN MY HAND...WHAT ARE THE CHANCES OF DRAWING THE ONE I NEED?
BUT IT'S IMPOSSIBLE!

AM I ...
AM I GOING TO LOSE ...?

YUGI!

HANG IN THERE, MAN!
DON'T GIVE UP UNTIL THE END!!

YUGI ...

DOOOM
DA
DA

DO IT NOW! PICK YOUR CARD!
YUGI !!
EEE
......
MMEH HEH HEH... YOU'RE JUST DELAYING THE INEVITABLE ...
NO MATTER WHAT CARD YOU DRAW, THERE'S NOTHING THAT CAN STAND AGAINST THE MIGHT OF THREE BLUE EYES WHITE DRAGONS!

THAT'S IT! DRAW THE CARD AND YOU CAN REST—IN PEACE!
REST FOR ETERNITY IN THE BLACKNESS OF DEATH!

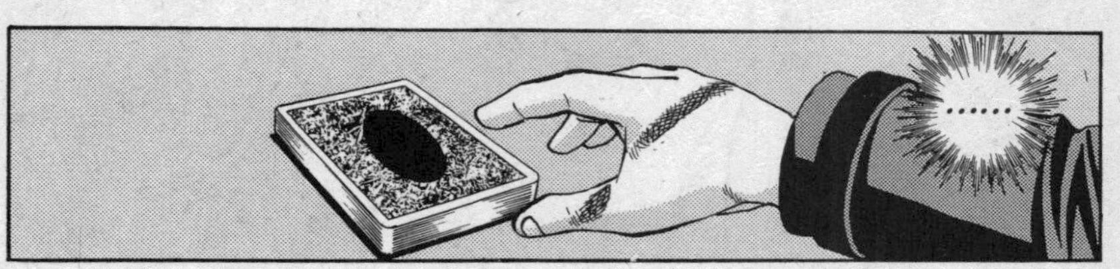
......

!

I SHOULD BE ABLE TO REACH THE CARDS...BUT THEY SEEM SO FAR AWAY ALL OF A SUDDEN!

DOOM

NO! IT'S NOT THE CARDS! IT'S ME!
I'M TRYING TO ESCAPE ...TO GET OUT OF DRAWING IT!

MY FEAR IS MAKING THE DISTANCE WIDER!

SHREE EEE

YUGI ...
IF WE'RE EVER ALONE, WE JUST HAVE TO THINK OF THIS SMILEY FACE ...
!

WE'RE HERE FOR YOU, YUGI ...

EVERYONE ...!

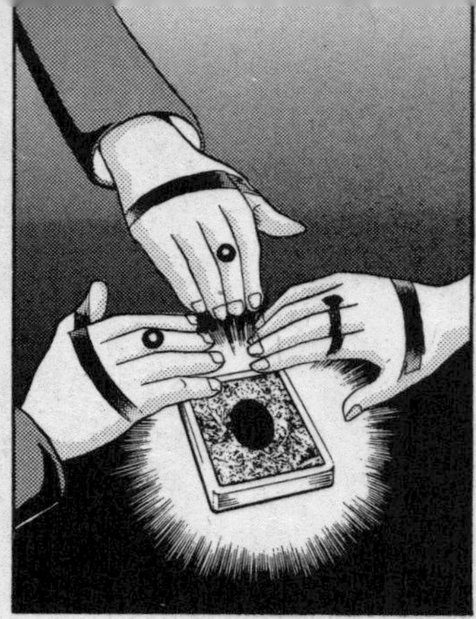

SWSH

MY FRIENDS ARE WITH ME ...

BAM

THANKS, EVERYONE...

I WON'T BE AFRAID ANYMORE.

MY NEXT CARD IS...
EXODIA THE FORBIDDEN ONE!
Exodia the Forbidden One
★★★★★★★★
An automatic victory can be declared by the player whose hand contains this card together with the Left Leg/Right Leg/Left Arm/Right Arm of the Forbidden One.
ATK/1000
DEX/1000
BA
WHAT ...?
....
BA
EXODIA ...?
I HAVE ALL FIVE CARDS!

EXODIA, AWAKEN!
RRRRMMM
!
RRR
IT CAN'T BE ...
THE EXODIA CARDS...THEY REALLY EXIST ...WHERE DID HE...WHERE DID HE GET THEM?
WHOOOM

DA DA
DORM

DADA
Y-
ZHU
ZHU
ZHU
Y-
Y-

SHH
RAGE INFERNO! EXODIA FLAME!
KSSHHH
EXODIA
ATK/INFINITE

SKREEE
EEEE

Y-...
Y-...
AAAA
A
AAA

BUT EVEN WEAK CARDS CAN JOIN TOGETHER SOMETIMES. AND *TOGETHER,* THEY CAN CREATE AN INFINITE POWER WHICH CAN DEFEAT ANY ENEMY!
YOUR BLUE-EYES WHITE DRAGONS WERE POWERFUL...
M...My Blue-Eyes White Dragons ...!
BA
UH.... UH...
IT'S OVER, KAIBA!
I WIN!
MM
Th-they just... just...
......
KAIBA • LIFE POINTS 0

Duel 40: A Piece of His Heart

IT'S TIME FOR YOU TO PAY FOR YOUR CRIMES!
AND FOR THE LOSER A PENALTY GAME!
Duel 40: A Piece of His Heart
BA-BMP
W-WAIT... I...
PENALTY GAME!! MIND CRUSH!!
HUOOM
AAAARRGGHH!!

READ THIS WAY
I'VE DESTROYED THE PART OF YOUR HEART THAT WAS FILLED WITH EVIL!
GOODBYE, KAIBA!
GAPE

AWRIGHT! YUGI DID IT! HE WON!!

YUGI!

YUGI ...

OR IS IT THE OTHER YUGI?

NO... IT DOESN'T MATTER WHICH ONE...

YOU'RE NOT THE SCARED LITTLE BOY YOU ONCE WERE!

YAAA
YY

THIS CAN'T BE...
WAY TO GO, YUGI!

HM ...

WHAT'S ALL THIS NOISE?
CAN'T YOU LET A BABY SLEEP, YOU @#*$!

HN!
!!

PLAY DEAD, PLAY DEAD...

TCH... MASTER KAIBA...?

NOW... GOTTA DO SOMETHING ABOUT THESE GOONS...

BUT AS LONG AS HE'S GOT THAT GUN...

I CAN'T PUT ANZU IN DANGER ...

CRAP... CAN'T TAKE ON TWO OF THEM ALONE...!

HUH ...?

CLO
NK
YERK ...

!!

READ THIS WAY

HONDA!!
YO!
THUD

THERE'S TOO MANY GUYS ASKIN' FOR A BEATING TO LEAVE THIS WORLD YET!!

KA

BAM

SHOOT ...

!

THAT'S ENOUGH!
!!

LET HIM GO!
M-
MASTER MOKUBA ...!

I SAID THAT'S ENOUGH! THE GAME IS OVER.

Y-YES SIR...
LEGGO ALREADY!

IS THAT KAIBA'S ...?
YEAH, HIS LITTLE BROTHER!
HE'S JUST AS BIG A CREEP AS THE OTHER ONE!

THIS "CREEP" SAVED MY LIFE.
HUH?!

I WAS LOCKED IN THAT ROOM FOR A WHILE, WITH THE BLOCKS DROPPING, UNTIL THIS KID TURNED 'EM OFF AND GOT ME OUT!
SO HE'S KAIBA'S BROTHER ...

HMPH!
DON'T TAKE IT PERSONALLY! I JUST OWED YUGI A FAVOR ...
...!

YUGI!

YOU DID IT, YUGI!

OH, YUGI!!

HONDA!!

GOOD JOB! WISH I COULD HAVE BEEN THERE!

YOU BET!

LET'S GO!

...!
MOKUBA ...

CAN YOU TELL ME SOMETHING? WHY DID KAIBA DO ALL THIS? WHY DID HE PLAN THIS REVENGE...?

IT ALL STARTED WITH THAT CHESS GAME ...

WHEN BROTHER WAS TEN AND I WAS FIVE... WE HAD ALREADY LOST OUR PARENTS...
MOTHER DIED SOON AFTER I WAS BORN ... FATHER DIED IN AN ACCIDENT WHEN I WAS THREE......

OUR RELATIVES USED UP OUR INHERITANCE, THEN LEFT US IN AN ORPHANAGE!

MOKUBA... DON'T CRY! I'LL MAKE A GOOD LIFE FOR US SOMEDAY!

LISTEN TO ME! IF YOU SHOW WEAKNESS, IT'S OVER!!
DON'T TRUST ANYONE!
MY BROTHER WAS ALWAYS SAYING THAT...

BUT LIFE AT THE ORPHANAGE WASN'T ALL BAD.
SETO TAUGHT ME CHESS.
WE LIVED TO PLAY EACH DAY ...

BUT THAT TIME... WHEN THAT PICTURE WAS TAKEN... WAS THE LAST TIME I SAW MY BROTHER SMILE.

NOT LONG AFTER THAT ...
HE CAME TO THE ORPHANAGE ... TO ADOPT AN HEIR...

GOZABURO KAIBA ...
SETO KNEW HE WAS THE PRESIDENT OF KAIBA CORPORATION... AND A WORLD GRANDMASTER OF CHESS.
MY BROTHER CHALLENGED HIM-

WHAT DID YOU JUST SAY?
HA HA HA HA HA!
IF I BEAT YOU IN CHESS, I WANT YOU TO ADOPT ME AND MY BROTHER!
HEH... YOU'RE AN INTERESTING KID...
!
AND SETO WON...
...BUT HE WON BY CHEATING!
AND SO OUR LAST NAME CHANGED TO KAIBA...
BUT THE LIFE WE BEGAN THAT DAY WAS THE OPPOSITE OF WHAT WE HAD HOPED FOR!
THAT MAN KAIBA WAS A MONSTER.
HE PUT MY BROTHER INTO A SPECIAL ACCELERATED SCHOOL PROGRAM.
DAY IN AND DAY OUT, HE FORCED HIM TO STUDY: FOREIGN LANGUAGES, SOCIAL STUDIES, ECONOMICS, GAME STRATEGY...
IT WAS LIKE ENDLESS TORTURE ...
BUT WHAT HE DIDN'T REALIZE WAS THAT HE WASN'T CREATING HIS HEIR...HE WAS CREATING A POWERFUL ENEMY!
KAIBA CORP. BOARD MEETING
SIX YEARS LATER

THE BOARD HAS SPOKEN! STARTING TODAY, KAIBA CORPORATION BELONGS TO ME!

HAVE I LEARNED WHAT YOU WANTED... *"FATHER"*?

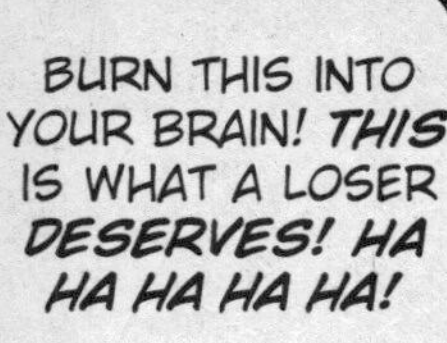

IF HE HADN'T CHEATED AT THAT GAME THAT DAY...
MAYBE I WOULD STILL HAVE A BROTHER.. THE WAY HE USED TO BE...

MAYBE HE WOULDN'T HAVE FORGOTTEN HOW TO SMILE...

MOKUBA ...

RIGHT NOW, KAIBA IS PICKING UP THE PIECES OF HIS HEART IN THE DARKNESS...

HUH ...?!!

HE'S REASSEMBLING THE SHATTERED PUZZLE OF HIS HEART!
BROTHER ...
ONE PIECE AT A TIME, WITH HIS OWN STRENGTH... SO THAT THIS TIME HE WON'T MAKE ANY MISTAKES...

YUGI ...
MY BROTHER WILL COME BACK, WON'T HE ...?
YES...
SOMEDAY... WHEN HE COMPLETES THE PUZZLE ...
HE WILL RETURN ...
I'LL WAIT FOR YOU FOREVER ...
I PROMISE, BIG BROTHER ...
FOREVER ......

HEY, YUGI!! I JUST GOT A CALL FROM HANASAKI AT THE HOSPITAL!
YOUR GRANDPA'S SURGERY WENT *GREAT!* THEY SAY HE'S THE HEALTHIEST COLLECTIBLE CARD GAME PLAYER THEY'VE EVER SEEN!
!!

GRANDPA'S OKAY!
THANK GOODNESS !!

ISN'T THAT GREAT, YUGI ??
YUP!
I WANNA GO SEE HIM RIGHT AWAY!
LET'S ALL GO TO THE HOSPITAL TOGETHER!
SPIN SPIN

I'M GOING TOO!!
THE NURSES AT THAT HOSPITAL ARE *HOT!*
YOU GO TO *SLEEP!*

BOY, IT WAS A LONG DAY, WASN'T IT?

HUH... COME TO THINK OF IT...
WHEN DID YUGI CHANGE BACK TO HIS USUAL SELF ...?

HEY, YUGI ...
ARE YOU ...

HM ...?
WHAT'S UP, JONOUCHI ?

AWW, IT'S NOTHING!

I KNEW RIGHT AWAY WHAT JONOUCHI TRIED TO ASK ME...

AFTER ALL ...

TODAY, FOR THE FIRST TIME, I CAN REMEMBER ALL THE BATTLES WE FOUGHT TOGETHER...

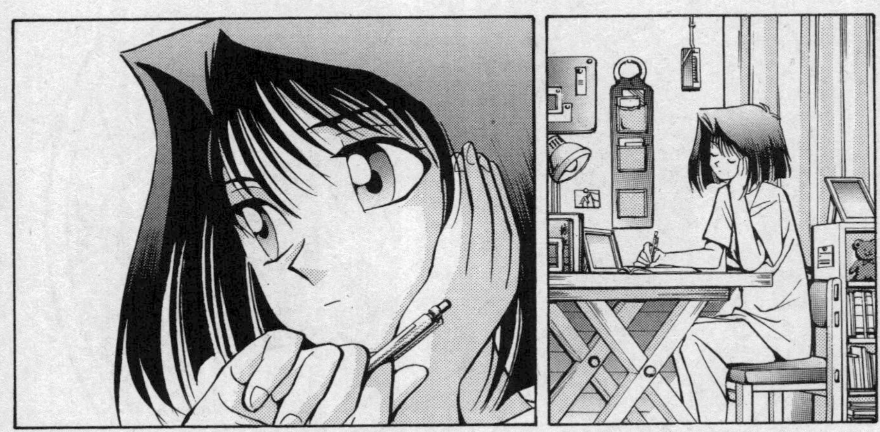

Duel 41: Let's Find "Love"!

Duel 41: Let's Find "Love"!

YUGI MUTOU!

YUGI
!
YOU'RE GOING TO BE *LATE!!*

OOOH! IF THAT BOY IS STILL ASLEEP...
STOMP
STOMP

CHK
YUGI
!!

DEEP
THOUGHT

YUGI...

WHAT ARE YOU DOING...?

WHY ARE YOUR SOCKS SPREAD ALL OVER THE FLOOR?

DOOM☆

MOM! DON'T TALK TO ME RIGHT NOW!

I'M TRYING TO CONCENTRATE!

GAME #1: SOCK CONCENTRATION

RULES
- GET A LOT OF IDENTICAL WHITE SOCKS.
- DRAW DIFFERENT SYMBOLS (HEARTS, STARS, POLITICAL INSIGNIA...WHATEVER!) ON THE BACK OF EACH PAIR OF SOCKS.
- MIX UP THE SOCKS AND SPREAD THEM OUT SYMBOL SIDE DOWN.
- USE YOUR SIXTH SENSE TO PICK OUT A PAIR OF SOCKS WITH THE SAME SYMBOLS AND YOU WIN!!

MORNING, YUGI!

I THOUGHT IT'D BE FUN TO WALK TO SCHOOL TOGETHER!

ANZU !!

YUP !!

WOW! I GET TO BE ALONE WITH ANZU ALL THE WAY TO SCHOOL!

SIGH... TODAY IS GOING TO BE A *DRAG*...

HUH ... WHY?

THE RESULTS FROM THAT ACHIEVEMENT TEST ARE BACK TODAY.

THEY'RE GOING TO PLASTER OUR NAMES OUT IN THE HALL BASED ON WHO GOT WHAT.

THAT'S RIGHT!

THE TEST SCORES ARE BEING ANNOUNCED TODAY! WOO HOO!

READ THIS WAY

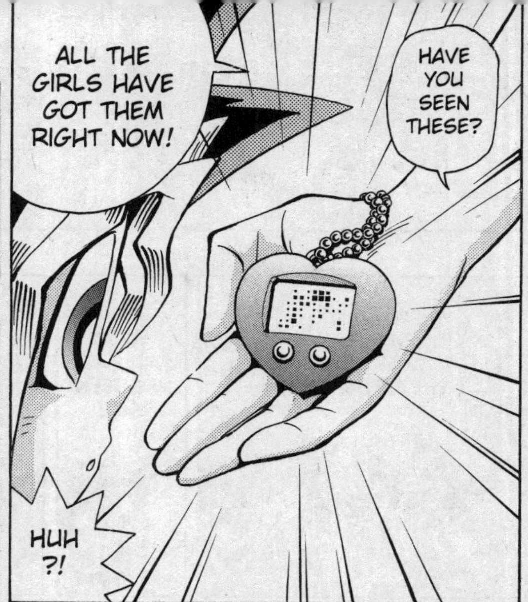

WHY DON'T YOU PUT IN YOUR DATA!
YOU BET!
HEH HEH ... SAY, YUGI ...
WANT TO SEE HOW WELL WE FIT TOGETHER?!
WHAAAA!!
BADUM
O-OKAY ...
NOW YOUR WAVEFORM HAS BEEN SET!
OKAY ...UM ...
BEEP☆
BEEP☆
ANZU GAVE ME A PRESENT!
ALL RIGHT!♡
COULD THIS MEAN ...

SMILE

OUR BIORHYTHMS MUST BE OFF TODAY OR SOMETHING!
I'M SURE THEY'LL RING NEXT TIME!

ACHIEVEMENT TEST RESUL
OH
THE ACHIEVEMENT TEST SCORES ARE POSTED!!

CHATTER
CHATTER
ACHIEVEMENT TEST RESU
YEAH! NUMBER 20! MY HARD WORK PAID OFF!
NO WAY! I DIDN'T EVEN MAKE THE TOP 100!
GAAH! DON'T POST THOSE NUMBERS!

OUTTA THE WAY!!

GAME #2:
ACHIEVEMENT TEST BINGO GAME

RULES

- FIRST, GO TO A JAPANESE HIGH SCHOOL.
- DRAW A 5X5 GRID ON A PIECE OF PAPER.
- PICK ANY NUMBERS FROM 1-50 AND WRITE THEM WHEREVER YOU WANT IN THE 25 BOXES. YOU CAN'T USE A NUMBER MORE THAN ONCE!
- NEXT, LOOK AT THE TOP 50 PEOPLE IN YOUR SCHOOL'S ACHIEVEMENT TEST RANKING AND COMPARE THEM TO THE NUMBERS IN YOUR BOXES. MARK BOYS AS BLACK SQUARES AND GIRLS AS RED SQUARES.
- THE PERSON WITH THE MOST HORIZONTAL, VERTICAL, OR DIAGONAL RED OR BLACK LINES WINS.

- NOW! BEFORE MOVING ON TO THE NEXT PAGE, TRY IT FOR YOURSELF!!
- WRITE ANY NUMBERS FROM 1-50 IN THE BOXES AT THE LEFT, BUT DON'T USE A NUMBER MORE THAN ONCE. WHEN YOU'RE DONE, GO ON TO THE NEXT PAGE AND COLOR IN THE BOXES AS SHOWN!!

NAMES NOT SHOWN TO PROTECT THE INNOCENT

1 RED	26 BLACK
2 RED	27 RED
3 BLACK	28 RED
4 BLACK	29 RED
5 RED	30 BLACK
6 BLACK	31 BLACK
7 RED	32 BLACK
8 BLACK	33 RED
9 RED	34 BLACK
10 BLACK	35 RED
11 RED	36 BLACK
12 BLACK	37 RED
13 BLACK	38 RED
14 BLACK	39 BLACK
15 RED	40 BLACK
16 BLACK	41 RED
17 RED	42 BLACK
18 BLACK	43 RED
19 BLACK	44 RED
20 BLACK	45 BLACK
21 RED	46 BLACK
22 RED	47 RED
23 RED	48 RED
24 BLACK	49 BLACK
25 RED	50 RED

TSURUOKA ...

WHAT A MEAN TEACHER!

HM!

WHAT ARE YOU HIDING IN YOUR CHEST POCKET!

HEY! WAIT--!

THE LOVE TESTER ANZU GAVE ME!!

YOU CAN'T BRING GAMES TO SCHOOL, YOU KNOW!
PLEASE GIVE IT BACK! IT'S NOT A GAME!
IT'S VERY IMPORTANT TO ME!!
HEY! GIVE THAT BACK TO YUGI!
YOU DON'T HAVE THE RIGHT TO TAKE PEOPLE'S THINGS JUST BECAUSE YOU'RE A TEACHER!
UNSKILLED SLACKERS LIKE YOU HAVE NO RIGHT TO TALK BACK TO A TEACHER!
GRR ...
WHADDAYA MEAN "UNSKILLED" ?!
EDUCATION IS A NOBLE PROFESSION! WE TEACHERS HAVE THE RIGHT TO DO ANYTHING TO SLACKERS LIKE YOU!
I COULD EVEN --
SMASH THIS THING!
!!

WE HAVE SKILLS!

SKILLS YOU COULD NEVER MATCH!!

YUGI!

I NEVER LOSE A GAME!!

BA

BAM★

NEVER!

STOP★

YOU NEVER WHAT...?!

IS THAT SO...
THEN WHY DON'T WE PLAY A GAME, EH?
THE RULES ARE SIMPLE!
I'LL HIDE THIS GAME SOMEWHERE IN THIS SCHOOL!
IF YOU CAN FIND IT WITHIN ONE HOUR, YOU WIN.
YOU GET YOUR KEYCHAIN GAME BACK!

30 MINUTES LATER...

SHF

59·30

NOW... THE SCHOOL GROUNDS ARE HUGE ...
I HAVE TO NARROW THE SEARCH AREA ...

YUGI'S GOOD, BUT...IT'S HOPELESS!
NO WAY THEY'LL FIND THAT TINY LITTLE THING ...

320

* LIKE MOST JAPANESE BUILDINGS, YOU'RE SUPPOSED TO CHANGE YOUR SHOES WHEN YOU ENTER A JAPANESE SCHOOL.

READ THIS WAY

AH ...
UM ...
YUGI ...

SNAP☆
!!
ANZU! THIS IS JUST WHAT I NEED!
BADUM♥

!!

YOU CAN'T COME IN HERE!
THIS IS THE TEACHERS' LOUNGE! STUDENTS AREN'T ALLOWED!
DO YOUR LITTLE TREASURE HUNT OUTSIDE!

YOU JUST CONFIRMED MY SUSPICIONS!
THE POCKET GAME IS *IN THIS ROOM!*

!!
WHA...

THE POCKET GAME IS HIDDEN SOMEWHERE YOU CAN'T REACH!
Y-YOU'RE WRONG!
IT'S NOT IN HERE!

SOMEWHERE WE CAN'T REACH... IN OTHER WORDS, SOMEWHERE WE CAN'T TOUCH.

I THOUGHT HARD!
WHERE WOULD *I* HIDE IT IF I WERE YOU!
FIRST, I WOULD USE THE *PRIVILEGES* OF A TEACHER!!
STUDENTS CAN'T RAISE A HAND TO A TEACHER.. THEY CAN'T EVEN *TOUCH* A TEACHER!

YOU CAN'T PROVE I HAVE IT WITHOUT TOUCHING ME!
HA HA HA HA!
NOW WHAT ?!
GG ... GG ...
GET THIS STRAIGHT! I'M A TEACHER, LIKE A **GOD** TO YOU! YOU WOULDN'T **DARE** TOUCH ME WITH YOUR **FILTHY** HANDS ...
I'D EXPEL YOU!!
IN OTHER WORDS, THE SAFEST PLACE IS ON YOUR OWN BODY!!

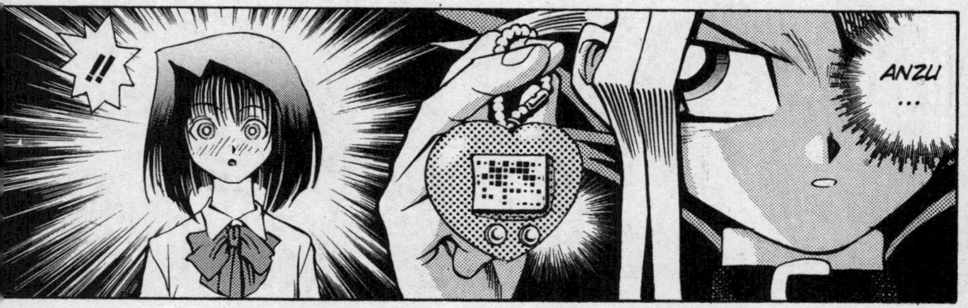

BIBEEP
BIBEEP
!

WHAT'S THAT SOUND ...?
BIBEEP
BIBEEP
... ?!

BIBEEP
BIBEEP
!!
HUH ...?!

THE SOUND'S COMING FROM HIS *HEAD!!*
THAT'S *GOTTA* BE THE POCKET GAME!
BIBEEP
BIBEEP
GET HIM, HONDA!
YEEP!

WITH THIS MUCH PROOF YOU *CAN'T* SAY WE CAN'T TOUCH YOU!!
WHY YOU-- !!
WRESTLE

HUH?!
GLEAM
!!

00:05
LOOKS LIKE WE WON, YUGI!

WHOA!
HE HID THE POCKET GAME INSIDE HIS WIG!!
BIBEEP
BIBEEP
EEEEEEEEEK!
PLEASE DON'T TELL ANYONE MY SECRET!

THANK YOU ...
... ANZU!

THE OTHER YUGI...
WHENEVER I SEE YOU...
I'LL HEAR THE SOUND OF THAT BELL AGAIN...
IN MY HEART...

Duel 42: Get the Million!!

* ABOUT $10,000 U.S.

READ THIS WAY

Duel 42:
Get the Million!!

HEH HEH HEH! AFTER THIS, I WON'T HAVE TO WORK MY BUTT OFF AT PART TIME JOBS ANY MORE!
HEY, YOU HAVEN'T WON THE MONEY *YET!*
GRRR! I'VE GOTTA WIN IT!
IF I WIN, I CAN PAY OFF MY OLD MAN'S GAMBLING DEBTS AND LIQUOR STORE TAB!
I WON'T HAVE TO RUN FROM THE COLLECTION AGENCIES ANY MORE! IT'S GONNA BE A **NEW LIFE!**
MY DAYS OF STRUGGLING ARE OVER!

YOU'VE BEEN WORKING TO PUT YOURSELF THROUGH SCHOOL FOR A WHILE, HAVEN'T YOU, JONOUCHI.
REMEMBER THAT PAPER ROUTE IN MIDDLE SCHOOL? EVERYONE CALLED HIM THE "LONE PAPERBOY!"

Programming Department

SO WHAT **SUCKER** ARE WE HAVING ON THE "GET THE MILLION GAME" TODAY?

On Air

HEY OUT THERE TO ALL THE FANS AT HOME!

IT'S TIME FOR **THE GET THE MILLION GAME!!**

THE GET THE MILLION GAME!

TA-DA

CLAP CLAP CLAP CLAP CLAP

DOOM

TODAY'S CHALLENGER IS THIS STRAPPING YOUNG MAN!

1,000,000 YEN!

16 YEAR OLD JONOUCHI FROM DOMINO CITY!

* ABOUT $1,000 U.S.

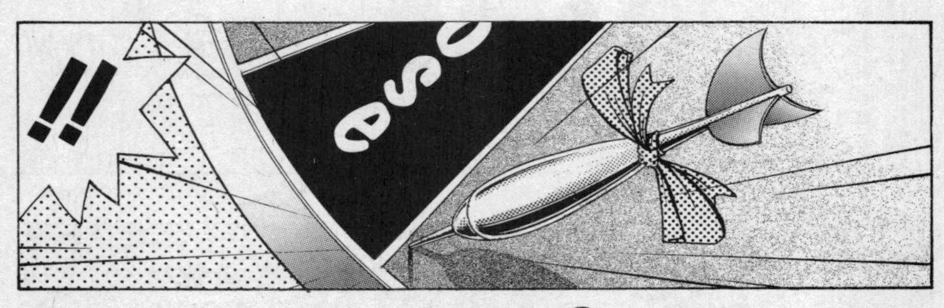

YOU WIN!
THAT WAS CLOSE ...
YOU GET ¥100,000 !!
AWW RIGHT !
CHACHING
GOOD JOB!
YOU'RE #1, MAN!
NOW THE STAKES GO UP AND SO DO THE RISKS! CAN YOU GET ¥500,000 YEN!?
FOR OUR SECOND GAME--

* ABOUT $5,000 U.S.

THE ELECTRIC HELMET!!

TADA

THE RULES ARE SIMPLE! BEFORE TIME RUNS OUT, THE CONTESTANT MUST RUN BETWEEN THE HIGH VOLTAGE WIRES WHILE WEARING THIS HELMET!

BUT *DON'T TOUCH* THE WIRES! THE *SLIGHTEST* BUMP AND THE METAL HELMET WILL CONDUCT A *DEVASTATING ELECTRIC SHOCK!*

I'LL DO IT!

SUCCESS!! HE WINS!!
THE CHALLENGER SUCCESSFULLY CLEARS THE SECOND GAME!!
HE WINS 500,000 YEN!
500
100

I DID IT! I GOT 500,000 YEN!
BA DUM

GOOD JOB, JONO-UCHI!
THAT'S THE STUFF!
YAAYY
ONE MORE STEP AND YOU GOT THE WHOLE MILLION!

WE'LL BE BACK WITH THE FINAL ROUND, RIGHT AFTER THIS WORD FROM OUR SPONSORS!

POP... IF I WIN THE MILLION YEN... I'LL PUT ALL OF THE PAST BEHIND US. WE'LL BE A REAL FAMILY AGAIN!
JUST YOU WAIT!

BOY, THIS IS REALLY TENSE!
I GOTTA GO TO THE BATHROOM!

HMM... WHERE'S THE BATHROOM?
WOW... I'M IN A TV STUDIO...
I WONDER IF I'LL MEET A STAR?

SO HOW ARE THE RATINGS?!
LOOKING GOOD, SIR!
GOOD.

SO IN THE NEXT ROUND IS THE WHEEL RIGGED TO *LOSE?*
YES SIR!
EVERY-THING'S READY!

HUH...?!

IF THERE'S ONE THING BETTER THAN SEEING A POOR PERSON STRUGGLING FOR MONEY—IT'S WATCHING THEM *FAIL* AT THE LAST MINUTE!
BWA HA HA HA HA HA!
SUFFERING *ALWAYS* TURNS A PROFIT!

WHAT A JOKE! *WHO* WOULD GIVE *MONEY* TO A *POOR* PERSON?!
WHO CARES? AS LONG AS I GET PAID! BWA HA!

WHAT DID HE JUST SAY ...!
ALL ALONG, THIS GAME SHOW WAS RIGGED...!
GRR...
HOW DARE HE USE JONOUCHI'S DESPERATE HOPES...
RMM
RMMMB
I'LL NEVER FORGIVE HIM!
FLASH
DA DUMMMM
NOW! IT'S TIME FOR THE FINAL ROUND!
IF JONOUCHI CLEARS THIS GAME, HE WILL WIN ONE MILLION YEN!
500

THE WHEEL OF FATE!!
DOOM
WELL, JONOUCHI? EITHER YOU *WIN* THE MILLION YEN--
OR YOU *FAIL* AND LOSE *ALL* THE MONEY YOU'VE WON SO FAR!!
¥1,000,000
Lose
Lotion
Box of Tissues
100
500
ONE MILLION YEN...
I'LL DO IT!!
IT'S AS GOOD AS MINE!
GO FOR IT, JONOUCHI!
KNOCK 'EM OUT!
500

NOW! THE WHEEL HAS STARTED SPINNING!!
HWOOOO
BA DUM BA DUM
IT WILL SPIN UNTIL JONOUCHI SAYS "STOP!"
ALL RIGHT! WHEN HE SAYS "STOP," YOU PRESS THAT BUTTON! YOU GOT IT?
YES SIR! I GET IT!
I PAINTED THE BUTTON RED TO BE SURE!
WHEN I PRESS *THIS* BUTTON, THERE'S *100% NO CHANCE* THAT THE WHEEL WILL WIN!
THERE ARE A LOT OF BUTTONS, BUT THERE'S NO MISTAKE THIS WAY!
SHF

SHOO!

ONLY **STAFF** ARE ALLOWED BACK HERE! GET OUT!

W-WHAT DO **YOU** WANT?!

BAM

ARE YOU FEELING **LUCKY?** THEN WHY DON'T WE **TEST** YOUR LUCK?

HEH HEH...

!

THERE'S A PAINT CAN ON TOP OF THE SCAFFOLDING, RIGHT?

AND HERE ARE TWO ROPES...

ONE IS TIED TO THE HANDLE OF THE PAINT CAN!

ULP...
HOW DID THIS BRAT LEARN THE SECRET...?!
....
TH-THERE'S NO CHOICE!!
ALL RIGHT! YOU! PICK A ROPE!!
Y-...
YES SIR...
OKAY... I'LL TAKE THE RIGHT ROPE......
THEN I'LL TAKE THE LEFT ONE!
YOU ALL SET?
READY... SET...
YANK
SLIP

KAPL
AAR-GLUB GLUB GLUB...
OP
YOU'LL GET PAINT ON MY CLOTHES!
UGH... YOU MORON!
!!
THERE'S RED PAINT ALL OVER THE SWITCHBOX!!
HUFF...
I HAVE TO PUSH THE BUTTON MYSELF...
HUH...?!
I CAN'T TELL WHICH IS THE RIGHT BUTTON!!
OH MY GOD--!
IF THE WHEEL STOPS ON THE WINNING SPACE...
THAT SHIFTLESS BUM WILL GET A MILLION YEN!
NOW YOU'RE SHOWING YOUR TRUE COLORS!
IT'S TIME FOR YOUR JUDGMENT!
RRMMB

PENALTY GAME! MIND ON AIR!!

DADA

MMM

AAGGHHH!!

NOW, AT THE CONTESTANT'S CALL!!

WHIRR

WHIRR

BANG
¥1,000,000
HE...HE WINS THE MILLION YEN!!
NO WAY... THIS NEVER HAPPENS...
I...I DID IT!! I'M A MILL-YEN-AIRE!
WHOA A

BWA HA HA HA HA!
GIMME YOUR MONEY!
WA HA HA HA
HEY ALL YOU BROKE, LAZY, WORKING CLASS COUCH POTATOES! GET AWAY FROM THE TV JUST LONG ENOUGH TO SEND ME YOUR CASH! CHECKS! MONEY ORDERS!
WE'RE DONE FOR!
APPARENTLY TRUE POVERTY LIVES IN THE SOUL!
ISN'T THAT RIGHT...MR. PRODUCER?!
SEVERAL DAYS LATER
WHAT'S WRONG WITH JONOUCHI?
THAT TV PRODUCTION COMPANY WENT **BANKRUPT**. NOW HIS CHECK IS NOTHING BUT A **WORTHLESS PIECE OF PAPER**...
WAAAAAAH!

BUZZ BUZZ

SPECIAL BONUS!

HONEYCOMB BOARD GAME!☆

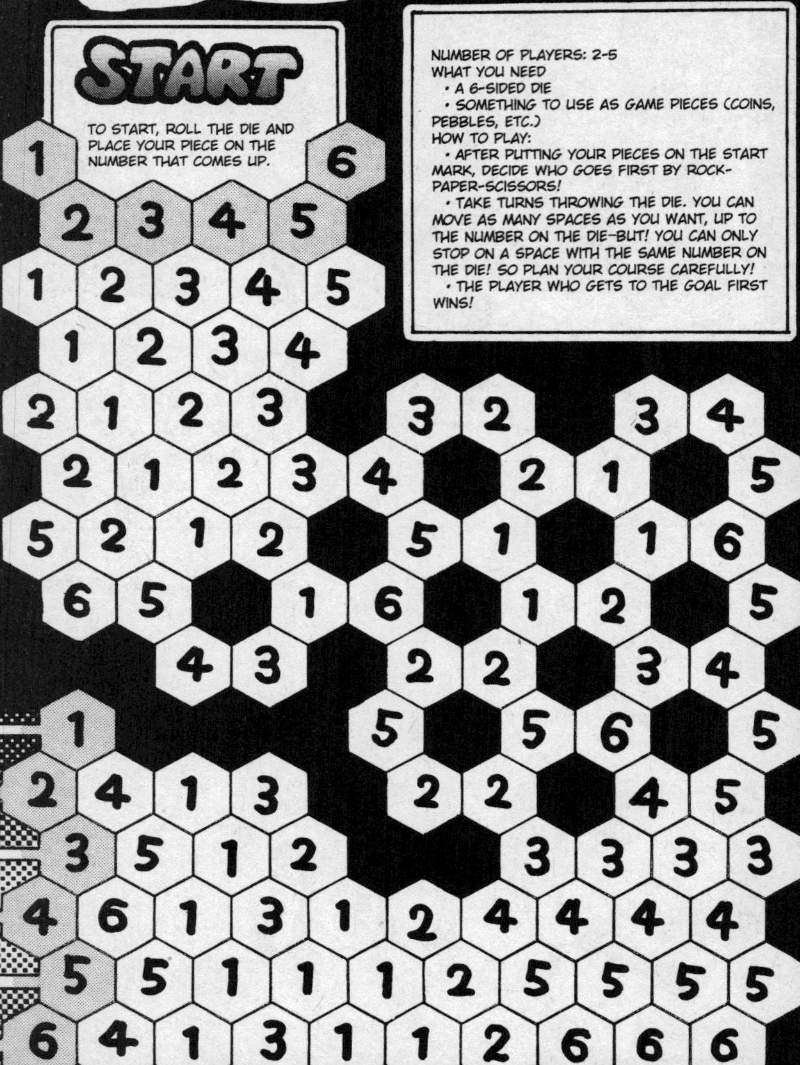

GOAL

MASTER OF THE CARDS

In Yugi's second duel with Kaiba, many classic **Yu-Gi-Oh!** cards appear for the first time. As **Yu-Gi-Oh!** fans know, the manga and anime version of the card game has simpler rules than the real-world version. Also, many of the card names are different between the English and Japanese versions. Here's a rundown of the cards in this graphic novel.

1. Hitotsu-me Giant
Known as "Cyclops" in the original Japanese. "Hitotsu-me" is Japanese for "one-eyed."

2. Winged Dragon, Guardian of the Fortress
This name is a literal translation of *toride o mamoru yokuryû*. In Japanese and Chinese mythology, dragons don't necessarily have wings, so it's understandable why this card is specifically called a *winged* dragon—or in Japanese, a *yokuryû*. (Dragons are *ryû* in Japanese and *long* in Chinese.) It doesn't have the same powers in the card game that it does in the manga.

3. The Wicked Worm Beast
This name is a literal translation of *jaaku naru worm beast*.

4. Saggi the Dark Clown
This name is a literal translation of *yami dôkeshi no saggi*.

5. Dark Energy
In the real-life game, this card is less powerful than in the manga, maybe because it'd be unbalanced otherwise.

6. Sangan
Known as "Critter" in the original Japanese, "Sangan" could mean "three eyes" in Japanese. This card doesn't have the same powers in the manga that it does in the actual game.

7. Gaia the Fierce Knight
Known as "Gaia the Dark Knight" in the original Japanese.

8. Blue-Eyes White Dragon
In the manga, this card is extremely rare. Kaiba had to steal and extort from collectors all over the world to get his three Blue-Eyes White Dragons.

9. Swords of Revealing Light
Known as *hikari no gofûken* ("Swords of Binding Light" or "Swords of Sealing Light") in the original Japanese.

10. Beaver Warrior
Known as "Ruizu" (or, to use another pronunciation, "Louise") in the original Japanese.

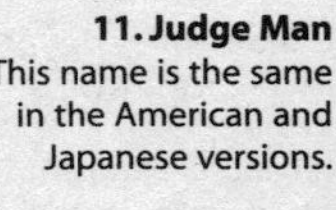

11. Judge Man
This name is the same in the American and Japanese versions.

12. Dark Magician
Known as "Black Magician" in the original Japanese.

13. The Exodia Cards
In the manga, according to Yugi's grandfather, no one has ever managed to use all five Exodia cards in a game. Perhaps they're rarer in the manga? Or perhaps deck-building skills aren't as advanced in Yugi's world?

ONE DAY I WENT SHOPPING IN TOWN. AFTER I FINISHED MY BUSINESS, I DECIDED TO GO TO A PACHINKO PARLOR. I WAS ABSORBED IN PLAYING PACHINKO WHEN ALL OF A SUDDEN I NOTICED *"AAAGGGH! MY BAG'S MISSING!"* INSIDE MY STOLEN BAG WAS MY WALLET, WHICH CONTAINED MY ENTIRE FORTUNE, AS WELL AS MY NOTEBOOK OF MANGA IDEAS. I'D BE VERY EMBARRASSED IF ANYONE SAW THAT NOTEBOOK. DARN IT! GIVE ME MY NOTEBOOK BACK, YOU DARN THIEF! SO THAT'S WHY I'VE FORGOTTEN ALL OF MY IDEAS.

–KAZUKI TAKAHASHI, 1997

SHONEN JUMP MANGA

Vol. 6

MONSTER FIGHT!

STORY AND ART BY

KAZUKI TAKAHASHI

THE STORY SO FAR...

Shy and easily picked on, 10th-grader Yugi spent most of his time alone playing games...until he solved the Millennium Puzzle, a mysterious Egyptian artifact passed down from his grandfather. Possessed by the puzzle, Yugi became *Yu-Gi-Oh*, the King of Games, and challenged bullies and criminals to weird games where the losers *lose their minds!* But against strange new games and new enemies, can Yugi protect his friends...or even himself?

DARK YUGI

武藤遊戯

YUGI MUTOU

The main character. When he solved the ancient Egyptian Millennium Puzzle, he developed an alter ego, the King of Games, which emerges in times of stress.

城之内克也

KATSUYA JONOUCHI

Yugi's classmate, a tough guy who gets in lots of fights. He used to think Yugi was a wimp, but now they are good friends. In the English anime he's known as "Joey Wheeler."

真崎杏子

ANZU MAZAKI

Yugi's classmate and childhood friend. She fell in love with the charismatic voice of Yugi's alter ego, but doesn't know that they're the same person. Her first name means "Peach." In the English anime she's known as "Téa Gardner."

獏良

RYO BAKURA

A transfer student at Yugi's school who shows up on page 565 of this graphic novel.

本田ヒロト

HIROTO HONDA

Yugi's classmate, a friend of Jonouchi. In the English anime he's known as "Tristan Taylor."

武藤双六

SUGOROKU MUTOU

Yugi's grandfather, the owner of the Kame ("Turtle") game store. His first name, "Sugoroku", is a Japanese game similar to backgammon.

Vol. 6

CONTENTS

Duel 43:
er Fight!! (Part 1)

HERE'S A GAME I THINK YOU'LL LIKE...

MONSTER FIGHTER!

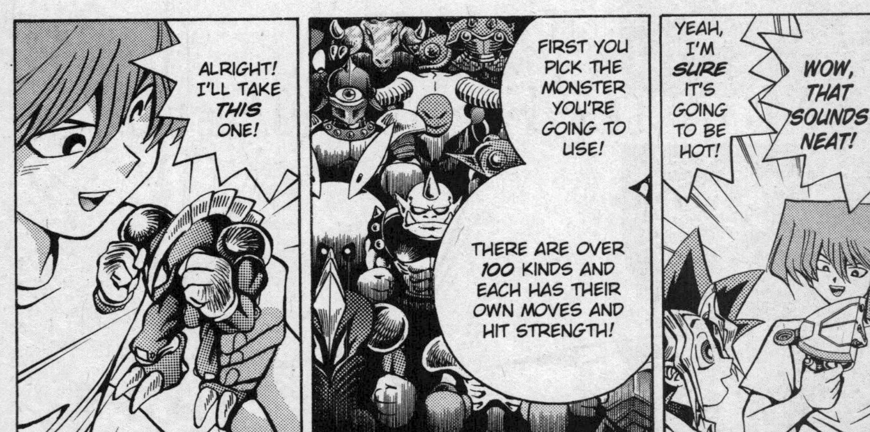

ONCE YOU'VE PICKED OUT YOUR MONSTER, YOU SET IT ON THE SPECIAL "FIGHTING GUN!"
YOU CONNECT THE MONSTER TO THE BASE WITH THE REMOTE CONTROL WIRE!
CHAK
THEN YOU LINK YOUR GUN WITH YOUR OPPONENT'S GUN AND YOU'RE READY TO BATTLE!
SO THAT'S YOUR MONSTER, YUGI!
YUP! HE'S PRETTY STRONG!
BEFORE YOU START, THE PLAYERS INPUT THEIR MOVE DATA!
THERE'S A SENSOR ON THE BACK OF THE GUN. YOU PUT THE BARCODE DISK ON IT, AND IT SCANS IT AND READS YOUR SECRET MOVES!
EACH MONSTER HAS DIFFERENT FINISHING MOVES!
ONCE THE GAME BEGINS, YOU WATCH YOUR OPPONENT FOR AN OPENING AND USE THE PUNCH, KICK AND GUARD BUTTONS TO DEFEAT HIM!
PUNCH
KICK
GUARD
FINISHING MOVE
THERE'S TWO WAYS TO WIN. YOU CAN KNOCK YOUR ENEMY OUT BY HITTING THEIR WEAK POINTS–*OR* YOU CAN FORCE THEM OUT OF THE RING WITH A CRITICAL HIT!

AWRIGHT, YUGI! LET'S BATTLE!

OKAY!

BATTLE START!!

BDSH
YOU DROPPED YOUR GUARD AND I KICKED YOU!
HIT TO YOUR WEAK POINT!
ACK! THAT HIT MADE THE GRIP VIBRATE!!
BDZT
BDZT
!!
WHEN YOU'RE HIT IN YOUR WEAK POINT, YOU CAN'T MOVE FOR TWO SECONDS!
YUGI! THIS IS YOUR CHANCE!
USE YOUR FINISHING MOVE!
OKAY!
I'M PULLING THE FINISHING MOVE TRIGGER!
CLIX
MACH TORNADO PUNCH!!
BASH
URK...
I DID IT! I WIN!
DO YOU EVER LOSE ANYTHING...?

READ THIS WAY
SO, WHAT DO YOU THINK?
IT'S AWESOME! I LOVE IT!
C'MON YUGI! LET'S SHOW EVERY-BODY AT SCHOOL!
OKAY!
THE NEXT DAY...
ZGAAAAA
CRITICAL HIT!
RING OUT! ALTI WINS!
DARN IT!
YOU GOT ME AGAIN!
ME NEXT!
WHAT'RE YOU PLAYING?
HEY, YUGI! WHAT GAME IS THIS?
IT'S CALLED MONSTER FIGHTER.
HEY, THAT LOOKS KINDA COOL.
I WANT TO GET ONE!
ME TOO!

WITHIN ONE WEEK, MONSTER FIGHTER WAS A BIG HIT AT SCHOOL.

THOOM

HEY, IS THERE A DUDE CALLED YUGI IN THIS CLASS?

BE CAREFUL, YUGI...
THAT'S KOJI "THE SPIDER" NAGUMO. HE'S GOOD AT GAMES, BUT THEY SAY HE STEALS THINGS FROM PEOPLE.

UM... IF THIS IS ABOUT MONSTER FIGHTER, OUR STORE IS STILL SOLD OUT...

I KNOW THAT! I DON'T GO TO THE STORE.

SEE?

OH! I GET IT.

YOU ALREADY HAVE ONE!

I CALLED YOU UP HERE...

YES...

THAT'S A GOOD BOY.

LET'S HAVE A BATTLE RIGHT HERE.

I'M A GAMER JUST LIKE YOU ARE.

I'M THE ONE WHO MADE THIS GAME SO POPULAR!

OKAY! LET'S DO IT!

HE WAS JUST LOOKING FOR SOMEONE TO PLAY WITH...

K-CHA-K

MY MONSTER IS WILD SPIDER!
JUST SO YOU KNOW, HE'S UNDEFEATED!
HUH? SO YOUR MONSTER IS ALTI?
NICE SCAPE-GOAT FOR A WEAKLING ...DUDE!

HUH ...?!
KCHK
KCHK
BY THE WAY, I FORGOT TO MENTION...
THERE'S THIS HOUSE RULE I ALWAYS PLAY WITH ...
WHOA!
NOT BAD!
KCHK
KCHK
SIMPLE! THE WINNER GETS THE LOSER'S FIGHTING GUN!
AND OF COURSE, THE LOSER'S MONSTER, TOO!
KCHK

WHAT ?!!
B-BUT THAT'S ...
NO WAY! I DON'T WANT TO, NAGUMO!
OH, LOOK OUT, DUDE! YOU'RE WIDE OPEN!
KCHK KCHK
HUH ...?!
FOOL ...
I SAID YOU'RE WIDE OPEN!
THWOK
URG ...
IT'S THE RULES! I'LL KEEP THIS!
WELL, I GOT A LOT OF OTHER APPOINTMENTS, SO I'VE GOTTA RUN, BUT ...
NEXT TIME WE FIGHT I'LL GET SERIOUS... HEH HEH...
OW ...
BAMM BB

WHAT?! MONSTER FIGHTER HUNTERS ?!

YEAH.
THERE'VE BEEN A LOT OF VICTIMS HERE AT SCHOOL!
THEY'RE SELLING THE GAMES ON THE BLACK MARKET!
WHO'S THE JERK DOIN' THAT STUFF?!
CLATTER
YUGI!
WHAT'S WRONG, YUGI!
NOT YOU TOO!
JONOUCHI...
I WANT TO ASK YOU FOR A FAVOR...

I STILL HAVE A GOOD STOCK...
AND IF I RUN OUT, I'LL JUST STEAL MORE!
I'M JUST A BRILLIANT ENTREPRE-NEUR!

HA HA HA! BUSINESS IS BOOMING!!
Monster Fighters ¥30,000

THANKS DUDE! COME AGAIN!
AWRIGHT! I FINALLY GOT ONE!

* ABOUT $300 U.S.

CLATTER
HUH... A CUST-OMER

I'VE GOT ANOTHER ONE, NAGUMO.
TRY AND STEAL THIS FROM ME TOO!

...?!

BAM
Y-YOU'RE THAT KID ...
YUGI ...
GLARE
IT'S A MONSTER FIGHTER ...
RETURN MATCH, NAGUMO!

K-CHA—K

DM DM DM
I DIDN'T THINK YOU'D ACTUALLY FIND ME...
YOU THINK YOU'RE PRETTY SMART, DON'T YOU? THERE MUST BE A BRAIN UNDER THAT HAIR!
THIS GAME IS THREE SETS.
THE FIRST TO TAKE TWO WINS!

JUST SO YOU KNOW, THIS MONSTER FIGHTER BATTLE...
...IS A SHADOW GAME!

HEH HEH... A "SHADOW GAME," HUH?
SO I GUESS THAT MEANS THERE'S NO RULES?
THIS TIME I'LL REALLY KNOCK YOU OUT!

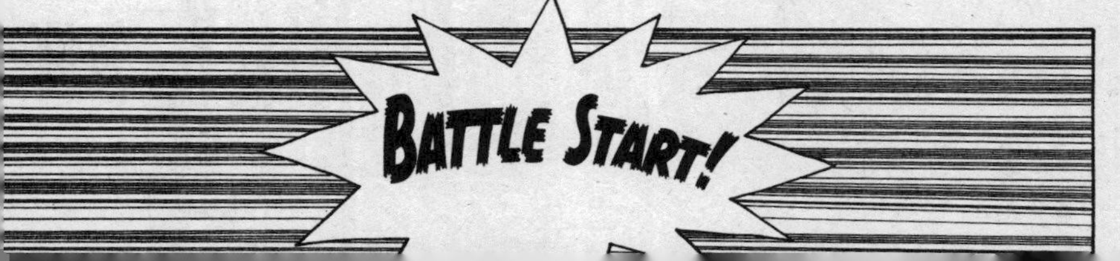
BATTLE START!

ZO-O-O-O-OM
WSH
I'LL TAKE THE FIRST PUNCH!
BISH!
CLICK
GUARD!

MIDDLE KICK!!
GUARD !!
SHHPP

1-2 PUNCH !
KCHK
KCHK
RIGHT LOW!

HEH... FOOL... HE'S PLAYING THE GAME SERIOUSLY ...

BASH
PUNCH !
GUARD !

PUNCH !
KCHK KCHK
KICK !
I'LL CLOBBER THIS KID AND TAKE HIS GAME GUN!

THIS GAME BATTLE IS JUST A WASTE OF TIME!
TAKE THIS!
WSH

WHEN YOU BREAK YOUR CONCEN-TRATION ...
YOUR MONSTER IS WIDE OPEN!
HUH ...?!
URK ...!
ZING
LEFT UPPER CUT!
CRITICAL HIT! RING OUT!
THWOCK
EEEYAAAAGGH!

WHA...

A CRACK IN MY FACE...!!

IN THIS GAME, THE MONSTERS WON'T BE DAMAGED...

BECAUSE...

WE ARE THE SCAPEGOATS FOR THE MONSTERS!

GAAHH!!

OWWWWW!!

FLOP FLOP

AAAGH! IT HURTS!

DON'T WORRY...

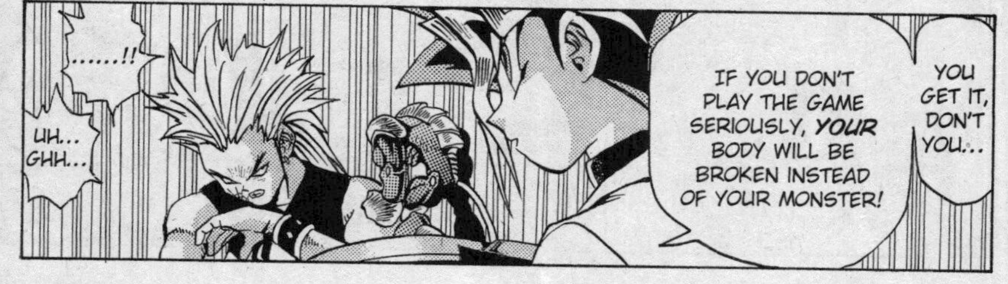

MONSTER FIGHTER ...THE SHADOW GAME!

URG ......

GAAHH ...

IN THIS GAME, **WE PLAYERS** TAKE THE DAMAGE INSTEAD OF THE MONSTERS!

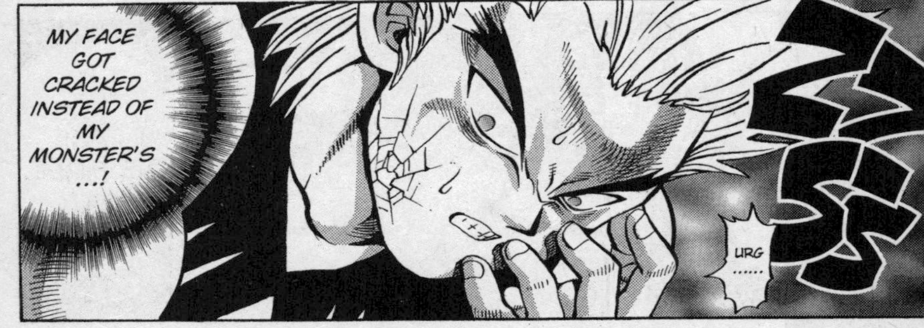

Duel 44: Monster Fight!! (Part 2)

Duel 44:
Monster Fight!! (Part 2)

READ THIS WAY

GRAB

... I SEE ...
IF I DON'T PAY ATTENTION TO THE GAME, *I'M* REALLY GONNA GET HURT...
GG... I GET IT!
BUT NOW IT'S YOUR TURN!!

THE GAME IS *THREE* SETS!
THE FIRST TO TAKE *TWO* WINS!
I TAKE THE *FIRST* SET!

NAGUMO'S MONSTER: ***WILD SPIDER***

WEAK POINT * FACE
SECRET ATTACK
* SPIDER DEATH TRAP

PUNCH STRENGTH
KICK STRENGTH
GUARD STRENGTH
ENDURANCE
POWER
SPEED

YUGI'S MONSTER: ***KILLER EMAADA***

WEAK POINT
* SIDE
SECRET ATTACK
* SPACE CANNON

PUNCH STRENGTH
KICK STRENGTH
GUARD STRENGTH
ENDURANCE
POWER
SPEED

YUGI! I'LL TELL YOU WHY I'LL ***NEVER*** LOSE THIS GAME.

I LEARNED TO FIGHT ON THE ***STREET!*** YOU CAN SEE IT IN MY MONSTER FIGHTER STRATEGY!

JUDGING DISTANCE, SKILLS AND TECHNIQUES, PSYCHING YOU OUT...

THERE'S NO WAY I COULD LOSE TO A GREEN KID LIKE YOU WHO'S NEVER BEEN IN A FIGHT!

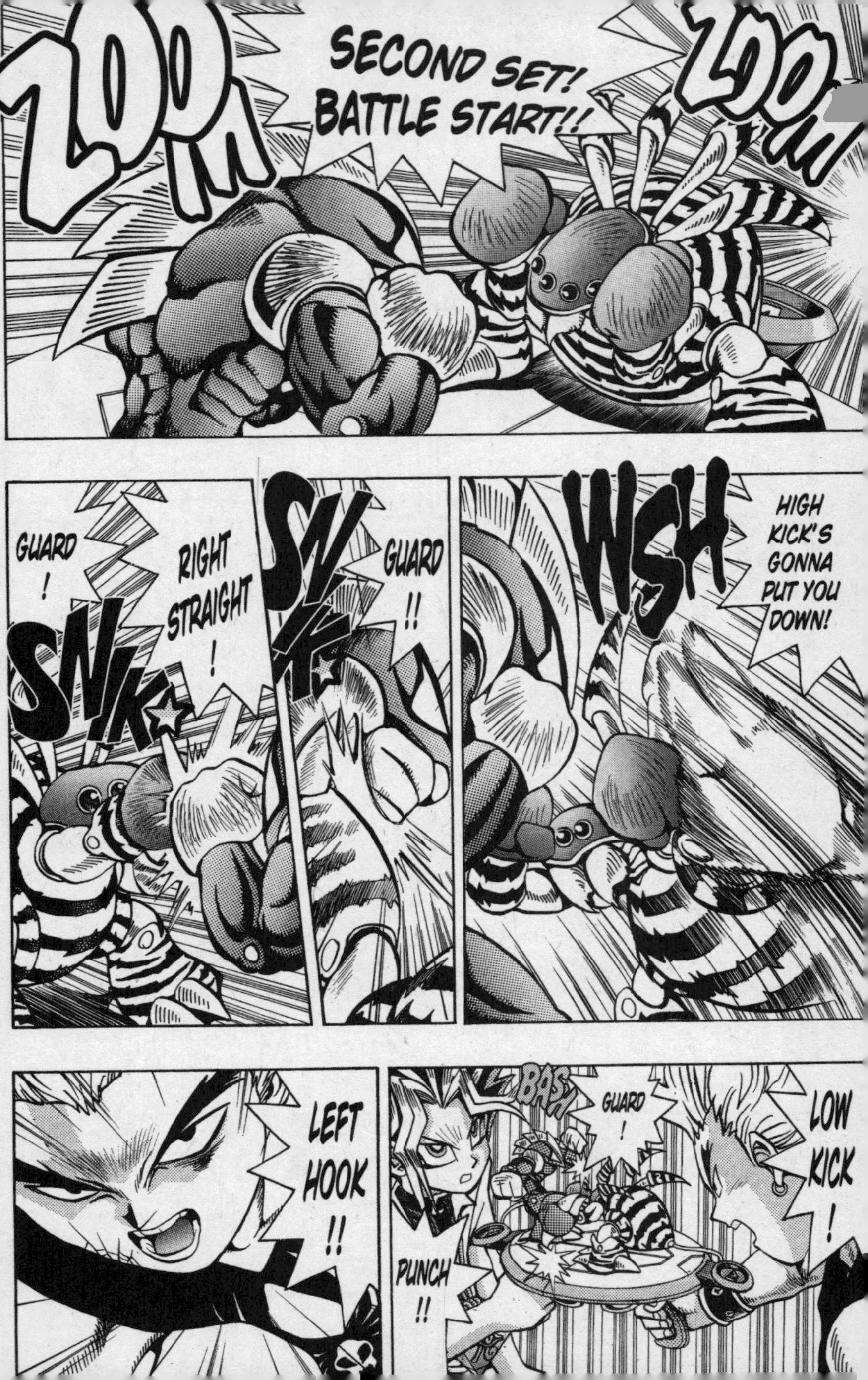

SECOND SET! BATTLE START!!

GUARD !
...!!
THIS LEFT HOOK IS A FEINT!
WSH
YAK
FOLLOWED BY AN INSTANT RIGHT STRAIGHT !!
CLICK
WHOOSH
TCH ......
I CAN'T RAISE MY GUARD IN TIME!!

FLOP
WHAT ?!!
HE FLIPPED OFF THE POWER AND WENT OUT OF BALANCE TO DODGE THE PUNCH!

NOW HE'S BACK UP...
BAM

1! 2!
JAB
JAB

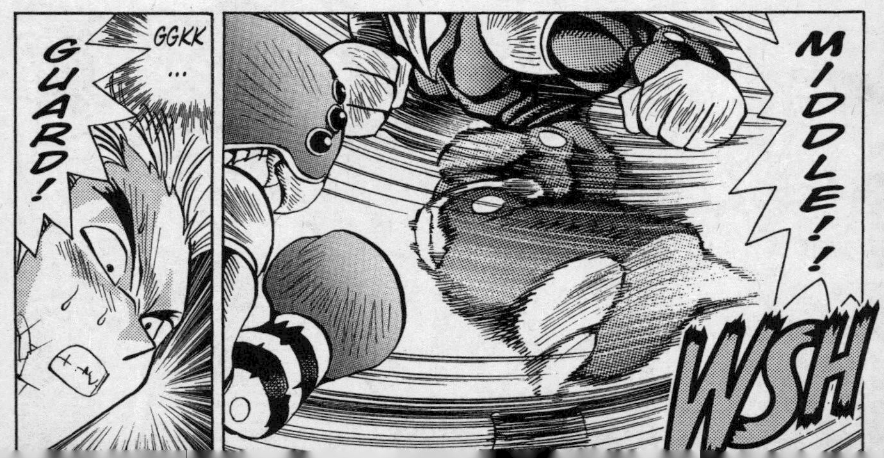
MIDDLE!!
WSH
GGKK ...
GUARD!

NO! THAT WAS A FEINT!!
IT STARTED AS A MIDDLE BUT IT'S REALLY A HIGH KICK!!
BSHH
THAT'S HIS WEAK POINT! HIT HIM!
FZZT
NO...THE GRIP'S VIBRATING! I CAN'T MOVE MY MONSTER!
BZZT BZZT
WILD SPIDER IS FROZEN FOR TWO SECONDS!!
CRAP...IF YUGI PULLS HIS FINISHING MOVE TRIGGER RIGHT NOW...
ZMZM
I'LL LOSE!
ZM ZM
I CAN'T LOSE TO THAT LITTLE BRAT!
D-GOOOM

GUK
...

YAH HA HA HA HA HA!! THIS IS HOW TO FIGHT!!
NOW THE TABLES ARE TURNED!
I WAS AIMING FOR HIM FROM THE START!

THIS IS MY CHANCE! WILD SPIDER'S FREEZE IS UNDONE! I'LL CROUCH DOWN AND GET CLOSE ......
SHP

AND PITCH HIM UP!!

NOW YOUR MONSTER IS A *FLY* IN A SPIDER'S WEB!!

READ THIS WAY
OPEN AIR COMBO!! SPIDER DEATH TRAP!
THOK THOK
THOK THOK
AAAGGGHHGGHHH!
HA HA HA HA HA! NOW THIS GAME IS EVEN!!
G... GUH ...
GASP ...
THAT ... CHEATER ...

HOW LOW CAN YOU SINK, NAGUMO!!

GWOOOO

HEH HEH...

NAGUMO... NOW YOU'VE REALLY... MADE ME... MAD...

GRIP

HM...

FLAP ☆

!

HEH HEH HEH ...

UNTIL NOW, THIS SHADOW GAME WAS LEVEL 1...

BUT FOR THIS FINAL SET, I'M ***RAISING*** THE "SHADOW MODE" TO LEVEL 3!

GET READY, NAGUMO!

HUH HUH HUH ...

"SHADOW MODE"... RIGHT... IS THAT SUPPOSED TO SCARE ME?

THE SHADOW GAME WILL REVEAL YOUR TRUE NATURE!

RRMMBB

FINAL SET ...

BATTLE START!!

DOOM

DOOM

HYOO
LET'S GO! RIGHT STRAIGHT!
CRK
GUARD!
UPPER-CUT!
BASH BASH
LEFT HOOK!
BODY!
SNIK
GUARD!
VSH
RIGHT HOOK!
GUH...!
LEFT STRAIGHT!
BSH
GUARD!
BSH
TCH......
THAT FRICKIN' BRAT... HE'S BLOCKING ALL OF MY ATTACKS!

LEFT LOW KICK!

CRACK

WOBBLE

!!

NO
...

I'VE LOST MY BALANCE
...

NOW!!
RIGHT STRAIGHT!!
HIT TO THE WEAK POINT! YOU'RE FROZEN FOR TWO SECONDS, NAGUMO!!
NO WAY! NO!
IF HE PULLS THE TRIGGER NOW, I'LL LOSE!!
YOU ASKED FOR IT, SUCKER!
I'LL KICK YOU IN THE STOMACH AGAIN!
URAAHH! I WIN!!

HUH ......?!
I-I CAN'T MOVE MY LEG ......
EH ...?
GRAB
GRAB
I TOLD YOU, NAGUMO! YOU CAN'T CHEAT IN THIS GAME!
LOOK AT YOUR LEGS!
W-WHAT THE ...!!
GRAB
GRAB
GRAB
GRABGRAB
THE MONSTERS HAVE GOT MY LEGS!!!

YIPE......
GRAB GRAB
EEP......
GRAB

THM
HUH ...?!

M-... MY WILD SPIDER TOO......!!
WH-... WHAT DOES THAT MEAN?!!

APPARENTLY, YOUR MONSTER WON'T SELL ITS SOUL TO EVIL!
ISOLATED AND FRIENDLESS! IT DOESN'T LOOK LIKE ANY OF THE MONSTERS ARE ON YOUR SIDE!
IMPOSSIBLE... THEN WHAT IS THIS MONSTER ON MY FIELD?!
YOU *EVEN* BETRAYED THE TRUST OF YOUR MONSTER...
THE *ONLY* MONSTER ON YOUR SIDE IN THIS GAME IS...
!!

DOOOH
UWAAAAAGGH!
NOW! I'LL CRUSH YOUR "MONSTER"!
BEHOLD YOUR INNER SELF, THE OTHER YOU, TWISTED INTO A SHAPE TO MATCH YOUR SICK DESIRES!
THE MONSTER CALLED YOUR SOUL!!
FINISHING MOVE!!
CLICK

SPACE CANNON!!
CHOOM
AAAAGHHHH!!

A PERSON CAN CHANGE THEIR SOUL INTO ANY KIND OF MONSTER...

BUT IN THE END...
...THE SHADOWS ALWAYS EAT THEM ALIVE!

Duel 45: 13 O'clock Terror!

Duel 45: 13 O'clock Terror!
THE AMUSEMENT PARK!!
Domino Park
ENT
Parking

READ THIS WAY

I CAN'T BELIEVE IT!!
ANZU ASKED ME OUT!!
COULD THIS MEAN...

UM... ANZU...
HM?
WHAT, YUGI?
THE TWO OF US GOING OUT...WOULD YOU SAY WE'RE ON A D-D-D...

HEY KIDDO!
THIS IS A HIGH SCHOOL TICKET.
YOU'RE STILL IN GRADE SCHOOL, RIGHT?
URK...

E-EXCUSE ME!
I MAY NOT LOOK IT, BUT I AM IN HIGH SCHOOL!

....

YA-HOO!
LOOK AT ALL THE RIDES!
WHAT SHOULD WE DO FIRST, ANZU?!

LET'S SEE...
IT'S A HOT SUMMER DAY...THE SUN'S SHINING...

SO WHY DON'T WE JUST...

SPLOOSH
AHA HA HA HA HA!
LET'S DO IT AGAIN!
C'MON YUGI!
O-... OKAY ...
GLITTER
BADUM

WHAT ARE YOU WAITING FOR?
COME ON!
EVEN THAT **BOMBER** WOULDN'T STAND THE POWER OF ANZU'S DYNAMITE BODY!!
BLUSH
IT'S SO BRIGHT ...
HM ...
......!!
YUGI ...?!
THE **OTHER** ONE...!!

READ THIS WAY

SQUIRT
WHA !!
...

WHADDYA THINK YOU'RE DOIN'!!
YOU LITTLE BRAT!!
WA HA HA HA HA !!

JUST MY IMAGI- NATION ...

THE ORDINARY YUGI IS LIKE A LITTLE KID...

WHAT CAN I DO ...
...TO MAKE THE YUGI I WANT APPEAR?

HEY, BABE!

YOU ALONE ?
WANT TO GET ON THE SLIDE WITH ME?

!!
I KNOW! MAYBE HE'LL APPEAR IF I'M IN TROUBLE!!

...!!
WHAT'S THE MATTER, ANZU?
GLARE
GLARE
HUH...?!
AIEEEEE!!
!!
ANZU!!
WHAT ARE YOU DOING?!!
PERVERT!
YIEEE!! HELP!!
WHAT'S THE BIG...
HUH...?!

READ THIS WAY

ATTENTION, PARK PATRONS.
THE POLICE HAVE RECEIVED A BOMB THREAT IN THE PARK. WE CAN'T GO INTO DETAILS FOR SECURITY REASONS, BUT...UH... PLEASE FOLLOW THE INSTRUCTIONS OF THE NEAREST POLICE OFFICER AND QUICKLY AND CALMLY PROCEED TO THE NEAREST EXIT. YOU CAN ALSO JUMP OVER THE LITTLE FENCES. THANK YOU.

THIS IS TERRIBLE!
I WONDER IF IT'S THE SAME BOMBER!!

ANZU! LET'S GET OUT OF HERE!
HMM... A BOMBER...

THAT SOUNDS EXCITING!
WHAT?! WE HAVE TO GET OUT OF HERE!

THIS SITUATION COULD BE MY CHANCE TO SEE THE OTHER YUGI...♡

WE GOTTA GET OUTTA HERE!
STAMPEDE
CALM DOWN, EVERYONE!!
IT'S THE BOMBER!!
AACK!
RUN

HUH...?
WHERE ARE YOU?!
ANZU...

THIS IS TERRIBLE! I'VE LOST ANZU!!

KEH HEH HEH ... I THOUGHT I'D GIVE YOU A ***HINT...***

LET ME TELL YOU ***WHERE*** THE BOMB IS SET. IT WON'T HELP YOU.

THREE PEOPLE'S LIVES ARE RIDING ON THIS GAME ...

IT'S HIM!

KEH HEH HEH ...

THE LOCATION OF THE BOMB IS ...

YUGI!
!

4
CLATTA
HERE! *UP HERE!*
3
ANZU!!
SHE'S ON THE FERRIS WHEEL!

CLATTA
I'LL MAKE YUGI ANXIOUS!
THEN MAYBE HE'LL COME OUT...

MAYBE I'LL GET TO SEE THE *OTHER* YUGI ...♡

THMP THMP
ANZU!!

THIS IS *BAD!* THERE ARE THREE PEOPLE RIDING THAT FERRIS WHEEL!
IN CARS #1, #3 AND #13!
GRR ... HE'S RIGHT ...

EX... EXCUSE ME!
MY FRIEND IS ON THAT FERRIS WHEEL... IS SOMETHING WRONG?!

THERE'S A BOMB PLANTED ON THAT RIDE!
12
13

DOOM
WHAT ?!!
ANZU !!

ALL RIGHT! THE WHEEL TAKES *10 MINUTES* TO MAKE A FULL TURN. AFTER THAT, THE BOMB *EXPLODES!* BUT YOU HAVE ONE LAST CHANCE!
LET'S PLAY A CARD GAME!
PANT
IF YOU'RE LUCKY, THERE WON'T BE ANY MORE BODIES...

GRR...!
THE BOMBER CHALLENGED US TO A *CARD GAME!!*
WHO'S A GOOD CARD PLAYER? IS THERE A *GAMER* HERE?
RRRMMMB

BAM
I'LL DO IT!
MMM
AH ...
THERE HE IS! ♡
HUH? YOU'RE THAT BOY...
GIVE ME THE CELL PHONE!

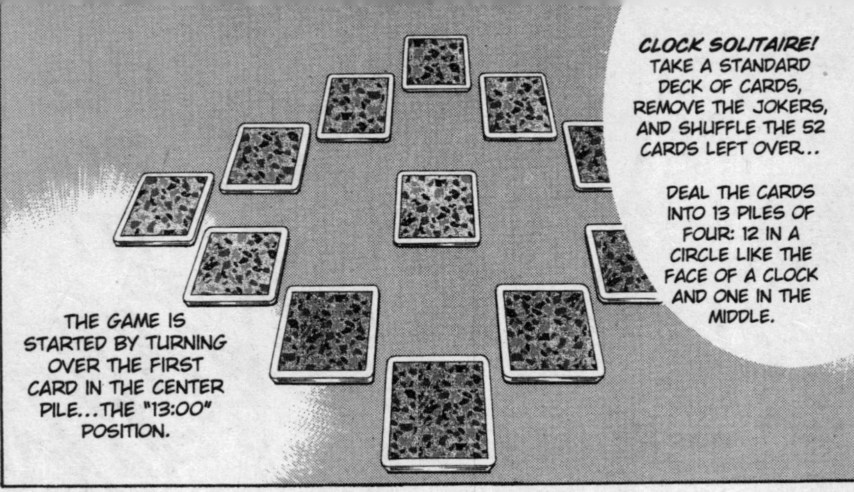
CLOCK SOLITAIRE! TAKE A STANDARD DECK OF CARDS, REMOVE THE JOKERS, AND SHUFFLE THE 52 CARDS LEFT OVER...
DEAL THE CARDS INTO 13 PILES OF FOUR: 12 IN A CIRCLE LIKE THE FACE OF A CLOCK AND ONE IN THE MIDDLE.
THE GAME IS STARTED BY TURNING OVER THE FIRST CARD IN THE CENTER PILE...THE "13:00" POSITION.

HERE I GO!!

THE FIRST CARD IS THE THREE OF SPADES.
SO I PLACE THIS CARD FACE UP UNDER THE 3:00 PILE.
THEN I TURN OVER THE FIRST CARD IN THAT PILE.
THE FOUR OF HEARTS...
I PLACE IT UNDER THE 4:00 PILE...
...AND FLIP THE TOP CARD!

NEXT, THE 10 OF DIAMONDS.
I PUT THAT UNDER 10:00.
THAT TOP CARD IS THE FOUR OF DIAMONDS.
NOW THERE ARE TWO CARDS UNDER THE PILE IN THE 4:00 POSITION.
THIS IS A SIMPLE GAME... AS ALL FOUR CARDS IN EACH HOUR PILE ARE TURNED OVER...
THE NUMBERS APPEAR ON THE FACE OF THE "CLOCK."

WHAT'S THE POINT? WHAT IS THIS MADMAN UP TO...?
THE FOURTH NUMBER FOUR CARD...
AND I'VE COMPLETED THE FIRST HOUR...
4:00 !!
YIEEE!
!
THE #4 CAR EXPLODED !!

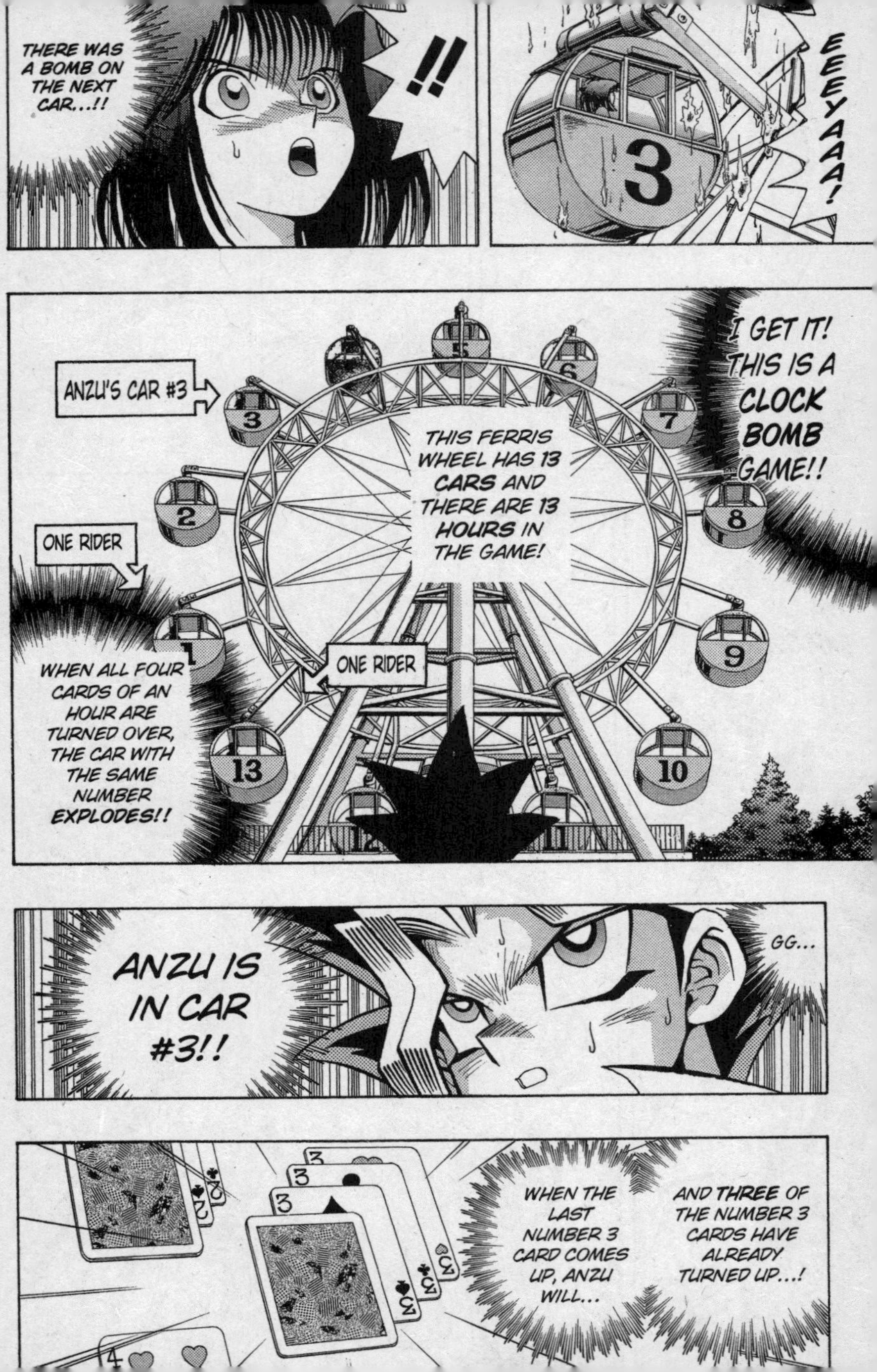

I GET IT! THIS IS A CLOCK BOMB GAME!!

THIS FERRIS WHEEL HAS 13 CARS AND THERE ARE 13 HOURS IN THE GAME!

ANZU'S CAR #3

ONE RIDER

ONE RIDER

WHEN ALL FOUR CARDS OF AN HOUR ARE TURNED OVER, THE CAR WITH THE SAME NUMBER EXPLODES!!

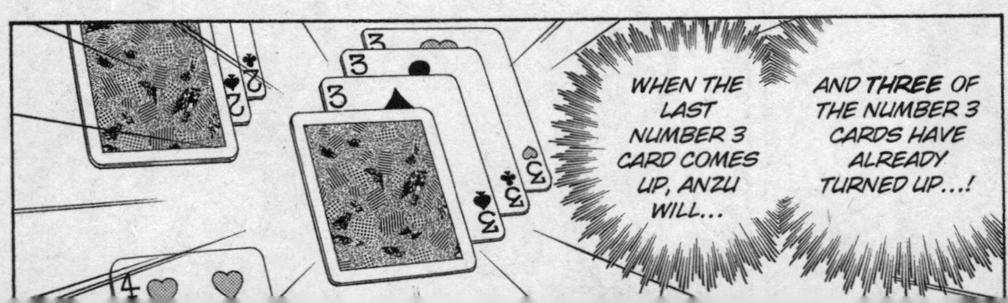

YUGI...
HELP ME!
NO MATTER WHAT...
I MUST SAVE ANZU!
KEH HEH HEH...
UNDERSTAND NOW? KEEP PLAYING! DO YOU REALLY THINK YOU'LL END THIS WITHOUT ANYONE GETTING HURT?
TCH...THE BOMBER MUST BE WATCHING MY CARDS AND TRIGGERING THE BOMBS!
10
BUT WHERE IN THE WORLD...
!
NOW THE 8:00 POSITION IS COMPLETE!!
7
9

IT'S OVER, CHIEF! SOONER OR LATER, ONE OF THE OCCUPIED CARS WILL EXPLODE!
HOW CAN THE BOY WIN THIS GAME?
THE 13:00 CARDS! KINGS GO IN THE MIDDLE OF THE CLOCK, SO I HAVE TO COLLECT THE FOUR KINGS!
I KNOW THE FULL RULES OF "CLOCK SOLITAIRE"! THERE IS ONLY ONE WAY TO BEAT THIS GAME!
YOU START FROM THE CENTER PILE, SO WHEN YOU DRAW THE FOURTH KING, YOU CAN'T DRAW ANY MORE AND THE GAME ENDS!
THAT'S HOW IT WORKS, RIGHT...? YES! AND THERE ARE TWO KINGS TO GO!
BRRM
BUT IF I DRAW THE LAST NUMBER THREE BEFORE THAT...
ANZU'S LIFE IS ...!
THERE GOES THE #2 CAR!
KABOOM
TCH ...

!!
SNAP
OKAY! THAT MAKES THREE KINGS!!
ONE MORE CARD!!
20 SECONDS LEFT!!
20 SECONDS TO THE HOUR ON THE ORIGINAL CALLING CARD! THEN ALL THE BOMBS WILL GO OFF!
THIS IS THE LAST CARD!!
PLEASE BE IT!
FIVE SECONDS!
BADUM
AN ACE?! USELESS!
G- G- G-

KING !!
BA
HE DID IT! THE FOUR KINGS ARE OUT!
WHOA
TIME IS UP!!
BAM
PHEW ...
OKAY!
LET'S EVACUATE THE THREE RIDERS!!
YUGI!!

LET'S GO!

YOU HAD ME WORRIED THERE......

OH RIGHT! DETECTIVE ...
WHAT IS IT?
YOU WANT TO KNOW WHERE THE BOMBER IS?

CHECK OUT THE PERSON RIDING IN CAR #13!

THERE WON'T BE A BOMB ON THAT CAR!
13
...!!
AND THAT'S THE ONLY PLACE IN THE PARK WHERE YOU CAN SEE MY CARDS AND SET THE BOMBS OFF!
CAR #13 IS THE ONLY SAFE CAR. THE PERSON PRETENDING TO BE A HOSTAGE IS THE BOMBER!

HEY, LET'S GET BACK TO OUR DATE!
~~~
~~~

YUGI
&
ANZU

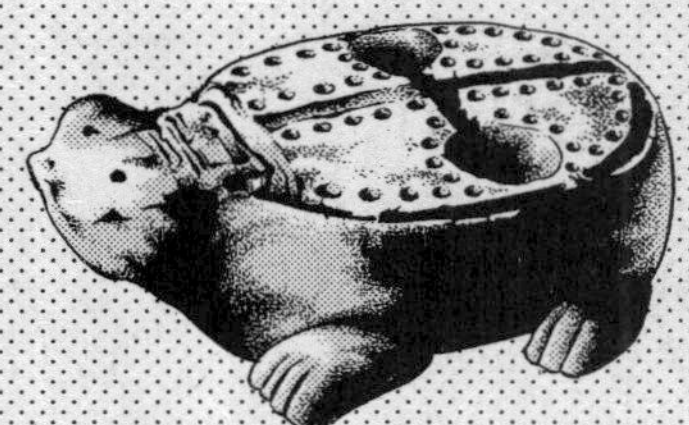

Duel 46: The Evil Dragon Cards (Part 1)

DOOM
GLOOM
HELLO, YUGI!
AH, IMORI!
YOU KNOW HIM, YUGI?
YUP! HE'S IN MY CLASS!

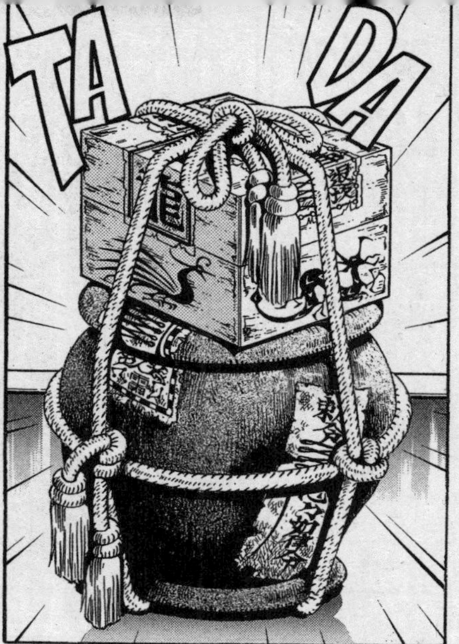
TA
DA

WHAT THE HECK IS THIS?!
SOME KIND OF STRANGE BOX...

HRM ?!
TH-... THIS IS...!!

MY GRANDFATHER WAS A GAME COLLECTOR. THE OTHER DAY, I DISCOVERED THIS JAR IN THE SHED ...
MY GRANDFATHER PICKED IT UP WHEN HE WAS IN MANCHURIA DURING WORLD WAR II!
I THOUGHT MR. MUTOU MIGHT KNOW WHAT IT IS ...SO THAT'S WHY I'M HERE!

IT DOESN'T LOOK LIKE A GAME...
IT LOOKS LIKE THOSE URNS YOU KEEP PEOPLE'S ASHES IN ......

CAN I OPEN IT, IMORI?
GO AHEAD! I HAVEN'T TOUCHED IT YET...

DON'T OPEN THAT!!
HUH ...?

READ THIS WAY

I'M SORRY FOR YELLING AT YOU... BUT YOU MUSTN'T BREAK THIS SEAL!

THIS IS AN ANCIENT CHINESE GAME CALLED *"DRAGON CARDS"*!
RMB RMB
I'VE HEARD RUMORS, BUT THIS IS THE FIRST TIME I'VE SEEN IT...

DRAGON CARDS?!

!?

IT'S WRITTEN THAT THE DRAGON CARDS WERE USED BY A TAOIST MASTER AS A FINAL TEST FOR FENG SHUI STUDENTS IN CHINA!
FENG SHUI? YOU MEAN THAT THING WHEN YOU REARRANGE FURNITURE?

FENG SHUI IS A FORM OF MAGIC THAT USES THE ENERGIES OF *NATURE!*
IT'S BEEN GRADUALLY SYSTEMIZED SINCE CHINA'S GOLDEN AGE, FOUR THOUSAND YEARS AGO.

WHY WERE THOSE DRAGON CARDS SEALED AWAY?

YOU KNOW ABOUT THE CONCEPT OF YIN AND YANG IN CHINESE PHILOSOPHY ...
YIN MEANS SHADOW, AND YANG MEANS LIGHT... IN OTHER WORDS EVERYTHING IN THE WORLD IS A BALANCE OF LIGHT AND DARK!

RIGHT NOW, THESE DRAGON CARDS ARE YIN–SHADOW!
THE SEAL SURROUNDING THE DRAGON CARDS IS YANG–LIGHT–CREATING A BALANCE!
IF THE SEAL ON THE DRAGON CARDS WERE BROKEN, THE YIN AND YANG WOULD CLASH CREATING A WARPED POWER!

!!

IMORI, WAS IT ...?
THESE DRAGON CARDS ARE SEALED AWAY ALONG WITH THE POWER OF THE SHADOWS!
PROMISE ME! YOU MUST NEVER BREAK THAT SEAL!
YES, OF COURSE !!

WOW, NOW I WANNA BREAK THE SEAL ...
STUPID! YOU'LL GET CURSED!

DRAGON CARDS ...
I WONDER WHAT KIND OF GAME IT IS...

HEH ...
POWER OF THE SHADOWS ...!!
RRMMB

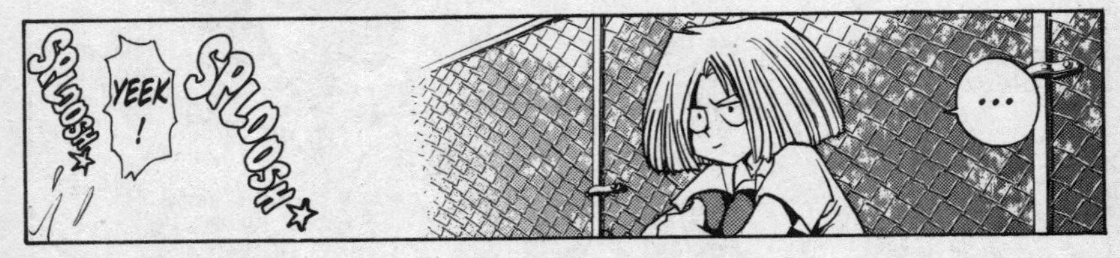

SUMMER WAS MADE FOR THE POOL!
GOOD FOR THE BODY! GOOD FOR THE HEART! AND EASY ON THE EYES!
THAT FELT GOOD!
HUH...
WHA...?!

!!
THERE'S A NOTE!

If you want your puzz
back, come by yourse
to room "C." Don't te
anyone about this. (If
you do I'll ditch the
zzle!)
– Messenger of
Darkness
MESSENGER OF DARKNESS?!

PANIC
THE MILLENNIUM PUZZLE IS GONE!!
PANIC PANIC

Room C
TMP

WHO IN THE WORLD ...!!

...
YUGI, WHAT'S WRONG?
ER...
IT'S NOTHING...

BANG
I'VE BEEN WAITING FOR YOU, YUGI!
IMORI !!
HEH HEH.

YOU USED TO BE BULLIED BY EVERYONE. BUT ONE DAY YOU GOT THIS MILLENNIUM PUZZLE AND GAINED THE POWERS OF DARKNESS...

ISN'T THAT RIGHT, YUGI?

!!

MY GRANDFATHER LEFT ME ALL SORTS OF BOOKS ABOUT GAMES...

AND BOOKS ON ANCIENT EGYPT...

AT FIRST I DIDN'T THINK THERE WAS ANY CONNECTION ...

BUT THEN I FOUND THE *SECRET* OF THE MILLENNIUM PUZZLE!

DOOM

TH-... THAT'S THE DRAGON CARDS!!

NOW IS THE TIME!
TO REMOVE THE SEAL!!

RUMBLE
HEE HEE HEH HEH ... I RELEASE THE SHADOW POWER ...

STOP, IMORI!
YOU MUSTN'T BREAK THE SEAL!!

BWA HA HA HA HA HA!
BRRMM
!!
RRM

AFTER MY VISIT TO YOUR SHOP, I DID SOME RESEARCH ON THE DRAGON CARDS...IN A TEXT ABOUT ANCIENT CHINA!
ACCORDING TO IT, ONCE THE SEAL ON THE DRAGON CARDS IS BROKEN, A SHADOW GAME *MUST* BE PLAYED OR THE PEOPLE OF THAT LAND WILL SUFFER ETERNAL *DISASTER!*
WHAT ?!!

THERE IS ONLY *ONE* WAY TO REPLACE THE SEAL ON THE DRAGON CARDS......
THE *LOSER* OF THE GAME MUST OFFER HIS *SOUL* TO THIS SOUL-EATING JAR TO CALM THE WRATH OF THE CARDS!
OFFER HIS SOUL ...?!?!
OO
Ss
ZZ
YUGI!
DON'T TRY TO BACK OUT!
YOU CAN'T ESCAPE THE DRAGON CARDS!!

OOOO
WHOO

READ THIS WAY

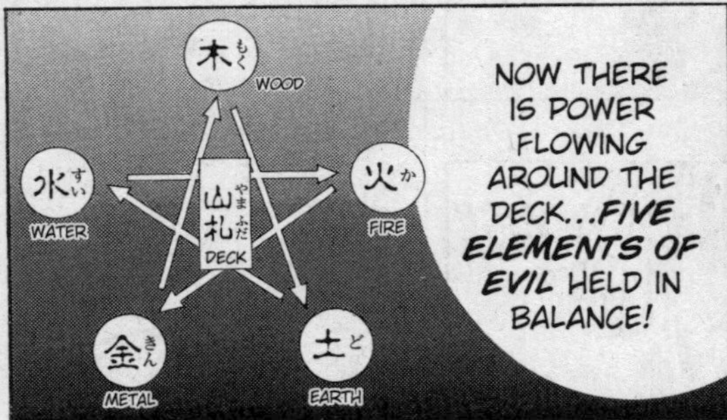

DA-DA-

NOW! GAME START!

DOOM

WITHOUT THE MILLENNIUM PUZZLE, AS YOUR PLAIN OLD SELF, THERE'S **NO WAY** YOU CAN BEAT ME!

SHP
I'LL DRAW THE FIRST CARD!!

HEH HEH HEH...A LEVEL 4 WATER DRAGON! THAT MAKES TWO IN MY HAND!
WATER 4
WATER 4
IF I DRAW ONE MORE, I CAN SUMMON A SHUI LONG—A WATER DRAGON!

I DISCARD ONE CARD I DON'T NEED!
METAL 1
I HAVE TO LAY IT FACE UP!
JUST LIKE OTHER CARD GAMES, YOU CAN READ YOUR OPPONENT'S HAND FROM THE CARDS THEY THROW AWAY!
SNP

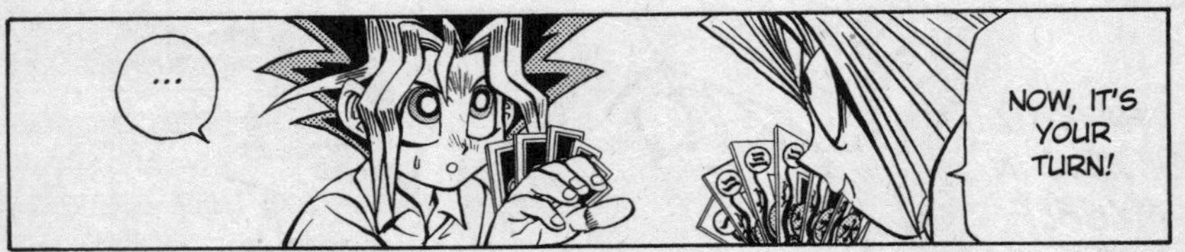
NOW, IT'S YOUR TURN!
...

!!
OKAY, THIS CARD LOOKS PRETTY GOOD!
FIRE 5

I'LL DISCARD THIS CARD!
HEH HEH...... I KNOW WHAT ELEMENT YUGI IS COLLECTING!

THE OBJECT OF THIS GAME IS TO COLLECT CARDS OF THE ELEMENT THAT WINS OVER YOUR OPPONENT'S ELEMENTS!

FIRE BEATS METAL! METAL BEATS WOOD, WOOD BEATS EARTH, AND WATER BEATS FIRE!

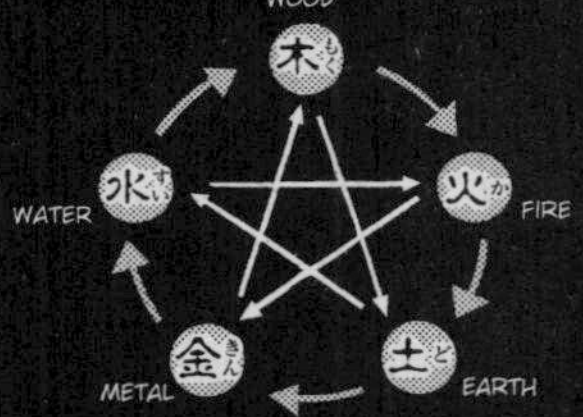

AND DIFFERENT ELEMENTS GIVE POWER TO OTHER ELEMENTS!

WOOD GIVES POWER TO FIRE, FIRE TO EARTH, EARTH TO METAL, METAL TO WATER, WATER TO WOOD!!

HA! I HAVE TWO WATER DRAGONS, LEVEL 3 AND 4!

YOUR DRAGONS ARE FIRE AND METAL! BAD MOVE!

SPLOOP
DRAGON BATTLE! JIAO LONG FU!
SSH
SSH
FLOOD ATTACK!
TWO SHUI LONGS– TWO WATER DRAGONS! MY FLOOD ATTACK WASHED YUGI'S DRAGONS AWAY!

I... I LOST...
HA HA HA HA HA! YOU KNOW WHAT'S NEXT, YUGI! PENALTY GAME!
YOU HAVE TO GIVE THE DRAGONS YOUR SOUL!
!!
GGK--
THOOP
AAGGGGH...
WSSSHT
YES! YES! THE DRAGONS ARE SUCKED INTO THE SOUL-EATING JAR ALONG WITH YUGI'S SOUL!!

FLOP
HA HA HA HA! I DID IT! I BEAT YUGI!
I... HUH?
HE GOT HIS HANDS ON THE MILLENNIUM PUZZLE!
!
FLASH
...
YU-... YUGI ...
!!
JUST IN TIME ...
RRMM
BB
IMORI ...
NEXT I'LL STAKE MY OTHER SOUL!!

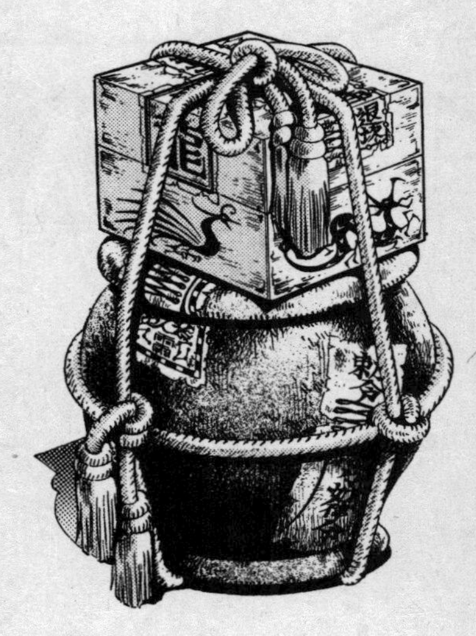

READ THIS WAY

YU... YUGI!!

RUMBLE

JUST IN TIME ...

IF I HADN'T SNATCHED BACK THE MILLENNIUM PUZZLE, MY SOUL WOULD BE ***ENTOMBED*** IN THE SHADOWS ***FOREVER!***

Duel 47: The Evil Dragon Cards (Part 2)

Duel 47: The Evil Dragon Cards (Part 2)

I GUESS I CAN'T BECOME THE GUARDIAN OF DARKNESS UNTIL I DEFEAT YOU, THE "BACK" YUGI ...

BAM
OKAY!
ONE MORE GAME!

RUMBLE

SSSZOOOO

BUT... WILL I GET MY SOUL BACK EVEN IF I WIN?

HEH HEH ...ARE YOU WORRIED?
THE SOUL OF YOUR "FRONT" SELF IS STILL SEALED IN THE SOUL-EATING JAR......

BUT THERE'S NOTHING TO WORRY ABOUT!
THIS JAR TAKES THREE MONTHS TO DIGEST ONE SOUL.
IF BY SOME EXTRAORDINARY FLUKE YOU ACTUALLY MANAGE TO WIN THE NEXT GAME, YOU'LL GET YOUR SPARE SOUL BACK GOOD AS NEW!

DADADADADA

GAME START!!

DADA

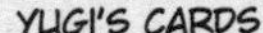

YUGI'S CARDS

IMORI'S CARDS

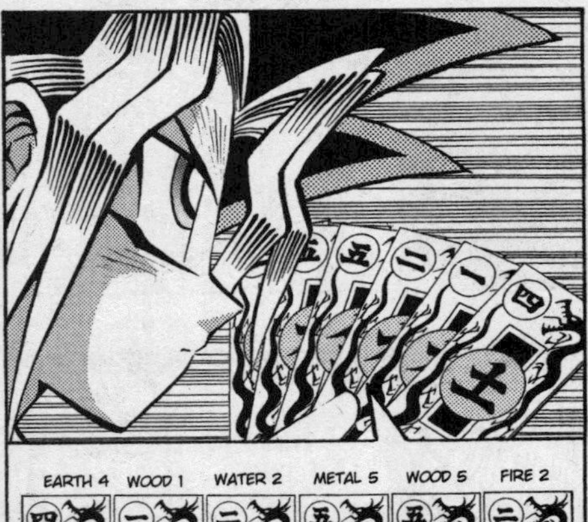

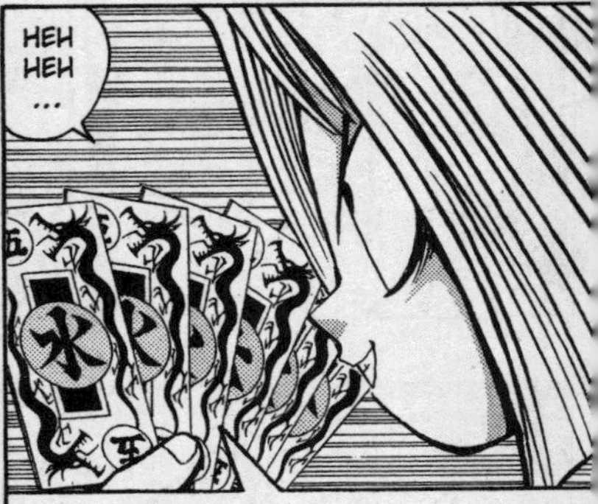

EARTH 4 WOOD 1 WATER 2 METAL 5 WOOD 5 FIRE 2

四 土 四 | 一 木 一 | 二 水 二 | 五 金 五 | 五 木 五 | 二 火 二

WATER 5 WATER 5 FIRE 4 WOOD 5 WATER 4 METAL

五 水 五 | 五 水 五 | 四 火 四 | 五 木 五 | 四 水 四 | 四

DRAGON CARDS RULES

THE CARDS REPRESENT DRAGONS OF THE FIVE CHINESE ELEMENTS (WOOD, FIRE, EARTH, METAL AND WATER). EACH CARD HAS A LEVEL FROM 1 TO 5, AND THERE ARE THREE DUPLICATES OF EACH CARD, FOR A TOTAL OF 75 CARDS.

AT THE START OF THE GAME, BOTH PLAYERS DRAW SIX CARDS. THEY KEEP DRAWING AND DISCARDING CARDS FROM THE DECK UNTIL THEY COLLECT TWO SETS OF THREE IDENTICAL CARDS. AFTER COLLECTING THE STRONGEST POSSIBLE SETS, EACH PLAYER SUMMONS TWO DRAGONS TO BATTLE. THE PLAYER WHO DEFEATS THE OPPOSING DRAGONS WINS.

WATER 5 WATER 5 FIRE 4 FIRE 4 WOOD 5 WOOD 5

NOW I HAVE THREE POTENTIAL SETS!

IF I DRAW ANY ONE OF THESE CARDS, I'LL BE ABLE TO SUMMON A DRAGON!

EARTH 4 EARTH 4 FIRE 2 WOOD 5 METAL 5 WATER 4

ONLY ONE CLOSE TO BEING A SET...

IT WILL TAKE SOME TIME BEFORE I COMPLETE MY HAND...

WATER 5

THREE "WATER 5"

THREE "EARTH 4"

WOOD 5

NOW I CAN SUMMON TWO DRAGONS!!

RUMBLE

THREE "WATER 5"

THREE "WOOD 5"

WHA ?!

HEH HEH HEH ... IN THIS GAME, YOU CAN MAKE SETS WITH THE CARDS YOUR OPPONENT ***DISCARDS!***

IT'S ***DANGEROUS*** TO DISCARD HIGH LEVEL CARDS TOWARD THE END OF THE GAME!

GGK ...

BECAUSE HE SUMMONED HIS DRAGONS FIRST, THEY GET **STRONGER** WITH EACH TURN IT TAKES ME TO COMPLETE MY SET!

!!

METAL 5

SUMMON DRAGONS !!
I'VE SUMMONED A LEVEL 5 WATER DRAGON AND A LEVEL 5 WOOD DRAGON!! A SHUI LONG AND A MU LONG!
I'VE SUMMONED A LEVEL 4 EARTH DRAGON AND A LEVEL 5 METAL DRAGON!! A TU LONG AND A JIN LONG!

WATER DRAGON LEVEL 5
WOOD DRAGON LEVEL 5
EARTH DRAGON LEVEL 4
METAL DRAGON LEVEL 5
ZD-D-D-D-D-D
DRAGON BATTLE! JIAO LONG FU!

HA HA HA! YUGI! I CAN'T BELIEVE YOU WERE STUPID ENOUGH TO SUMMON ANOTHER METAL DRAGON!
DID YOU FORGET THAT IN OUR LAST BATTLE, MY WATER DRAGON DROWNED YOUR METAL DRAGON IN AN INSTANT!
GO, WATER DRAGON!!
DESTROY THE JIN LONG! UNLEASH THE DELUGE!
BRRMMMM
FIVE
SHUI LONG (WATER DRAGON) SPECIAL ATTACK: FLOOD •CAN FREELY CONTROL WATER TO BLAST ENEMIES. IT HAS THE ABILITY TO RUST METAL.
FLOOD ATTACK!!
SHOOSSH

READ THIS WAY
SPLSSHHHH
YOU CAN'T GET ME WITH THE SAME TRICK TWICE, IMORI!!
DD
EARTH DRAGON !!
TU LONG
(EARTH DRAGON)
SPECIAL ATTACK:
GROUND SHATTER
• MOVES THE EARTH BY CONTROLLING THE "DRAGON'S BREATH" WITHIN THE SOIL. IT CAN ABSORB THE ELEMENT OF WATER INTO ITS BODY.
MM
GROUND SHATTER!
RR
RRMMB
WHA ......!

THE EARTH DRAGON RAISES THE GROUND AND DAMS THE FLOOD ATTACK TO PROTECT THE METAL DRAGON!!

SHBAAAA

AS LONG AS THE EARTH DRAGON IS THERE, YOUR WATER DRAGON'S ATTACKS WON'T WORK!!

EARTH GIVES POWER TO METAL AND METAL IS PROTECTED BY EARTH!

RELATIONS OF THE FIVE ELEMENTS

もく 木 WOOD
か 火
ど 土 EAR
きん 金 METAL
すい 水 WATER

EARTH EMPOWERS METAL

THE WOOD DRAGON IS GETTING BIGGER!

WHERE'S IT GETTING THAT POWER?!

KRK KRK KRK

HEH HEH HEH...FROM THE WATER DRAGON, OF COURSE!

JUST LIKE A SAPLING SOAKS UP WATER AND GROWS INTO A GREAT TREE!

GWOOO

WOOD 木
FIRE 火
EARTH 土
METAL 金
WATER 水

GASP ...!

THIS IS BAD! HE'S GOING AFTER THE EARTH DRAGON...!!

D-D-D-D

SHWIRL

THE WOOD DRAGON'S SHOOTS ARE ENTERING THE EARTH DRAGON!!

THUK

WOOD 木
FIRE 火
EARTH 土
METAL 金
WATER 水
強 STRONG
弱 WEAK

DOOK

DOOK

DOOK

NOW, BACK TO WHERE WE WERE! THE WATER DRAGON ATTACKS THE METAL DRAGON AGAIN!
FLOOD ATTACK !!
BPR MMM
SHOSSSH
NOW THE EARTH DRAGON CAN'T MOVE IN TO HELP!
NO! METAL DRAGON !
!!
SPLO
OOOSH
HA HA HA HA! IT TOOK THE FLOOD STRAIGHT ON!
THE METAL DRAGON IS DEAD! AND NOW, YUGI, YOU TOO ARE-
HUH?!

THOOM

FEH...STILL THERE...THE METAL DRAGON IS STILL ALIVE!

THAT'S IT! THE FLOOD ATTACK WAS **WEAKENED** BECAUSE THE WATER DRAGON GAVE ITS POWER TO THE WOOD DRAGON!

SNK

SNK SNK

BUT LOOK!! IT WORKED AFTER ALL! THE METAL DRAGON'S BODY IS **RUSTING!**

SNK SNK

WOBBLE

SNK SNK

METAL DRAGON !!

GIVE ME THE LAST OF YOUR POWER !!

GWOOOO

WOBBLE WOBBLE

!!

WHAT ...!!

K-SHING
I-IMPOSSIBLE ...IT USED ITS AXE-WINGS! IT TOOK FLIGHT!
SHP
GO!
DO IT, METAL DRAGON !!
CRACK
OOO
VHOOO
OH... OH NO!
IF METAL HITS WOOD, IT'S GOING TO...
FLOOD ATTACK !!

KA-CHO
AXE-WING SLASH!!!!!!
YES! THE WOOD DRAGON IS DOWN!
SPLA
SHOOSH
GLUK
GLUK
JIN LONG ...METAL DRAGON... YOU GAVE YOUR LIFE TO SAVE YOUR COMRADE...

AND NOW THE EARTH DRAGON IS BACK!!
BA
BAM
NO... NEVER...
G-GO! WATER DRAGON!!
FLOOD ATTACK!!
GROUND SHATTER!!
RM RM RM RM RM

RMB
RMB
THE EARTH ELEMENT DAMS THE FLOW OF WATER AND ABSORBS THE NEGATIVE ENERGY!
WEAK WOOD FIRE WATER METAL EARTH STRONG
N-NO! THE WATER DRAGON IS SINKING INTO THE CRACKS IN THE EARTH!
RM
I LOST ... EVERY-THING ...!
IMORI! HERE'S YOUR PENALTY GAME!
NORMALLY I TRY TO COME UP WITH SOMETHING ORIGINAL, BUT...NOW IT'S YOUR TURN TO FEED YOUR SOUL TO 25 RAVENOUS DRAGONS!
BANG
GGK ...

READ THIS WAY

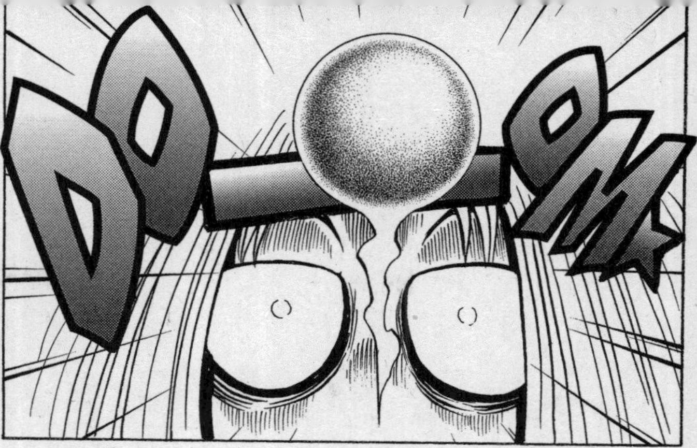

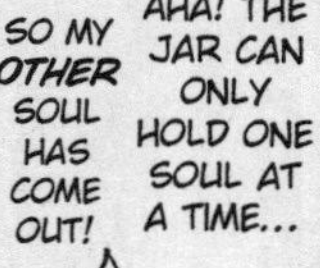

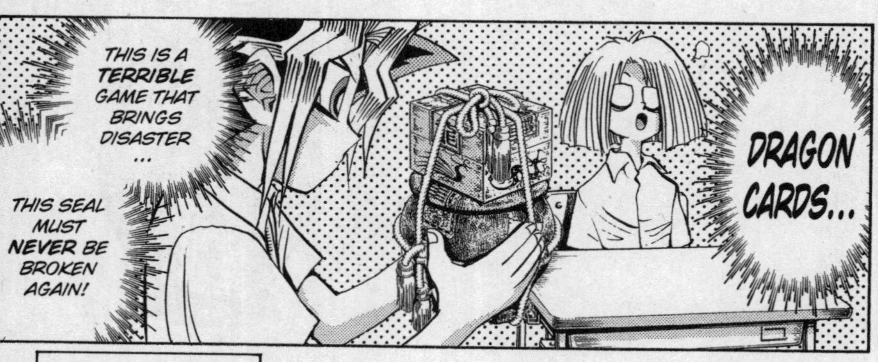

GAME OVER

罰ゲーム★
…
勅令
急々加律令

Duel 48: Jonouchi! Soul Battle! (Part 1)

"SUPER YO-YO?!"

BAM ☆

YUP!

IT'S THE ***HOTTEST*** STREET ITEM RIGHT NOW!

YO-YOS! EVERY-BODY WANTS SOME!

YOVEGA FIREBOY
Fireboy
BONSAI 1997 MADE IN USA

READ THIS WAY
WHOA! IT WENT TO THE END OF THE STRING AND SPUN AROUND!
AND IF YOU PUT IT ON THE GROUND WHILE IT'S IN "SLEEP MODE"...
TA
DA
PARADE THE POOCH!!
WHIRRR
WHAT! THAT'S JUST THE OLD "WALK THE DOG!"
WAHA
URK...
YOU'RE JUST SHOWING OFF, GIVING IT A NEW NAME!
D... DARN IT...
TH... THEN I'LL SHOW YOU SOMETHING *REALLY* COOL...
I'VE NEVER TRIED THIS, BUT...
LOOP THE LOOP!!
WSH
WSH
WSH
ACK! LOOK OUT!
DUCK! DUCK FOR YOUR LIVES!

HUH ...?

GET RID OF THAT THING!!

HMPH.
I DON'T EVER WANT TO SEE ANOTHER YO-YO AGAIN AS LONG AS I LIVE!

NEZUMI !

WHAT'S YOUR PROBLEM, NEZUMI?
WHAT KIND OF *WEIRDO* HAS A THING AGAINST YO-YOS?
YO-YOS ARE FUN...WHY DON'T YOU TRY...?

HUH ...
AH...
WHAT HAPPENED TO YOUR FACE...?

HMF!
YOU SEE THIS BRUISE?!

HAVEN'T YOU HEARD ABOUT THE ATTACKS AROUND HERE...?
ATTACKS ...?!
YO-YO ATTACKS!
THERE'S A GANG USING YO-YOS TO MUG KIDS AT OUR SCHOOL!

WHAT?!
YOU MEAN THAT BRUISE IS FROM...?!

YEAH.

I WAS WALKING ALONE AFTER DARK THE OTHER NIGHT WHEN ALL OF A SUDDEN...

THESE THREE GUYS SURROUNDED ME! THEY TOLD ME TO HAND OVER ALL MY MONEY!

WHEN I SAID NO AND TRIED TO GET OUT OF THERE...
THEY TOOK OUT THESE YO-YOS AND...

THUK

READ THIS WAY

WHAT!!

!

I WAS SO MAD...!

HOW DARE THOSE JERKS USE YO-YOS TO STEAL FROM LITTLE KIDS?!

ROAR

RR

I WISH THEY WERE HERE RIGHT NOW! I'D SHOW 'EM!

READ THIS WAY

I'LL GO WITH YOU, JONOUCHI.
NAH, THERE ARE ONLY THREE DUDES... I CAN HANDLE 'EM ON MY OWN!

OH! UH...
COULD YOU COME TOO, YUGI?
IT'S JUST 'CAUSE... I HATE TO BE AROUND FIGHTS...
I'D FEEL BETTER IF SOMEONE LIKE YOU WAS THERE.

OKAY!
I'LL GO WITH YOU!
BURN
I'LL TEACH THOSE JERKS A LESSON...

THOSE WHO LAUGHED AT YO-YOS...
...WILL CRY AT YO-YOS!
BWOOOSH
WHATEVER THAT MEANS...

DOOOM

IT'S JUST AROUND THE CORNER UP AHEAD.
THIS IS A SCARY NEIGHBORHOOD ...THERE'S NO HOUSES OR SHOPS OR ANYTHING...
BY THE WAY, NEZUMI...

READ THIS WAY

(IF YOU DON'T REMEMBER, CHECK OUT *YU-GI-OH!* VOL. 2!)

JONOUCHI USED TO HANG WITH HIRUTANI IN MIDDLE SCHOOL. BUT WHEN JONOUCHI DIDN'T WANT TO COME BACK TO HIS GANG, HIRUTANI BEAT HIM UP...BAD! HE'S A REAL THUG!

!
JU
MP
!!

THMP

GET BACK, YUGI!

CRAP...THIS ISN'T JUST THREE GUYS! THERE'S A *BUNCH* OF THEM!

SHWIRRL

YO-YOS !
...!

SHWIRR

YA HA HA HA!

TMP

CIRCLE AROUND THEM! GET THEIR BACKS!

COME ON, YUGI!
JONOUCHI!

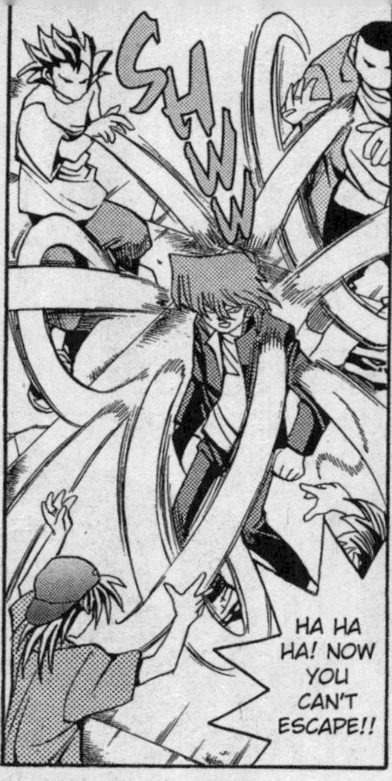
HA HA HA! NOW YOU CAN'T ESCAPE!!

THESE GUYS...... THEY KNEW WE WERE COMING...
THEY PLANNED THIS ATTACK!

WSH
GG...
WSH
WSH

HEH HEH HEH......
NOW YOU CAN'T MAKE A MOVE...
HOW DOES IT FEEL, JONOUCHI?

HEH HEH ...
TAKE ONE STEP, AND YOU ENTER THE NET OF FLYING YO-YOS...AND COME OUT WITH BROKEN BONES AND MISSING TEETH!
JONOUCHI !
HIRUTANI !!
IT'S YOU... YOU'RE BACK!

WSH
SORRY TO DISAPPOINT YOU, **BOSS MONKEY!** I DON'T THINK I'D LIKE IT IN YOUR **CAGE!**
WSH
HEH ......
I FORGOT. THE FIRST THING I'VE GOT TO DO IS STOP YOU MOUTHING OFF.
CHECK **THIS** OUT!
BAM
GUH ...
YUGI!!
DO IT !!
GRAB
CLANK
CLAT CLAT CLAT CLAT

YUGI !!

ULK ...

JONOUCHI ...DON'T DO WHAT HE SAYS...

UH ......

...

WELL, JONOUCHI! YOU CAN'T MOVE AN INCH! WHAT'S YOUR CHOICE?
SWEAR TO JOIN MY GROUP...
OR WATCH THIS KID DIE RIGHT BEFORE YOUR EYES!

GRR ...
YUGI!
SHWW
D-DON'T DO IT... JONOUCHI ...

G-G-

!
WHAT ...!

FEH ...
HIRUTANI ...
WHADDYA MEAN, I CAN'T MOVE ...?

TMP
HE MOVED!
HE WENT INTO THE YO-YO MURDER NET!
THK
THK
THK
THK
URG...
THK
THK

THK
THK
THK
CRK
CRK
THK
YUGI!
I'M COMING!
J-JONOUCHI...
TCH......
WHAT...?! WHY'D HE DO IT?!
YOU'RE GONNA DIE, JONOUCHI!

ANYONE WHO STANDS STILL AND WATCHES A FRIEND *DIE*...
DOESN'T HAVE A *RIGHT* TO LIVE!

JO... JONOUCHI ...
SNAP
SKCH
...... YUGI ...

JUST WAIT, I'LL GET YOU DOWN...

J-...
... HUP !
WHZ
WHZ
GET THE HOOK OFF YOUR NECK!

@#$% !
JONOUCHI ...YOU BAS...
DOOM

YOU'RE GOING TOO *EASY* ON HIM! HIT HIM *HARDER!*

HIRUTANI... THE PAIN OF THESE BRUISES ......

IS NOTHING COMPARED TO THE PAIN OF BETRAYING MY FRIEND !!

BAM

Duel 49: Jonouchi! Soul Battle! (Part 2)

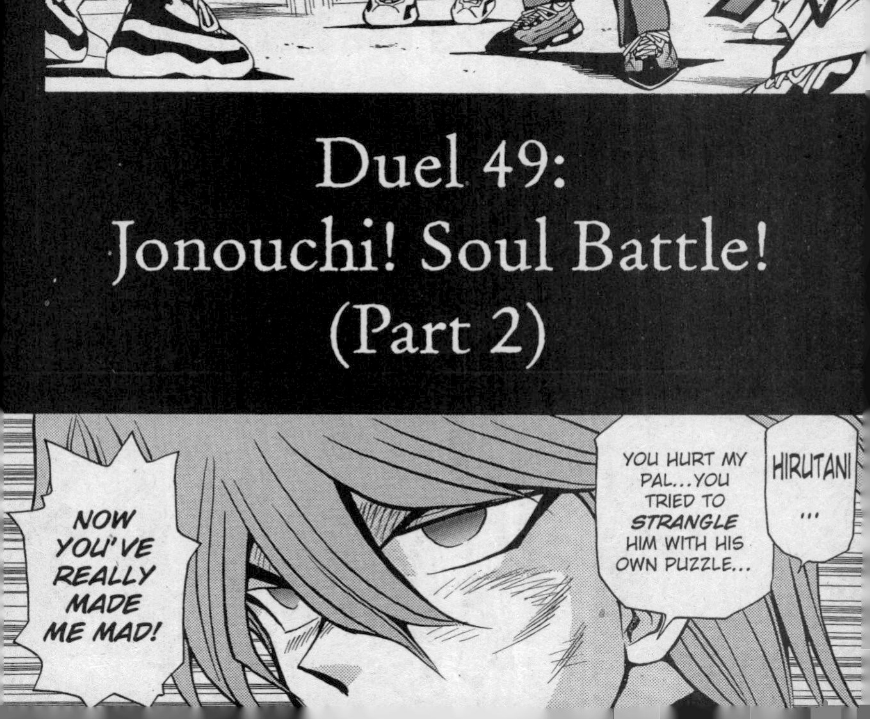

HEH HEH HEH ......
BEFORE YOU TALK BIG, WHY DON'T YOU LOOK WHERE YOU ARE?

EVEN *YOU* SHOULD REALIZE YOU'RE IN A *NO WIN* SITUATION!

......

HEE HEE HEE ...
WE'RE GONNA "WALK THE DOG" ON YOUR DEAD BODIES!
WSH
WSH

TOO MANY THUGS! TOO MANY YO-YOS!
NOWHERE TO RUN! THIS IS BAD...

WHAT SHOULD I DO...?

JONOUCHI... I'M GOING TO GIVE YOU ONE MORE CHANCE.
IF YOU SWEAR TO JOIN MY GROUP, I'LL LET YOU LIVE!

HIRUTANI!

JONOUCHI WILL NEVER JOIN YOU AGAIN!
HE DOESN'T CARE HOW MUCH YOU THREATEN HIM!
BAM

THAT'S RIGHT!
HEAR THAT, BOSS MONKEY?
THAT'S WHAT A REAL FRIEND WOULD SAY!

...

KILL THEM!!

SHW★SHW

SWSH

AGGH...

G-G-G-

JONOUCHI!

YOU STAY BACK, YUGI!!

!

THAT'S IT!

YUGI! LET ME BORROW THE MILLENNIUM PUZZLE!

HUH...?!

OKAY, IT'S YOURS!!

WHAT'S JONOUCHI GOING TO DO WITH IT...?

BAM
THIS IS JUST WHAT I NEED TO TURN THE TABLES!
COME AND GET ME, YOU CHIMPS!
OOK OOK!
KRUSH
GET HIM!
VWM VWM
HUH ...!
WH... WHAT?! HE'S SWINGING THAT NECKLACE!
VWM

WHAT ARE YOU TRYING ?
WNG
WNG
BWA HA HA HA! NICE TRY, BONZO!
DO YOU THINK I'M SWINGING THIS FOR *FUN?*
!?
DON'T YOU SEE IT YET?
YOUR YO-YOS *AREN'T* COMING BACK...
!
WHAT?!
BABAM
'CAUSE I'VE GOT 'EM!

NICE!!
HE USED THE CENTRIFUGAL FORCE OF THE PUZZLE TO CAPTURE THE YO-YOS!
HEH HEH... AND NOW I CAN TAKE THESE...
AND HANG THEM ON THIS HOOK...
AAGGHHHHH!
I-IT HURTS ...!
MY FINGER'S GONNA FALL OFF!
DAH HA HA HA HA! "HUMAN HANGING YO-YO TECH"!

READ THIS WAY
WHAT ?!
THANKS, YUGI!
HERE'S YOUR PUZZLE BACK!
SNK
RMMB
DOOM
YUGI!
ALL RIGHT, JONOUCHI! IT'S PAYBACK TIME!

YOU TAKE HIRUTANI, JONOUCHI!!
I'LL TAKE THE REST OF THEM!
AWRIGHT!!
TMP
AFTER THEM!!
DON'T LET THEM LEAVE HERE ALIVE!!
THEY'RE GOING UPSTAIRS!
TMTMTM

THERE HE IS! ON THE ROOF!!

MORON... THERE'S NOWHERE TO RUN UP HERE!
HEH HUH HUH HUH ...
A YO-YO ?!!
HE'S FAST ...!!
LET'S START THE GAME !
SNA
P

THE RULES ARE SIMPLE! THE LAST ONE STANDING ON THE ROOF, WINS!
MAKE YOUR MOVE!!
FINE WITH ME!
GET AROUND HIM!
HIRU-TANI.
!
LET'S SETTLE THIS ONCE AND FOR ALL!
HEH HEH... I'VE HEARD YOU SAY THAT BEFORE...
BACK IN MIDDLE SCHOOL...AT THE START OF OUR BEAUTIFUL FRIENDSHIP!
REMEMBER HOW WE USED TO FIGHT 'TILL WE WERE BOTH ON THE GROUND? NOBODY WON...
THAT WAS BEFORE YOU WERE SO SCREWED UP IN THE HEAD...
TODAY, I'M NOT HOLDING BACK!
HEH HEH...

LET'S GO!!

SHWW

HEH HEH HEH!

SHWIRL

TAKE THIS!
WSH

TMP
POK
POK

SHEESH ...
RUN ALL YOU LIKE, STARHEAD! SOONER OR LATER, OUR YO-YO NET IS GONNA TAKE YOU DOWN!

POK
POK
THAT'S IT! FORCE HIM TO THE *EDGE!*
HA HA HA HA! NOWHERE TO RUN, LOSER!
!

READ THIS WAY

HA HA HA! YOU'VE FALLEN INTO OUR *TRAP!*
NOW YOU HAVE A CHOICE! LET US YO-YO YOUR *FACE* OFF...
OR *JUMP* OFF THE EDGE!
HEH HEH HEH ...
YOU'RE THE ONES WHO HAVE FALLEN INTO A TRAP!
!!

WHA ...!
CRK
CRK
NO WAY ...!
SO THAT'S WHAT HE WAS DOING ...!
CRK
CRK
CRK
YOU DON'T AIM YO-YOS AT *PEOPLE*!
YOU AIM THEM AT THE GROUND!
THINK ABOUT THAT...IN THE HOSPITAL!

CRASH

AAAGGGGHHH!

THUDDD

I WONDER HOW JONOUCHI'S DOING...

THWAK

URK ...

WHAT'S THE MATTER, HIRUTANI ?!

YOU'VE GOTTEN PRETTY **FLABBY!**

MUST BE **EASY** ON TOP OF **MONKEY MOUNTAIN** !

CRAK

TCH ...

TOSS
!!
TAKE THIS!

NOW YOU DIE!
HEH HEH HEH... UNLIKE YOU, I'VE GOTTEN SMARTER!

@#$*!
AGGH ...!
GOT GLASS IN MY EYES...

WAP
GAAH
...

CRAP... I CAN'T SEE...

HEH HEH HEH ...
I'LL PLANT THIS BROKEN GLASS IN THE BACK OF YOUR NECK...AS A VICTORY FLAG TO SHOW I WIN!
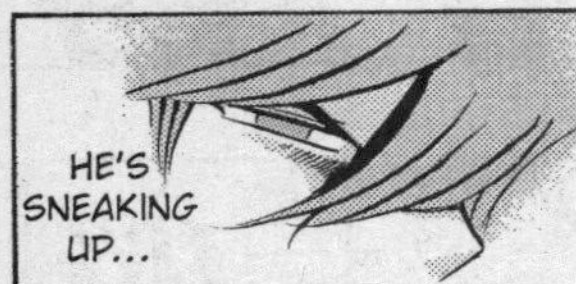
WHERE IS HE? HE'S GOTTEN QUIET...
HE'S SNEAKING UP...

CRNK
...

CRNK

DIE!!!!!

YOU IDIOT!
THE GLASS YOU TOSSED IS TELLIN' ME WHERE YOU ARE!
RAAHHH!!
THWOK
AGGH ...
AAH ...!
SKID SKID

OW
...
EYES
ALL
WATERY
...

GRAB
ACK
...!

WELL,
HIRUTANI?
WANT TO SEE
MY "YO-YO
TECH" SINCE
YOU'RE
THERE?

SHWIRLL

PARADE
THE
POOCH
!!
Y'KNOW,
WALK
THE
DOG!
SHWIRLL
!

BOINK
OW!

AAAAGGHH!!!

SNAP
I GOTTA CONFESS ...THAT'S THE ONLY TRICK I KNOW...
STILL PRACTIC-ING THE *OTHERS* ...

YUGI!
JONOUCHI! YOU'RE ALL RIGHT!

HEY, WHERE DID THAT LITTLE RAT NEZUMI GO, ANYWAY?!
GOOD QUESTION ...
WHEN I FIND HIM I'M GOING TO KICK HIS BUTT!

I'M SORRY, YUGI... GETTING YOU CAUGHT UP IN MY PROBLEMS AGAIN.
YOUR PROBLEMS ARE MY PROBLEMS ... JONOUCHI ...

Duel 50: Millennium Enemy 1: The Mysterious Transfer Student

Duel 50: Millennium Enemy 1: The Mysterious Transfer Student

NOW WHERE SHOULD WE HAVE YOU SIT...
AH, NEXT TO JONOUCHI IS OPEN...
THAT'S ME! OVER HERE!
EWW! BE CAREFUL, BAKURA!
DON'T LET JONOUCHI POLLUTE YOU!
ME POLLUTE HIM?! WHY I OUGHTTA--
NICE TO MEET YOU, JONOUCHI!
YO, SAME HERE! LET'S BE FRIENDS, HUH?
SMILE
BAKURA, THESE ARE MY BUDS!
HI, I'M YUGI.
THIS IS HONDA AND ANZU...
NICE TO MEET YOU!
WOW, YUGI... YOUR FAMILY RUNS A GAME STORE?
DO YOU LIKE GAMES, BAKURA?
YES, VERY MUCH!
I ESPECIALLY LIKE BOARD GAMES AND TABLETOP GAMES...
MY FAVORITE IS A GAME CALLED MONSTER WORLD...HAVE YOU HEARD OF IT?
WOW... MONSTER WORLD!

READ THIS WAY
WHAT KIND OF GAME IS "MONSTER WORLD"?

MONSTER WORLD IS A COMBINATION BOARD GAME AND ROLE-PLAYING GAME! YOU KNOW, LIKE "HOBGOBLIN" OR "MAZES AND MONSTERS"!
DARK MASTER
ONE PERSON PLAYS THE "DARK MASTER" AND THE MONSTERS, AND THE OTHER PEOPLE PLAY A GROUP OF ADVENTURERS. TOGETHER THEY ACT OUT A STORY USING MINIA-TURES ON A PLAYING FIELD.
THE DARK MASTER (D.M. FOR SHORT) WINS IF HE DEFEATS THE ADVENTURING PARTY. THE ADVENTURERS WIN IF THEY BEAT THE DARK MASTER. HE'S SORT OF LIKE THE BOSS MONSTER OF THE GAME.
ADVENTURERS (CHOOSE FROM DIFFERENT RACES AND CLASSES TO MAKE YOUR CHARACTER)

THE NEAT THING ABOUT "MONSTER WORLD" IS THAT THE BOARD IS MADE OF INTERCONNECTING BLOCKS THAT CAN BE ARRANGED IN DIFFER-ENT WAYS. YOU CAN BUY MORE BLOCKS AND EXPAND IT.
THERE ARE FORESTS AND MOUNTAINS, VILLAGES AND CASTLES. BY ARRANGING THEM IN DIFFERENT WAYS, YOU CAN COME UP WITH A DIFFERENT ADVENTURE EVERY TIME!

I'M *IMPRESSED*, YUGI! YOU KNOW A LOT ABOUT GAMES!
NAAH ...

THAT SOUNDS LIKE FUN!
HOW ABOUT WE *ALL* PLAY MONSTER WORLD TOMORROW!
HUH, BAKURA ?
UH ......

O-OKAY ...
...
HUH? BAKURA DOESN'T REALLY SEEM INTO IT...

UM...BY THE WAY, THERE'S SOMETHING I'VE BEEN WONDERING ABOUT...
WHERE DID YOU GET THAT *PENDANT,* YUGI...?
...
OH, THIS?
IT'S CALLED THE MIL-LENNIUM PUZZLE!
IT CAME FROM THE TOMB OF AN EGYPTIAN PHARAOH!
WOW, CAN I SEE IT?
ACTUALLY, I ALSO ...
!
ZNNG
OW ...
WHAT'S WRONG, BAKURA?!
UH... NO... IT'S NOTHING ...
HERE'S THIS BACK ...
WHAT'S RONG WITH ME? MY HEST HURT ALL OF A SUDDEN...

HEY, JONOUCHI!
DON'T HOG BAKURA ALL TO YOURSELF!
VWIP
WHAA?

HEY, CUTIE! LET US SHOW YOU AROUND THE SCHOOL! ♡
ER...
WE'VE ALREADY STARTED A FAN CLUB FOR YOU! ♡

...
GUYS LIKE BAKURA HAVE ALL THE LUCK!
UNLIKE YOU!

BAKURA SEEMS LIKE A NICE GUY!
YEAH!
HE'LL BE A GOOD FRIEND!

WE'LL HAVE TO PLAY MONSTER WORLD SOMETIME!

CROWD CROWD
THIS IS THE MUSIC ROOM!
THERE'S THE BATHROOM!

AND NEXT IS...
UH-HUH ...I SEE...
I'M NOT GOOD WITH GIRLS...

HMPH!

HEY, YOU!
YOU THINK YOU CAN WALK AROUND THE HALLS WITH A FLOCK OF GIRLS?
WHOSE CLASS ARE YOU SUPPOSED TO BE IN?!
UH-OH... IT'S MR. KARITA, THE P.E. TEACHER ...!
...
HMPH ...
YOU'RE THE NEW KID WHO JUST TRANSFERRED IN, AREN'T YOU...
I HEAR YOU HAD SOME PROBLEMS AT YOUR LAST SCHOOL...
!!
HOWEVER, THERE'S RULES AT DOMINO HIGH, MISTER!
LIKE THIS HAIR!!
YANK
AH ...
LONG HAIR FOR BOYS IS AGAINST THE RULES!
YEEK! YEEK! OH, BAKURA!
PLEASE DON'T HURT HIM!
LISTEN, MISTER FASHIONABLE! OR SHOULD I SAY "LITTLE MISS FASHIONABLE"?
I WANT YOU TO HAVE A CREW CUT BY TOMORROW!
THEN I'LL TREAT YOU AS A STUDENT OF THIS SCHOOL!
BWA HA HA HA!
HE'S AWFUL!
ARE YOU OKAY, BAKURA?
YES ...
I'M... I'M FINE.
I'M SORRY, BUT COULD I BE ALONE FOR A WHILE?

READ THIS WAY

UHN ...

WHAT'S **WRONG** WITH ME...? MY CHEST JUST KEEPS HURTING...

EVER SINCE I TOUCHED YUGI'S PENDANT...

DA DOOM

TO MY PENDANT ...

READ THIS WAY

YOU DON'T WANT TO...?
NO, THAT'S NOT IT!
I *WANT* TO PLAY THE GAME WITH ALL OF YOU!

THE THING IS...

AT MY LAST SCHOOL, I *USED* TO GET TOGETHER WITH MY FRIENDS TO PLAY ROLE-PLAYING GAMES...
BUT WHEN I DID, A *STRANGE* THING WOULD HAPPEN...

PEOPLE WHO PLAYED GAMES WITH ME WOULD *LOSE CONSCIOUSNESS.* THEY'RE *STILL* IN A COMA IN THE HOSPITAL...

YOU MAY NOT BELIEVE ME, BUT IT'S TRUE...

!!

THAT SORT OF THING KEPT HAPPENING, SO PEOPLE STARTED AVOIDING ME...
THAT'S WHY I KEPT CHANGING SCHOOLS...
NOW I'M LIVING IN AN APARTMENT BY MYSELF, AWAY FROM MY FAMILY...

I *WANT* TO BE FRIENDS WITH YOU!
AND I *WANT* TO PLAY GAMES BUT...

I MADE A DECISION...
I DON'T WANT TO LOSE ANY MORE FRIENDS...
SO YOU SHOULDN'T GET TOO CLOSE TO ME...

WELL... I'LL SEE YOU...
AH!

BAKURA!

PEOPLE GOING INTO COMAS BECAUSE OF A GAME? THAT CAN'T BE POSSIBLE...CAN IT?

Amane,
w is school? How are
d mother? Your brother
his new school today. I'
en there a little while
ery first day I
ends. They ask
my apartm
forward

H-HA HA HA HA...

THAT VOICE AGAIN!!
!!
SO... YOU CAN HEAR MY VOICE NOW, CAN YOU?
WHO'S THERE ?!

...!!

I GUESS FROM NOW ON, I'LL BE ABLE TO **SPEAK** WITH MY HOST...

TRULY A DAY TO REMEMBER! H-HA HA HA...

BECAUSE OF YOU, I'VE FINALLY FOUND THE BEARER OF THE MILLENNIUM PUZZLE...

H-HA HA HA...NOW YOU CAN'T TAKE ME OFF...

TH-THE PENDANT...

I'VE DECIDED TO KEEP YOU AS MY PERMANENT HOST!

DOOOM

YOU MEAN THIS PENDANT...!

FLAP

WHO AM I? I'VE BEEN WITH YOU FOR A LONG TIME...HIDING WITHIN YOU...

AND WITHIN THE RING OF WISDOM, THE MILLENNIUM RING...

THE MILLENNIUM RING?!

GET OUT! GET OUT OF MY BODY!!
NOW, NOW...DON'T BE SO COLD. BELIEVE ME WHEN I SAY, IT FEELS GOOD IN HERE! IN YOU!

AND INSTEAD OF PAYING RENT, I GRANT YOUR WISHES! WHY, I'VE GRANTED THEM ALMOST EVERY DAY...
HUH ...?!

DIDN'T YOU THINK THIS WHEN YOU WERE PLAYING THOSE GAMES...?
"HOW FUN THIS IS"! "I WISH I COULD PLAY GAMES WITH MY FRIENDS FOREVER" ...!
I GRANTED THAT WISH FOR YOU!

WH... WHAT ARE YOU TALKING ABOUT...
Y-... YOU CAN'T MEAN THOSE...
WELL... YOU'LL REALIZE SOON ENOUGH ...

IN ANY CASE, THIS IS MY CHANCE TO GET MY HANDS ON THE MILLENNIUM PUZZLE!!
IF I LET THIS OPPORTUNITY GO BY, I DON'T KNOW HOW LONG I'LL HAVE TO WAIT FOR ANOTHER ONE...

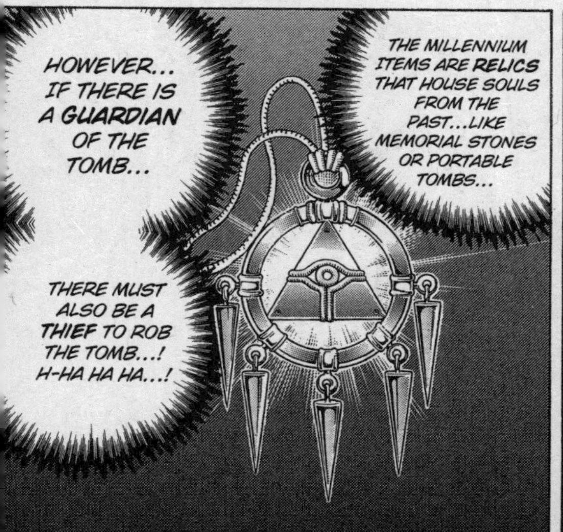
THE MILLENNIUM ITEMS ARE RELICS THAT HOUSE SOULS FROM THE PAST...LIKE MEMORIAL STONES OR PORTABLE TOMBS...
HOWEVER... IF THERE IS A GUARDIAN OF THE TOMB...
THERE MUST ALSO BE A THIEF TO ROB THE TOMB...! H-HA HA HA...!

NOW... SINCE I'M FEELING GOOD TONIGHT, LET ME PAY MY "RENT"...
WH-WHAT ARE YOU UP TO?!
H-HA HA HA...SO YOU WANT A CREW CUT?
RMMB
YOU MAY NOT BELIEVE IT, BUT I CARE FOR MY MASTER...THAT GYM TEACHER SWORE AT YOU, DIDN'T HE...?
!!
DON'T ...!
RRMMBB
SLEEP, RYO BAKURA. SLEEP...
DOOM
WHOOOOO

CHOOM
PENALTY GAME !!
YEE ...
I'VE SEALED YOUR SOUL INTO THIS *MINIATURE!*
H-HA HA HA HA!
FROM NOW ON YOU'LL ACT YOUR PART AS A *LIVING PIECE* IN MY CAMPAIGN WORLD!
THUD
GYAAAGGHH!

THE NEXT DAY...

BAKURA DIDN'T COME TO SCHOOL TODAY...

YES ...?

BANG

YO!

Y-YUGI!
GUYS ......

WE CAME OVER TO PLAY WITH YOU, BAKURA!
LET'S ALL PLAY MONSTER WORLD TOGETHER !!

NO!
GET OUT OF ...

DOOM
...THE HALL AND COME ON IN!
I'M SO GLAD YOU COULD ALL MAKE IT...
RIGHT THIS WAY...
DON'T MIND IF I DO!
SORRY WE DIDN'T CALL AHEAD...
...
DID BAKURA'S **EXPRESSION** CHANGE ALL OF A SUDDEN...?
MUST BE MY IMAGINATION...

MONSTER WORLD, THE ADVENTURE BOARD GAME! THIS IS MY CUSTOM BATTLE BOARD!
TA
DA
WOW! COOL!
OR SHOULD I SAY...A SHADOW GAME?! H-HA HA HA...!
DADADOOM
NOW, LET'S DO SOME ROLE-PLAYING!

Duel 51: Millennium Enemy 2: Monster World

Duel 51:
Millennium Enemy 2: Monster World

WELL, ARE YOU READY TO START PLAYING?
YEAH!
AWW RIGHT!
DA
DA
DOOM
YUGI...I'LL WIN THIS SHADOW GAME... AND I'LL TAKE YOUR MILLENNIUM PUZZLE!

LET ME EXPLAIN THE RULES.

THE PLAYERS ARE SPLIT INTO TWO GROUPS: THE "D.M.," OR DARK MASTER, ON ONE SIDE AND THE ADVENTURERS ON THE OTHER.
THE DARK MASTER CONTROLS THE MONSTERS AND EVIL CREATURES THAT LURK THROUGHOUT MONSTER WORLD. HIS ROLE IS TO STOP THE ADVENTURERS BY PLAYING THEM TO THE BEST OF HIS ABILITY!
THE ADVENTURERS WORK AS A TEAM. EACH PERSON CHOOSES THEIR CHARACTER'S RACE, CLASS AND ABILITY SCORES. THEY WORK TOGETHER TO BEAT THE DARK MASTER!

THE DARK MASTER HAS TO DEFEAT ALL OF THE ADVENTURERS TO WIN.
I'LL BE THE DARK MASTER, OF COURSE!

FOR THE ADVENTURERS TO WIN, THEY HAVE TO FIND THE "BOSS MONSTER," THEN DESTROY HIM!
SO WE GET TO KILL THINGS?
YOU CUT RIGHT TO THE POINT!
MONSTER WORLD COMBINES ELEMENTS OF A BOARD GAME AND A ROLE-PLAYING GAME!
BAKURA'S TAKING THE PART OF THE GAME MASTER IN AN RPG!

READ THIS WAY

"ROLE-PLAYING GAME"?

YOU MEAN LIKE VIDEO GAMES?

VIDEO ROLE-PLAYING GAMES ARE MORE COMMON *TODAY*...

BUT THE *ORIGINAL* ROLE-PLAYING GAMES WERE PLAYED AROUND A TABLE.

WHAT ARE TABLETOP ROLE-PLAYING GAMES? BASICALLY IMPROV ACTING WITH RULES. THE "GAME MASTER" PREPARES A STORY AND CHALLENGES. THE "PLAYERS" ACT OUT THE PARTS OF THEIR OWN CHARACTERS, AND THE "GAME MASTER" ACTS OUT THE PARTS OF EVERYONE ELSE. TOGETHER, THEY TALK THEIR WAY THROUGH AN IMAGINARY ADVENTURE.

THAT'S RIGHT!

AND DO YOU KNOW THE TRUE MEANING OF ROLE-PLAYING?

?

RACE LIST

HUMAN	AVERAGE WISDOM, STRENGTH AND SPEED.
ELF	HIGH WISDOM AND CHARISMA. MAKE GOOD MAGICIANS. LOW STRENGTH.
HALF-ELF	A HUMAN-ELF CROSSBREED.
HOBBIT	SMALL BUT VERY FAST, AND WELL-MUSCLED FOR THEIR SIZE. MAKE GOOD THIEVES.
PIXIE-FAIRY	HIGH WISDOM, ABLE TO FLY, ONE OF THE "MAGICAL RACES."
DWARF	LOW WISDOM, BUT HIGH STRENGTH AND CONSTITUTION.
BIRDTAIL	A RACE OF BIRD PEOPLE. ABLE TO FLY. HIGH CHARISMA.

CLASS LIST

WARRIOR	BEAST TAMER
MAGICIAN	BARD
PRIEST	ENCHANTER
MARTIAL ARTIST	DIABOLIST
MAGIC GUNMAN	ILLUSIONIST
MERCHANT	THIEF

HONDA
CHARACTER NAME: HIROTO
RACE: HUMAN
CLASS: MAGIC GUNMAN
WEAPON: MAGIC GUN
EQUIPMENT: CLOAK
MAGIC BULLETS
ABILITIES:
SPEED 18
WISDOM 10
STRENGTH 14
COURAGE 19
LEVEL 1 HIT POINTS 23

ANZU
CHARACTER NAME: ANZU
RACE: ELF
CLASS: MAGICIAN
EQUIPMENT: ELF'S STAFF
ELF'S CLOAK
ELF'S HAT
ABILITIES:
SPEED 20
WISDOM 17
STRENGTH 9
COURAGE 14
LEVEL 1 HIT POINTS 18

JONOUCHI
CHARACTER NAME: JOEY
RACE: HUMAN
CLASS: WARRIOR
WEAPON: SHORT SWORD
ARMOR: LEATHER ARMOR
LEATHER SHIELD
ABILITIES:
SPEED 16
WISDOM 8
STRENGTH 20
COURAGE 21
LEVEL 1 HIT POINTS 25

YUGI
CHARACTER NAME: YUGI
RACE: HALF-ELF
CLASS: BEAST TAMER
WEAPONS: NONE
EQUIPMENT: ELF CLOAK
ABILITIES:
SPEED 17
WISDOM 18
STRENGTH 9
COURAGE 18
LEVEL 1 HIT POINTS 22

WOW! YOU MADE THESE FIGURES LOOK JUST LIKE US!
YES, I PRIDE MY GAMES ON MY ATTENTION TO DETAIL.
I'LL ENTER YOUR CHARACTER DATA INTO THE COMPUTER FOR REFERENCE.
THESE NUMBERS WILL MAKE ALL THE DIFFERENCE WHEN YOU GET INTO A LIFE-OR-DEATH FIGHT!
AS THE "MASTER," I MAKE THE CRUCIAL ROLLS!
ALL RIGHT, IT'S ALL READY!
PLACE YOUR PIECES ON "START"!
TA DA
LET THE ADVENTURE BEGIN!
LET'S DO IT, GUYS!!

GAME START!

DODODO

MIN

DO

ONE OF THE FACETS OF THIS GAME IS THAT YOU DON'T KNOW WHERE THE ENEMY MONSTERS ARE HIDING!
THE MONSTERS WILL APPEAR DEPENDING ON THE PLAYERS' ACTIONS...OR SOMETIMES, BY *RANDOM CHANCE!*

COME TO THINK, WE DON'T KNOW MUCH ABOUT THIS WORLD!
LIKE WHO'S THE ENEMY OR WHAT'S THE POINT OF THE GAME!

THE TOWN!
YOU GO TO A *TOWN* TO GET INFORMATION IN AN RPG, DON'T YOU?!
THERE'S EVEN A TAVERN!

ANZU'S RIGHT!
LET'S GO TO THE TOWN FIRST!!

VERY GOOD!
YOU TAKE FIVE TURNS TO ENTER THE VILLAGE ...

KAPOK☆
BAN

WOW!
YOU TAKE OFF THE VILLAGE MODEL, AND THERE ARE PEOPLE INSIDE!
LOOK AT THE DETAIL!
OKAY! LET'S PULL UP TO THE BAR AND GET SOME NEWS!

HEY, YOU! OLD MAN!
AS YOU CAN SEE, WE'RE HIGHLY SKILLED ADVENTURERS!
ANY WAY FOR US TO MAKE SOME DOUGH?
YOU START WITH MONEY ...?

GLANCE

AT THOSE WORDS, THE VILLAGER SENDS A GLANCE YOUR WAY AND SIGHS AS HE SPEAKS...

"IF MONEY COULD SOLVE OUR PROBLEMS, I'D GIVE YOU ALL I'VE GOT..."
"BUT BEFORE YOU COULD CLAIM YOUR REWARD, YOU'D BE DEAD!"
WITH THAT, THE OLD MAN MOVES AWAY FROM THE BAR..

HEY, HOLD ON THERE, OLD TIMER!
SOUNDS LIKE YOU GOT A STORY! WE'RE ALL EARS!
CLAK
CLAK
THIS DIP IS TOTALLY INTO IT ...

HEARING THOSE WORDS, THE OLD MAN OPENS HIS MOUTH AND SAYS IN A HEAVY TONE ...

"UNTIL A FEW YEARS AGO, THIS VILLAGE WAS PEACEFUL...BUT THEN THE DARK LORD ZORC ASSASSINATED THE KING AND CHANGED THE CASTLE INTO A DEN OF EVIL!"
"AFTER THAT, MONSTERS BEGAN APPEARING IN OUR PEACEFUL VALLEY. MANY OF MY FELLOW VILLAGERS HAVE FALLEN PREY TO THEM."

WHAT?! THEY CAN'T GET AWAY WITH THAT!
AWRIGHT, DUDE! WE'LL TAKE CARE OF ZORC!!

SO LET'S SEE SOME GOLD PIECES! COUGH 'EM UP!
HOW MEAN!
THIS GAME BRINGS OUT YOUR BAD SIDE!

HEY, YUGI... IS THERE A SPEAKER IN THERE? IT SOUNDS LIKE THE OLD MAN'S REALLY TALKING ...
NO, NO ...

IN A TABLETOP RPG, CHARACTERS OTHER THAN THE ADVENTURERS ARE ACTED OUT BY THE GAME MASTER. THEY'RE CALLED "NON-PLAYER CHARACTERS."
THEN BAKURA MUST BE THROWING HIS VOICE ...
I GUESS ...

"HEAR ME, ADVENTURERS! BEFORE YOU START ON YOUR JOURNEY, YOU SHOULD TALK TO THAT MAN IN THE CORNER..."
"HE CAN TELL YOU THE SAFEST ROUTE TO ZORC CASTLE!"

HEY!
HUH ...?
!
BWAHAHAHAHA
LOOK AT THAT VILLAGER FIGURE!
AH!
HE LOOKS JUST LIKE KARITA FROM GYM!!

HUH... DID THAT FIGURE JUST TALK?
DUH! AS IF!

NOW PLAY YOUR PART...

B-BUT...

HELP...

YOU WILL ACT THE ROLE OF VILLAGER "D" FOREVER!

DOOM

PLAY YOUR PART... OR DIE!

"Z-ZORC CASTLE... IS TO THE NORTH... OUTSIDE OF THE VILLAGE..."

OKAY, GOT IT!

"B-BUT STAY OUT OF THE FOREST... IT'S FULL OF MONSTERS..."

OKAY, LET'S SKIP TOWN AND START HACKING!

LET'S ROLL! DON'T STOP FOR ANYTHING!
THM
THM

ALL RIGHT... YOU'VE JUST ENTERED AN AREA WHERE THERE'S A DANGER OF A RANDOM ENCOUNTER ...

FROM NOW ON, THERE'S A *JUDGMENT ROLL* EVERY TURN TO DETERMINE IF MONSTERS WILL APPEAR!

WITH THESE 10-SIDED DICE!
BANG

10-SIDED DICE...!

I'VE NEVER SEEN DICE LIKE *THAT* BEFORE...

THE AREA YOU'RE IN RIGHT NOW HAS A MONSTER ENCOUNTER RATE OF 30%!

THE ROLL IS DONE WITH TWO 10-SIDED DICE!
THE WHITE DIE IS THE *ONES* COLUMN...THE RED DIE IS THE *TENS* COLUMN...SO YOU GET A NUMBER BETWEEN ZERO AND 99!
IF THE OUTCOME IS FROM 31-99 THEN YOU'VE *AVOIDED* MEETING ANY MONSTERS.

I MAKE THE ROLL!
BA
NG
THE JUDGMENT ROLL IS 21!
THAT'S LOWER THAN 30...
THAT MEANS THAT A MONSTER APPEARS!!
DO
OM
A LEVEL 3 GOBLIN!
HA HA HA HA! WE FOUND A MONSTER!

ALL OF THE BATTLES ARE DECIDED WITH THESE 10-SIDED DICE!!

WITH A PERCENTILE ROLL!

NOW, YOU GO FIRST! TAKE YOUR SHOT!

OH-KAY!

THE WARRIOR ROLLS!

YAAAH!

DROP

BASED ON THE WARRIOR'S LEVEL, SPEED AND WEAPON, I CALCULATE THAT THE WARRIOR'S SHORT SWORD KILLS THE GOBLIN ON A ROLL OF 40 OR LESS!
HOODY HOO!
GRAAAH!
OKAY! THE GOBLIN GOES DOWN!
THE CLOSER YOU ROLL TO DOUBLE-ZERO, THE MORE DAMAGE YOU DO TO THE ENEMY!
GOOD MOVE, "JOEY"!
BWA HA HA HA HA
BUT ON THE OTHER HAND, IF YOU THROW A FUMBLE, A 99, YOU HAVE TO TAKE A PENALTY...
THE PENALTY TO BECOME A MINIATURE IN MY GAME WORLD... FOR THE REST OF YOUR LIVES! H-HA HA HA HA!

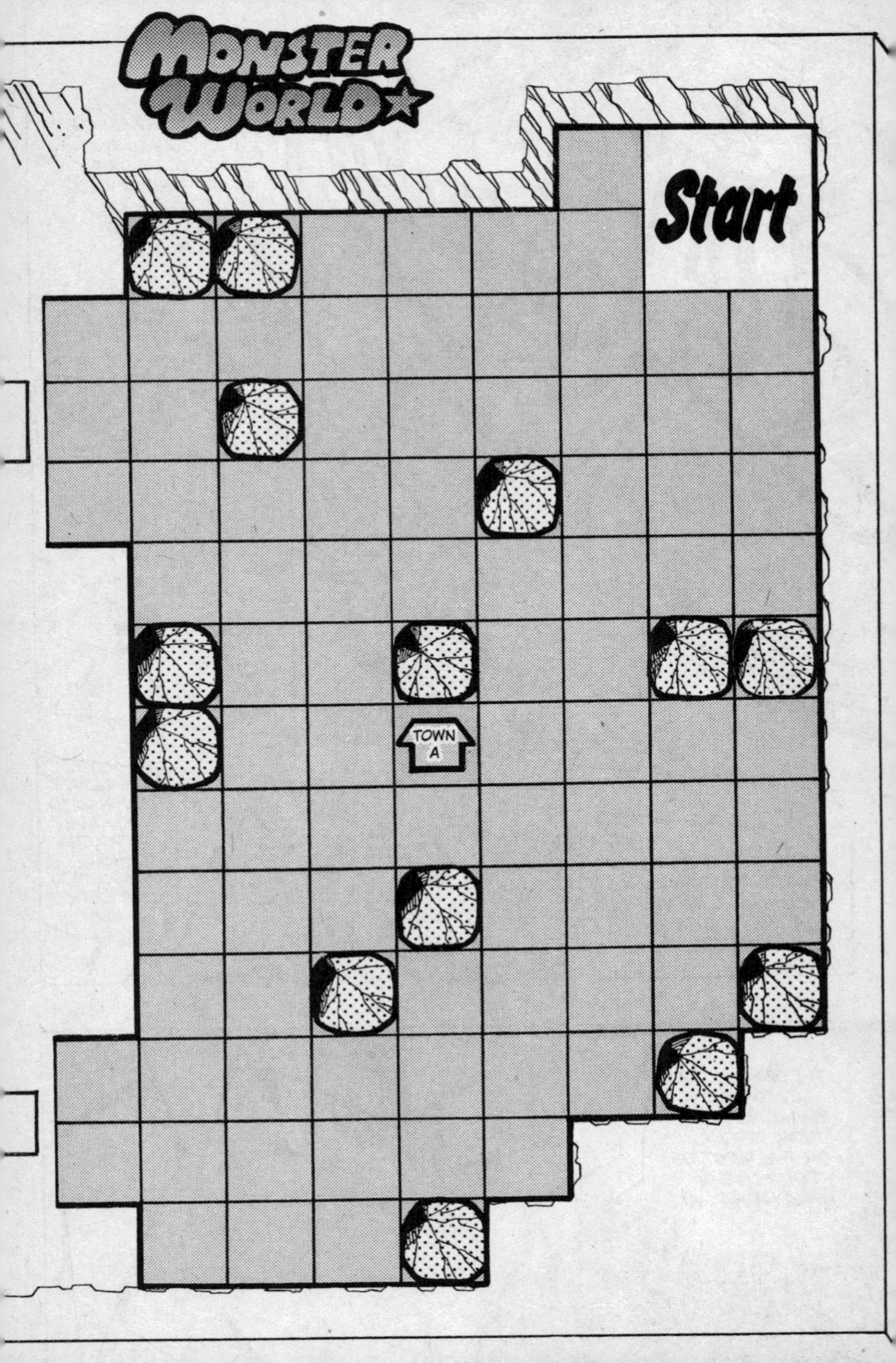
MONSTER WORLD
Start
TOWN A

TO FIND OUT HOW TO PLAY, TURN TO THE NEXT PAGE!
TOWN B
CASTLE ZORC
ZORC AREA
TOWN C

MONSTER WORLD BATTLE GAME

PLAYERS: TWO (ONE HERO, ONE GAME MASTER)

THE HERO!

WHAT YOU NEED:

* FOUR SIX-SIDED DICE (TWO PAIRS OF TWO DIFFERENT COLORS)
* ONE MARKER (FOR THE HERO)
* TWO PHOTOCOPIES OF THE GAME BOARD ON PAGE 604-605 (ENLARGED PHOTOCOPIES WOULD BE GOOD). ONE IS THE FIELD CHECK SHEET FOR THE GAME MASTER (SEE PAGE 607). THE OTHER IS THE BOARD TO PLAY THE GAME ON!
* A CALCULATOR

THE STORY OF MONSTER WORLD

ONCE THERE WAS A PLACE CALLED MONSLY KINGDOM. PEOPLE LIVED IN PEACE HERE, WHERE THE LAND WAS GREEN AND BOUNTIFUL AND COLORFUL BIRDS FLEW UNDER COTTON-CANDY CLOUDS.

BUT ONE DAY, THE SKY TURNED BLACK AND AN EVIL SHADOW FELL ACROSS THE LAND. THE DEMON KING ZORC HAD AWAKENED FROM HIS LONG SLEEP! CREATING MONSTERS TO DO HIS BIDDING, HE LORDED OVER THE PEOPLE WITH GREAT CRUELTY. AFTER MANY YEARS OF DARKNESS, PEOPLE BEGAN TO CALL MONSLY KINGDOM...

MONSTER WORLD!!!

THE PEOPLE LIVED IN FEAR AND CURSED THEIR LIVES. BUT THEN ONE DAY A HERO CAME FORWARD. BEARING THE LIGHT OF HOPE IN HIS SWORD, HE SET OUT TO DEFEAT ZORC.

THE QUEST BEGINS TO CONQUER ZORC CASTLE! THE BATTLE BETWEEN THE DEMON KING AND THE HERO IS ABOUT TO BEGIN!

PREPARATIONS BEFORE PLAYING

* THE PLAYERS DECIDE WHO WILL BE THE HERO AND WHO WILL BE THE GAME MASTER BY ROCK-PAPER-SCISSORS.
* THE GAME MASTER CONTROLS ZORC AND THE MONSTERS!
* BEFORE THE GAME BEGINS, THE GAME MASTER TAKES THE FIELD CHECK SHEET (A PHOTOCOPY OF THE BOARD) AND PUTS SYMBOLS FOR THE MONSTERS ON THE SQUARES. (SEE BELOW.) DON'T SHOW THE FIELD CHECK SHEET TO THE HERO! YOU CAN ONLY PUT A LIMITED NUMBER OF MONSTERS ON THE FIELD CHECK SHEET, BASED ON THEIR TYPE:

* GOBLIN (HP 100) ----- 10
* GARGOYLE (HP 150) ----- 5
* DRAGON (HP 200) ----- 5
* LAND MINES ----- 5
* ZORC (HP 500) IS PLACED IN THE ZORC AREA (IT'S ALL ONE BIG SPACE).

* YOU CAN'T PLACE MONSTERS ON MOUNTAINS OR TOWNS.
* YOU CAN'T MOVE THE MONSTERS, LAND MINES OR ZORC ONCE THE GAME BEGINS! THE HERO HAS TO GO TO THEM INSTEAD!

RULES FOR PLACING MONSTERS ON THE FIELD

* YOU CAN'T PLACE MONSTERS OR LAND MINES IN BOXES DIRECTLY NEXT TO EACH OTHER. YOU CAN PLACE THEM DIAGONALLY, THOUGH!

DRAG	GOB	GARG	
		DRAG	
		MINE	

NO

DRAG			
	GOB		DRAG
		GARG	
	MINE		

YES

WHEN THE GAME MASTER FINISHES PLACING HIS MONSTERS ON HIS FIELD CHECK SHEET, THE GAME STARTS!!

HOW TO PLAY

* THE HERO CHOOSES THE LEVEL OF THE GAME. THE HIGHER THE LEVEL, THE HARDER IT IS FOR THE HERO! (SEE PAGE 609)
* THE PLAYERS EACH TAKE TWO DIFFERENT-COLORED DICE (SO THAT NEITHER OF THEM HAS TWO DICE OF THE SAME COLOR).
* THE HERO PLACES HIS MARKER ON THE START MARK AND IT'S ***GAME START!!***
* THE HERO MOVES BY THROWING A SINGLE DIE. SHE CAN MOVE IN ANY DIRECTION SHE WANTS, BUT NOT DIAGONALLY. HOW FAR SHE CAN MOVE IS DETERMINED BY WHAT SHE ROLLS.

⚀ ⚃ ——— ONE SPACE

⚁ ⚄ ——— TWO SPACES

⚂ ⚅ ——— THREE SPACES

(THE HERO CAN'T MOVE THROUGH MOUNTAINS OR OFF THE MAP.)

* THE GAME MASTER CHECKS THE SPACES THE HERO MOVES THROUGH ON HIS FIELD CHECK SHEET. IF THE HERO MOVES THROUGH OR STOPS ON A SPACE WHERE A MONSTER IS PLACED, THE GAME MASTER ANNOUNCES A BATTLE, AND THEY FIGHT AT THAT SPACE!

BATTLE SYSTEM

* THE GAME MASTER LETS THE HERO KNOW WHAT TYPE OF MONSTER SHE HAS ENCOUNTERED!
* THE PLAYERS BOTH THROW ONE DIE. THE ONE WITH THE HIGHER NUMBER GETS TO ATTACK FIRST. (ROLL AGAIN IF IT'S A TIE.) THEN, THE ATTACKING PLAYER THROWS HER TWO DIFFERENT COLORED DICE. DECIDE BEFORE ROLLING THE DICE WHICH COLOR IS THE TENS AND WHICH COLOR IS THE ONES! HER OPPONENT (THE HERO OR THE MONSTER) LOSES THAT NUMBER OF HIT POINTS.

FOR EXAMPLE: ⚀ ⚂ ——— 13 POINTS

⚄ ⚅ ——— 56 POINTS

IF THE PERSON WHO WAS ATTACKED HAS MORE THAN 0 HIT POINTS LEFT, IT'S ***THEIR*** TURN TO ATTACK! DO IT OVER AGAIN BUT WITH THE SIDES REVERSED. THIS GOES ON UNTIL ONE PLAYER REACHES 0 HIT POINTS...AND DIES!

IF THE HERO ROLLS DOUBLES ON HIS ATTACK (LIKE 00 OR 33), THEN IT'S A CRITICAL HIT! THE MONSTER TAKES 100 POINTS OF DAMAGE AND THE HERO'S HIT POINTS GO UP BY 100 POINTS. (MONSTERS AND ZORC CAN'T MAKE CRITICAL HITS!)

* AFTER THE HERO DEFEATS A MONSTER, HE THROWS TWO DICE (LIKE IN THE EXAMPLE) AND ADDS THAT NUMBER TO HIS HIT POINTS. (THIS IS SEPARATE FROM THE HIT POINTS YOU GET IF YOU ROLL A CRITICAL HIT.) THERE'S NO UPPER LIMIT TO THE HERO'S HIT POINTS!
* AFTER THE HERO DEFEATS A MONSTER OR LAND MINE IN A SPACE, SHE CAN'T GO BACK AND FIGHT THE SAME MONSTER AGAIN. THE GAME MASTER MUST CROSS IT OUT ON THE FIELD CHECK SHEET.

WINNING THE GAME

* THE HERO MUST MOVE HIS MARKER TO THE ZORC AREA AND WIN THE FINAL BATTLE WITH ZORC TO WIN THE GAME.
* THE GAME MASTER MUST DEFEAT THE HERO TO WIN! THE GAME MASTER ONLY LOSES IF ZORC'S HIT POINTS GO TO 0 OR LESS.

OTHER RULES

* THE HERO CAN GET MORE HIT POINTS BY STOPPING AT A TOWN. HOWEVER, HE CAN ONLY GO TO EACH TOWN ONCE.

  TOWN A ----- GAIN 200 POINTS
  TOWN B ----- GAIN 150 POINTS
  TOWN C ----- GAIN 100 POINTS
* IF THE HERO STEPS ON A LAND MINE HE LOSES 100 HIT POINTS.
* THE HERO'S LEVEL DETERMINES HER STARTING HIT POINTS.

LEVEL	1	2	3
HERO HP	400	300	200

☆ ADVICE FROM YUGI!!

A PREMIUM BOX SET OF THE FIRST TWO STORY ARCS OF ONE PIECE!

A PIRATE'S TREASURE FOR ANY MANGA FAN!

STORY AND ART BY EIICHIRO ODA

BAROQUE WORKS
ONE PIECE

ONE PIECE
EAST BLUE AND BAROQUE WORKS BOX SET — VOLUMES 1-23

Comes with EXCLUSIVE POSTER and the ROMANCE DAWN mini-comic!

As a child, Monkey D. Luffy dreamed of becoming King of the Pirates. But his life changed when he accidentally gained the power to stretch like rubber...at the cost of never being able to swim again! Years later, Luffy sets off in search of the "One Piece," said to be the greatest treasure in the world...

This box set includes VOLUMES 1-23, which comprise the EAST BLUE and BAROQUE WORKS story arcs.

EXCLUSIVE PREMIUMS and GREAT SAVINGS over buying the individual volumes!

WWW.SHONENJUMP.COM

RATED T FOR TEEN
ratings.viz.com

VIZ media
www.viz.com

Kuroko's BASKETBALL

TADATOSHI FUJIMAKI

When incoming first-year student Taiga Kagami joins the Seirin High basketball team, he meets Tetsuya Kuroko, a mysterious boy who's plain beyond words. But Kagami's in for the shock of his life when he learns that the practically invisible Kuroko was once a member of "the Miracle Generation"—the undefeated legendary team—and he wants Kagami's help taking down each of his old teammates!

THE HIT SPORTS MANGA FROM SHONEN JUMP IN A 2-IN-1 EDITION!

viz media · SHONEN JUMP

DRAGON BALL SUPER
STORY BY Akira Toriyama ART BY Toyotarou
Goku's adventure from the best-selling classic manga *Dragon Ball* continues in this new series written by Akira Toriyama himself!
Ever since Goku became Earth's greatest hero and gathered the seven Dragon Balls to defeat the evil Boo, his life on Earth has grown a little dull. But new threats loom overhead, and Goku and his friends will have to defend the planet once again!
RATED T FOR TEEN
VIZ media
viz.com
SHONEN JUMP
DRAGON BALL SUPER © 2015 by BIRD STUDIO, Toyotarou/SHUEISHA Inc.

RATED
T
FOR
TEEN
ratings.viz.com

VIZ
media